Section on Public Administration Works

GOVERNMENT INNOVATION

Translation by Celorio Morayta, servicios especializados de idiomas:
Nicholas Papworth (head translator), Elaine Jones, Maurice Harrah
and Gonzalo Celorio Morayta

RAMÓN MUÑOZ GUTIÉRREZ

Government Innovation

The Good Government Paradigm in the Administration of President Vicente Fox

FONDO DE CULTURA ECONÓMICA

First edition, 2004

Muñoz Gutiérrez, Ramón
Government Innovation. The Good Government Paradigm in the Administration of President Vicente Fox / Ramón Muñoz Gutiérrez. – Mexico : FCE, 2004
465 pp. ; 23 x 17 cm – (Colec. Administración Pública)
ISBN 968-16-7624-6 (hardcover)

1. Public Administration 2. Mexico – Politics and Government – 2001 – 3. Fox, Vicente I. Ser II. t

LC JF1355 Dewey 350 M482i

Comments and suggestions: editor@fce.com.mx
www.fondodeculturaeconomica.com
Tel. (55)5227-4672 Fax (55)5227-4694

ISBN 968-16-7624-6 (hardcover)

Printed in Mexico

To my wife Claudia and my children José Ramón, Ana Claudia, Julio Iván and Juan Pablo: with love and gratitude for accompanying me on my journey through life and politics.

Acknowledgments

To President Vicente Fox Quesada, for his leadership and personal commitment to government innovation and quality, but above all for his unwavering conviction to work for the establishment of democracy in Mexico.

To all Mexican men and women working in every corner of the country and beyond its borders to build a more prosperous and democratic Mexico for our children.

To all the members of the many innovation and quality networks who, with talent and enthusiasm, have gradually changed the face and reputation of the Federal Government.

To all the public servants who work day after day, with zeal and dedication, to build a Good Government.

Table of Contents

CHAPTER 6
INNOVATIVE PRACTICES 183

Foreword

In the early nineties, a number of governments in the developed world were sufficiently responsive to realize that their citizens demanded changes, that government structures had fallen into discredit as a result of their inefficiency and gigantism. They understood that whereas large corporations were making radical innovations to compete more effectively by raising their quality and thus improving possibilities of keeping their customers satisfied, government administrations remained stagnant and failed to contribute solutions to the difficulties citizens encountered in their dealings with public institutions.

The first alarm call came in the mid-eighties from the British and United States governments, which launched attacks in both words and deeds against the complexity and inefficiency of their own bureaucracies. Meanwhile, the governments of developing countries were incapable of carrying out sweeping reforms to make them more efficient.

Two decisive developments were taking place in the new global reality. On the one hand, civil society was becoming increasingly active and participatory, and the new information technology was facilitating communication and organization. Furthermore, globalization was setting new standards in social interrelations and providing citizens with new tools for information and observation of their rights and obligations and for new forms of democratic interaction. On the other, the demands made by markets, investments and capital flows could not fall to the private sector alone, even though its structures were moving forward in leaps and bounds. It was that very progress that emphasized the need for governments to widen and improve their response capacity in all spheres. The old structures were incapable of responding to the new needs imposed by globalization.

Society and the private sector were literally putting governments all over the world up against the ropes. How were they to act, respond to and satisfy the new demands?

A number of governments, supported by forward-thinking experts in public administration and aided by others from the field of private enterprise, set themselves the task of reflecting and acting on the best way to make innovations in the public administration in their respective countries.

It was obviously not just a question of directly and indiscriminately applying the ideas and systems of private enterprise to public management. Every government is "fenced in" by its country's own political life, by its characteristics as a nation, both historically and in terms of infrastructure, and also by the level of its citizens' political awareness.

The course of this evolution has been heightened over the past ten years: earlier models, centralized, bureaucratized, inertial, are being replaced by new forms of participatory democracy and by government innovation. Government leaders are incorporating new ideals and democratic practices into the manner in which governments serve citizens, and they themselves are also benefiting from the reforms as a result of the new communication with citizens and the attainments in efficiency, productivity and quality.

Clearly, only countries with an effective public administration, sound political and economic institutions, appropriate social policies and committed leadership can assure an integration into the world economy that benefits the largest number of inhabitants.

In a country such as Mexico, with its history of public administration, its leadership in Latin America and its role in the world economy, government innovation was essential; it lay not only in the realm of duty, but within the bounds of urgency.

President Vicente Fox took it upon himself to initiate and also spearhead that transformation process in the Federal Government in Mexico. His commitment, as he himself stated, was to achieve *a world-class government, one of total quality... with the goal of replacing traditional patterns of public management with the most advanced administrative and technological systems.*

The Mexican government found itself having to work along two parallel lines in administration: one, reducing backlogs while dealing with day-to-day tasks; and the other, changing, innovating and transforming in order to place Mexico at the forefront in the new paradigm of Good Government.

To that end, the Model for Innovation and Quality in the Federal Public Administration was promoted as a great paradigmatic umbrella, and at the same time the INTRAGOB Model was applied in order to attain quality levels that would make the public administration competitive by international standards. Ramón Muñoz, entrusted by President Fox with overseeing the process of innovation and quality in the Mexican government, gives an account in this book of the process carried out and of some of the most significant results obtained, especially in institutions with the most direct dealings with citizens. This process has, of course, not been easy and has required a determined political will, as is no exception in other countries, either.

I think it is also important to highlight the structure of this book, for it leads the reader—whether a beginner or someone experienced in the field—to an understanding of the reasons that have prompted governments to undertake their innovations, and also gives us a clear reference as to how the transformation process began to take shape; but Muñoz very cogently places special emphasis on the needs and democratic thrust of the changes, not only on their pragmatic and utilitarian application. Subsequently, he details the structure of the Agenda for Good Government being applied in Mexico, which summarizes and conceptualizes the central objectives of the innovation in its six action lines. This Agenda will undoubtedly serve as an example for many countries that are only now embarking on their government transformation. Mexico's innovative experience has been extremely interesting and exemplary and has caught the attention of very diverse countries, particularly in Latin America.

Building a good government is an essential condition for shaping a responsible, efficient public administration, but above all, a powerful means to build relations of trust, joint responsibility and participation between citizens and government.

Although introducing innovations in public administration is urgent for democracy and relations in the globalized world, the process must be studied as a means of implementing a new paradigm in internal relations in an effective government's public administration and between the latter and the citizens.

Governmental Innovation: the Paradigm of Good Government in the Administration of President Vicente Fox is a work that highlights the notion that innovation must necessarily lead us to a broad, clear concept of quality. To innovate is to improve, change, transform, reinvent —in each case as applicable—the context, needs and past performance, but in addition this must be done with quality, taken to mean effectiveness and efficiency, savings in resources of all kinds, customer service—citizens, children—honesty, transparency, the entire set of attributes that leads precisely to the exercise of Good Government, which in Mexico's case turned into a priority.

Governmental Innovation: the Paradigm of Good Government in the Administration of President Vicente Fox is a book which will undoubtedly enrich the bibliography of the most valuable experiences in the new public administration worldwide, while at the same time stressing the importance of combining clear objectives and political will, which are essential to any process of change.

Guido Bertucci
Director of the Division for Public Economics and Public Administration
Department of Economic and Social Affairs
United Nations

Introduction

Good Government is a binding commitment when governing under a democratic mandate. The main purpose of Good Government is to gain citizens' trust. When President Vicente Fox took office in December 2000, ending an authoritarian regime, he faced a collosal challenge: promoting change within the framework of a presidential democracy that operates in the form of divided government and with a true revolution in citizen expectations. Vicente Fox, the candidate of Alianza para el Cambio (Alliance for Change), won the presidential election, but no party obtained an absolute majority in Congress. The Revolutionary Institutional Party (PRI) remained as the foremost political force in both chambers.

When people analyze, state their view and judge the current government's performance, this important strategic consideration tends to be overlooked.

In the past, when the Mexican authoritarian regime prevailed, the Chief Executive had the leading voice in the design of public policies. He could do this with relative ease in view of the enormous power concentrated in him. The President likewise dominated both his party —the PRI—and Congress. He had access to all the cards of power. Accountability was merely pretense.

Democracy, however, is a very different political system. At the heart of democracy, like a sacred treasure, lies freedom. Octavio Paz said it was the regime of relative opinions. Absolute truths in the realm of politics have begun to collapse. Playing this game involves respecting a series of values and rules related to people's rights, care of the environment, accountability and making public management transparent, raising the level of public debate, allowing citizens to participate in decision-making that will affect their lives...

To meet these challenges it was important to begin the transformation of government structures and the entire public apparatus. The public administration was trapped in a design based on organization systems devised during the era of the industrial revolution and its instruments were in line with a political system that citizens had shunned at the polls.

So the only alternative was to bet on **innovation.** The questions were: in what direction?, how fast?, with what kind of organization?, with what instruments? In response to this we designed the Strategic Model for Government Innovation and Quality. President Fox approved it in January 2001. It was a guide that would serve as a map in conducting the process of change. It was by no means the last word, for we are all well aware that the best model is reality itself, and as Francis Bacon held: *"time is the most innovative factor of all."*

In order to simplify the strategy for change and the transformation of the public administration and focus the results in the area of Good Government, the Presidential Agenda for Good Government was designed and widely disseminated.

This book gives an account, "halfway down the road," of truly "innovative" stories of men and women in public service who have worked in teams to steadfastly transform their fields, using leading-edge technology, so as to gradually change the face and reputation of public duty. Many success stories are in the making in other areas of the Federal Government. They will become public in due course.

At first there was talk of a "silent revolution" in referring to this whole process of change toward innovation and quality. Today this process is being lived *out loud,* to paraphrase Emile Zola. The presentation of the Stockholm Challenge award to the Mexican Government headed by President Fox, in the category of electronic government, undoubtedly attests to this. But above all, the acid test, the ultimate test, is Mexican citizens' rating.

In June 2001 the Madrid-based Center for Sociological Research published a very interesting study of opinions and attitudes entitled: *Twenty-five years later. Recollections of the Franco regime and the transition to democracy by year 2000 Spaniards.* When asked "what do you think is the most important component for there to be democracy?", 39% of those surveyed replied: **the right to say what one thinks.**

I wouldn't know what Mexicans would reply to this and other questions on the democracy lived during President Fox's mandate, but I am certain that among the good things they would talk about, several would have to do with the qualities of Good Government, transparency, services rendered with quality and delivered quickly, more professional public servants and more honest practices. All of this within a setting of tolerance and great respect for others' opinions. Freedom to say, responsibly, what we think.

Chapter 1

Democracy and Good Government

The Shared Hope

At a glance it would seem that most of the countries in the world have left ideological conflicts behind—there is no need here to include other more ancient ones of a different nature, such as those with deep religious roots—in order to set out on a course coincident with liberal, constitutional democracy. After the fall of the Berlin Wall, a watershed in recent history, what remained of the Cold War concluded, ending the bipolar world, and the confrontation between communism and democracy came to an end. Russia itself and the Eastern European countries have hastened their internal democratic lives and are making major efforts to adjust to the new demands of international coexistence, in which trade, the economy and markets play a fundamental role, but also in which growing social participation in internal and external affairs is a key factor. Perhaps the most obvious example of that new phenomenon is the recent addition of a further 12 countries—most of them in Eastern or *Communist* Europe—to the European Union. Does anyone remember what the *Iron Curtain* was all about?

In the last 20 years most of the countries of the world have moved closer to liberal democracy, whether by recovering it or by gaining access to it. While this is happening, do they also have to make the effort to fit into a wider concept of democracy? Do the new demands of democracy also pose new challenges for governments?

It is interesting to reflect on what Fareed Zakaria has called "The Rise of Illiberal Democracy." According to the author, even though the concept of democracy has spread throughout the world, it would appear to coexist with a group of countries that in fact limit individual freedoms, but hide behind elections to defend their democratic outlook or practice. Zakaria believes that the shield of "illiberal" democracy can help authoritarian, intolerant, racist or fundamentalist regimes to come to power. Their rise to power is legitimized by democratic practice, but this does not mean that full democracy exists in their societies.

Robert Kaplan holds a similar view in his essay *Was Democracy Just a Moment?,* in which he gives an account of authoritarian regimes which to a greater or lesser extent protect themselves with democracy. He considers that the disappearance of communism in Eastern Europe is not a guarantee that democracy in the world is assured for life, and makes reference to other important movements, including the Enlightenment, which also disappeared despite their virtues.

These legitimate concerns, when many countries are only just going through the transition to democracy or have not yet succeeded in consolidating it, are precisely the ones that lead us to thinking about the strength and value of a Democracy that broadens or expands the limits of traditional democracies, largely as a result of the effects of globalization and the new information and communication technologies and their value in social mobilization.

The Universalization of Liberal Democracy

Despite the different viewpoints debated after World War II, in the fifties and especially in the third wave of democratization at the end of the twentieth century, liberal democracy is the most widely accepted political model in the world today, and the exceptions notwithstanding, it may be said that it is fully accepted in the western hemisphere.

Very diverse countries, among them a few in Latin America, including Mexico, are advancing toward the consolidation of democracy. Such a consolidation involves the institutionalization of democratic practices and the extension not only of those practices, but also of a democratic culture, in such a way that it becomes a virtually irreversible way of life.

Here it is important to quote how two authors, Huntington and Del Aguila, summarize in five brief principles the essential values of liberal democracy as a system of government:

1. Leaders are appointed through periodic, fair elections;
2. Elected leaders are not subject to the will of internal or external factual powers (army, businesspeople, etc.);
3. The vote is secret and virtually all adults can vote or be voted for;
4. There is freedom of speech and association;
5. The right of information exists.

However, if we talk about a democratic culture, a democratic way of life extended throughout society, then these principles broaden and pave the way for what might be called the *Expansion of Democracy:*

1. Democracy, that is, collective decision making by democratically elected representatives;
2. Tolerance, whereby competitors are viewed as political adversaries with whom to compete, not as personal enemies to be destroyed; here, the aim is to avoid messianic populism—usually self-imposed—as well as moral condemnation of opponents—which can lead to physical elimination of contenders (both tend to be the two sides of the same coin);
3. Plurality, which implies not only tolerance for other positions, but also defense and even furtherance of political diversity;
4. Legality, that is, respecting the law and channeling differences through peaceful institutional proceedings;
5. Participation, that is, updating democratic practices by exercising them on a daily basis, as well as a sense of joint responsibility in public affairs;
6. Respect for human rights (freedom, integrity, etc.);
7. Transparency, that is, the right to information;
8. Accountability;
9. Equality of opportunities, or *inclusion;*

10. Honesty and efficiency (insofar as this implies care of the commonweal because it has an impact on the use of society's resources).

Democracy that Expands

Following those principles, the role of the State has also changed. Its role as the sole, omnipotent guiding force, formerly played by the government, has been diluted and transformed, and has lost its traditional strength, leaving part of its "power" in the hands of citizens and numerous sectors of civil society which anticipated the issues of government improvement, inter-group relations, the role that should be played by political parties and congresses or parliaments; society has asked itself these questions and in many cases has also sought, anticipatively, its own answers. Civil society and the productive sectors in general have understood in advance of the government, as in other eras in history, the need to make changes and have applied pressure to that end. The citizens themselves, expressing their disappointment and disapproval of government conduct—from arbitrary administrative acts to dishonesty and corruption—were the ones who "nixed" them and prompted them to change.

> *Democracy that expands is sustained above all by a sort of new global awareness that goes beyond national spheres; an awareness of what can be done and what is wanted, from care of the environment to respect for human rights, from respect for plurality to competition that offers quality options; a new global awareness that remains alert to what occurs beyond its limits.*

Trade and financial exchanges have taken on prime importance; these flows appear to be the determining factors of globalization or of its key features; nonetheless, new horizons have opened up in all fields of human endeavor: scientific, educational, artistic, sociological, psychological, and social coexistence. Globalization continues to afford enormous possibilities for coexistence in the process of formation and assimilation; hence the importance of the practice of Democracy coupled with a hyperactive role by society. Globalization is far from reaching its completion; starting just over a decade ago as a result of progress and of the use of the new information technologies, it is bound to shape human and social relations and those between States at the outset of this century.

The world is full of new expressions of democracy. As of the eighties—Huntington pinpoints the start of the "third wave" of democratization in 1975—the feeling arose in many countries that the parliaments, the bodies of peoples' representatives, were not sufficient and fell short by far of reflecting people's true and deepest social concerns. If the political parties were undergoing a crisis—a crisis they have yet to surmount and which they must promptly confront if they are to modernize themselves—the same had happened to congresses.

In his book *Can We Live Together?*, sociologist Alain Touraine points out that "the democratic spirit is not limited to one particular domain, the domain of politics. It wants to spread to all aspects of social life: to business and to schools or hospitals, to cities and to associations, to the courts and to political assemblies. What binds institutions together is the fact that all of them—each in its particular sphere—have to answer the same question: How do we combine the unity of a social entity with the diversity of its components – the interests, opinions and values of its members?" A key role has undoubtedly been played by the defense of human rights in the world, an awareness that began to spread in the late seventies and has grown exponentially with globalization.

Moreover, we should acknowledge the growing complexity of societies which are becoming less and less homogeneous, and in which a concept of national culture merely saves a modicum of common features which in turn include very diverse cultural expressions. The complexity of modern societies also gives rise to differences and to needs that have to be met in the market, not only consumption but also what might be called "government attention." Such needs have to do not only with the delivery of services of all kinds or attention to backlogs or age-old problems, but also with the particular demands of specific groups.

Due to a lack of clear, timely responses, civil society gradually found the means to express itself, to make itself heard in a respectful but also firm, organized manner. Non-Governmental Organizations (NGOs) undoubtedly attest to this as a new worldwide expression.

Today, the Democracy that expands has not destroyed the concept of representative democracies, but it has unsettled the latter by extending it. The citizen appears to say: *I elect you, but I participate too, I'm not leaving it all in your hands*. Before there was a demand for solutions to specific problems; now citizens want to take part in the solutions, they want to participate in their design, their execution and, above all, in overseeing and appraising their results.

One case that merits special attention concerns the media and citizens' growing awareness of the right to be informed. It no longer suffices to believe that governments inform or that the media also do so: new rules for ones and the others have been demanded everywhere and, while governments legislate on the matter to eliminate obstacles to knowing the truth, the media have seen the need—demanded by audiences—to make explicit the codes of ethics that give greater certainty to their news contents. Although this trend began in the late seventies, today it seems to be a growing imperative. It is important to understand that such changes have been the product of news corporations that were sensitive to the demands and interests of their customers. But just as in other fields of social coexistence, these corporate changes have prompted changes in government rules; in the final analysis all of this is due to the new democratic life.

And that participation, that need for democratic expression, is already crossing the barriers of the strictly national sphere to become a sort of worldwide participation: *what happens to you concerns me; I support you*. Today, therefore, many central government decisions are subject to international scrutiny, not only by ad hoc agencies, but also by social agencies for which one of the expressions and possibilities afforded by globalization are openly stating their views, creating support and information networks, etc. Democracy today has new bastions and niches such as civil liberties defense movements, which are so strong and important that their local power enables them to come into immediate contact with multiplier cooperation groups throughout the world. Just over 20 years ago such movements were not in evidence even in the democracies that were supposedly the most advanced.

Therefore, in today's democracy the term "joint responsibility" is taking on increasing importance and meaning. Many governments apply it and want it, but they should be aware that it is not a generous gift but the result of social demands. Do governments want jointly responsible societies or do all societies want to be jointly responsible? In both cases it can be said that some do, some do not; some have begun to value its advantages, but the fact remains that it is a term that came out of society and should gain strength over the coming years; the time this takes will depend only on the degree of countries' democratic progress.

While this was taking place, governments came up against mounting difficulties in implementing their policies, as society viewed them not only critically and distrustfully, but at times even indifferently, an indifference which led to a lack of social participation in their results. Trust in governments had been undermined: as huge, complex organizational structures they were lagging well behind the new demands.

Good Government

For Przeworski, what makes democracies sustainable is their institutions and their performance; in other words, when they promote desirable goals and when at the same time, their institutions are capable of confronting the ensuing crises if those goals are not met. This author, however, does stress that a democracy's capacity or effectiveness is a significant factor in its consolidation, since "without an effective State there can be no democracy." Added to this there is all the recent thinking on the crucial importance of strengthening the capacity of institutions, the State and the government to solve public problems, as well as the discussion at international level on the need to promote *Good Government.*

Thus, today the practice of democracy implies monitoring of government administration, compatibility of interests and aspirations beyond borders, extensive social participation and joint responsibility in the implementation and appraisal of public policies. It leaves no gaps for the authoritarian exercise of power that still exist in traditional democracies; hence the concept of Democracy is far from exhausted: it is simply expanding and changing. Almost two decades ago a major current of government *Innovation* or *Reinventing* government started in the world, based on principles of efficiency, competitiveness and quality that were above all democratic.

Those pioneering governments in the drive to transform public administration were sufficiently visionary and daring to invite thinkers behind the substantial changes effected in private enterprise to reflect urgently on the matter. It was essential to hit upon a different course, practical, with palpable results, one which would combine the best features of two administrative tendencies. In the end, this resulted in more flexible, efficient governments and a citizenry—a *clientele*—satisfied with public-sector goods and services. Admittedly, the solutions adopted by private enterprise were not entirely compatible with the requirements of government innovation. Back in 1986 Deming warned of the problem, and later Halachmie, in 1995, was more categorically opposed. As is usually the case, the extreme positions were outdone by reality. In practice it became possible to reach a compromise and to prove that even though the same views might not coincide completely, the differences were not irreconcilable, either: to innovate, one had to reconcile.

On the other hand, trying to find a single, transferable model was unworkable; so the idea was to devise a set of factors and measures that would set each government on the road to the solution that best suited it and was viable in its own context, depending on its specific needs and its own historical, social and political circumstances.

When the process had been under way for a decade—and in some countries, such as Australia, for more than fifteen years—*Reinventing* government or government *Innovation* became a growing trend throughout the world, especially in countries with an expansive democracy, which are also facing new challenges and obligations. The changes made have the virtue of benefiting both parties equally: internally, governments become more efficient, streamlined and competitive, which in turn helps them in their relations externally—with citizens and in international exchanges—and society obtains more, improved benefits by receiving a faster response with much less red tape.

In the discussion on the size or strength of the State, which in the final analysis directly affects the size or strength of government, there appears to be agreement on one practically irrefutable point: a State —or government—is strong insofar as it promotes development and inclusion; the more efficient, productive and responsive a government, and the more capable of stimulating creativity and respect for freedom, the stronger (or sounder) it will be; a *Good Government* guided by these premises is appreciated and valued by the citizens it serves in the first place; but also, in the new global interrelations, it becomes a government appreciated and respected by its counterparts and even by the citizens of other countries.

But shaping a *Good Government* is by no means a finite task. It should in fact be viewed as a continuous process, and even more so considering the speed of change in today's world. No solution is definitive or permanent. Any country, having embarked on the Innovation process, should realize that it is also undertaking a process of ongoing change that requires a high degree of oversight, creativity, objectivity and capacity to adapt.

A *Good Government*, in addition to being effective, efficient, productive and democratic, must necessarily be honest and transparent and keep its own ethic intact, for it must inspire trust in its citizens and in those who come to it from abroad seeking either productive investment opportunities or cooperation in international policies.

In conclusion, Democracy requires *Good Government* in order to find expression, and a *Good Government* should spur that democracy in order to keep its status.

Chapter 2

World Trends in Government Innovation

In the new international coexistence, which is dynamic and demanding as well as competitive, governments at all levels must transform themselves in order to adapt to present and particularly future demands, for after all, everything has only just begun. This takes on special importance when the majority of countries have to fight to reduce poverty, and that fight is a priority.

The development of new market relations needs changes in the paradigms of relations between citizens and the Federal Government, but also between citizens and local authorities

The new practices of democracy compel governments to be more open and participatory, which entails convening and involving different stakeholders in society in planning, negotiation and decision-making processes. In view of the components and demands of globalization, these social sectors may also be external, which demands of governments greater openness and capacity for dialogue and, in fact, competitiveness even in interlocution, particularly when attracting foreign investment is involved.

Such demands have led governments to seriously question their operating structures and the role of bureaucracies, as well as to launch innovative processes of relations, communication and information; in a nutshell, of productivity and efficiency.

For years there was talk of administrative modernization to meet the need to improve government processes, whether to downsize the bureaucracy, optimize budgets or simplify methods and structures. In the late seventies Mexico went through just such a process, but in practice it was not very significant.

Needs detected in the past have now been compounded by the

new requirements resulting from globalization and the new democratic paradigm. B. Dillinger, one of the World Bank's foremost analysts, has pointed out that the development of new market relations needs changes in the paradigms of relations between citizens and the Federal Government, but also between citizens and local authorities.This involves a new concept, or perhaps the intensification of an innovative practice in the decentralization of States, currently a gargantuan task for many governments, with enormous backlogs. Certainly one of the paradoxes of globalization is strengthening local authorities and the impetus each can give to their development needs and goals. In view of their proximity to social and economic problems within their own spheres of action, local authorities can take new development trends into account.

A change of this nature implies a change in the most elementary practices in the relations between government and citizens stemming from citizens' manifest dissatisfaction with the laggardly response of their central and local administrations.

Globalization and expressions of citizen discontent evidenced governments' backwardness in the face of the momentous changes that had shaken the world. This became particularly obvious in the countries of Eastern Europe, which in just a few years have moved from a lack of freedoms and the most absolute centralism, to global competitiveness, democracy and the need for reform of the State. Another case in point is Latin America, which, with variations and understanding its own context, is experiencing the need to step up its innovation after decades marked by dictatorships, populist policies, indebtedness, inefficient governments, growth of government deficits, etc.; we could cite many reasons, but what is important is to appreciate that the change is actually taking place, at uneven speeds, but that is also a result of the forceful reality of the starting point.

The steps taken prior to the situation we are experiencing placed special emphasis on the privatization of state-owned enterprises, an important but insufficient measure, and on downsizing the bureaucracy, which in due course ends up in new personnel being hired; budget methods underwent changes and reforms, budgets by program arose in many countries, but the results were still far from satisfactory, to the extent that relations between government and citizens continued to deteriorate even further.

Here it is worth quoting a reflection by Gowher Rizvi from Harvard University, who has stated that:

> The challenges to governance cannot be solved by isolated experiments or mere tactical shifts in policies. Instead, they can be solved only through ceaseless and fundamental redesign of practice and policy that engages citizens and delivers services in completely new ways.

The changes that took place were superficial and therefore short-range. Perhaps it was not the right time, or the necessary tools were not in place.

It would be absurd to consider the changes that preceded the new paradigm of Quality Government useless; they should in fact be viewed as the forerunners of a reform which, in the final analysis, today amounts to a whole innovation process rapidly being carried out throughout the world, for the same reasons: providing better responses and bringing government closer to the people. It is a demand of global societies, the need for which had already been felt since the eighties, and it became a matter of urgency in the mid-nineties. Sometimes it is impossible to realize how much time elapses for an "idea" to be put into practice.

In light of the different paradigms contained within the overall paradigm of Good Government—a concept and practice toward which all current innovation is directed—we should take a look at similar concerns that arose in the sphere of private enterprise, apparently so far removed administratively, operationally and conceptually from public administration.

Reinventing Government

Here we should draw attention to various coinciding events that precipitated innovation in public administration. We cite them only

In talking about the public administration today there is a language that would have even caused laughter among theoreticians and analysts. This new language comes from private initiative. It is now beginning, not without difficulties, to permeate not only the traditional bureaucracy, but even civil society, where it is also encountering resistance

because of their importance, without attempting to present a historical sequence; they are coinciding events which turned out to be singularly important to the changes being undertaken.

In 1988 a group of top-level European companies came to the conclusion that they should make not only new but different efforts in favor of their own management and product quality. That year, 14 chemical, automotive, food and electronics corporations, and also an airline, created the European Foundation for Quality Management (EFQM), which was endorsed by the then European Commission. At present it has more than 800 members in 38 countries. That was how the European Model for Business Excellence came about, but above all it was a genuine transformation process for certain companies that sought to raise their competitiveness in the face of the drive by Japanese and US corporations. We draw attention to this fact because to a great extent it was a project that had a bearing, a few years later, on the European Union's debates on government quality and the need for innovation in its institutions.

A little earlier, Ronald Reagan in the United States and Margaret Thatcher in Great Britain launched attacks on their own countries' bureaucracies, with special emphasis on downsizing the government apparatus in order, supposedly, to thin it down and thus make it more efficient. The primary measures and concepts were also gradually applied in other parts of the world. The results, however, fell far short of expectations, for slimming down elephants made them neither more productive nor more efficient, and far less capable of providing service with quality, a word almost unheard of at the time when speaking of the public administration.

Perhaps the start of the innovative transformation being experienced should be situated in the mid-nineties. In the United States, Bill Clinton called for a crusade for *reinventing government*. The discussion at that time did not center on its size but on its operation and related problems, on ways to make it more efficient, and in particular, closer to citizens' needs. It was then that the word "quality" suddenly made its appearance in public administration theories and became a paradigm of Good Government.

Clinton offered to *put the customer first* (taking citizens to be customers) in giving them a professional, high quality, efficient, economical and ethical government.

Great Britain, for its part, following the attempts begun by Margaret Thatcher, placed special emphasis on the career civil service so as to restructure the very concept of bureaucracy and ensure that civil servants performed their duties with renewed responsibility and pride. This radical transformation involved a series of substantive changes in administrative procedures as a whole and in dealings between government and citizens.

Hafiz Pasha, Director of the United Nations Development Programme (UNDP) for Asia-Pacific, takes as a forerunner Total Quality Management (TQM), a method used in the United States as of World War II in the defense industry which years later reached local administrations in the United States, particularly in California, which is hardly surprising if we bear in mind the state's industrial power on a world scale.

TQM focused on measuring production-control variants and was adopted, modified and substantially expanded by the Japanese in their enterprises. Now, TQM is related especially to change in organizations in which quality and customer satisfaction are the basic driving forces.

There is a need to innovate at government level, but each country has its peculiarities, its internal realities and balance of power—we will not go into a discussion now about what should be and what is—and therefore its own time frames

In talking about the public administration today there is a language that would have even caused laughter among theoreticians and analysts. This new language comes from private initiative. It is now beginning, not without difficulties, to permeate not only the traditional bureaucracy, but even civil society, where it is also encountering resistance. Words like flexibility, productivity, competitiveness, quality and customers are now common currency in the countries that have taken the greatest strides in government innovation. Governments at the forefront in government innovation looked to private corporations and the consultancy firms that designed their methods, processes and systems so that they might contribute new ideas stemming from their own experiences, in order to reconcile or even compare them to public-administration theoreticians' ideas. Finally, the combined efforts and political will brought into play redefined concepts and suggested new possibilities, strategies and action lines, as well as critical paths.

Elaine C. Kamarck, of Harvard University's Center for Global

Innovation, summarizes the intertwinement that took place between public and private management as follows:

> The reform movement in the public sector was enhanced by the ideological triumph of market models in the private sector. But other changes in the private sector were also taking their toll on traditional bureaucracy. Most importantly, new information technology was changing the private sector so quickly that the experience of citizens in the private sector and in the public sector was increasingly divergent.

Government innovation and the objective of Quality Government are under way throughout the world, driven also by international agencies concerned over the needs and costs of economic and human development, as well as the fight against poverty, but above all spurred on by citizens and their demands in the new democratic paradigm.

The New *Requirements* of Government

Look at the service function of public administration, of governments, in the simplest possible way. Managing is costly. And the costs have to be commensurate with the benefits, especially in the case of public policy. These policies range from comprehensive support for marginalized groups or sectors or those in specific activities, to the way to carry out procedures for starting up a business or the facilities required to attract foreign direct investment. The more the application of those policies is efficient, higher quality and at a lower cost, the more they will benefit the customers to whom they are directed.

How can this be done?

There are no single formulas. As a matter of fact, part of the reason why some of the policies of multilateral or supranational agencies have failed is because at the time they did not take into account specificities, contexts, and historical and social realities that still prevail today. There is a need to innovate at government level, but each country has its peculiarities, its internal realities and balance of power—we will not go into a discussion now about what should be and what is—and therefore its own time frames. It may be said that applying new decentralizing practices in countries with a deeply-rooted local-government culture, such as Germany or the United States, is not the same as applying them in countries with a strong history of centralism. Machines cannot be forced, for that produces uneasiness and inefficiency in operators if they perceive that the machine might go out of control or... break down.

Perhaps a few elementary questions would be useful as a starting point: *Is my government fit enough to swim in the turbulent waters of the defense of human rights if it does not practice them internally? Can my government compete for foreign investment if its rules are unclear and it has a high degree of corruption? Can my government be efficient and address social demands if it is concerned about patronage and the results of the forthcoming elections?* Of course there are also positive questions, but both types should question what needs to be achieved, why and for what purpose.

It is most important to have a clear sense of past experiences, study their successes and failures, know what one has available, know what one wants with what one has and ultimately, have the certainty that there are sufficient tools to ensure that, on the basis of all of the above, what one seeks to achieve is both viable and better.

If one has a clear idea of the foregoing, the new trends can reveal basic paradigms and premises that coincide and can be turned into actions based on the realities of the starting point.

To effect changes in governments, the World Bank made the following recommendation in its 1997 annual report, *The State in a Changing World*:

> Government innovation means "subjecting state institutions to greater competition, to increase their efficiency. It means increasing the performance of state institutions, improving pay and incentives. And it means making the state more responsive to people's needs, bringing government closer to the people through broader participation and decentralization."

The New Paradigms

However, the new global reality, economic and financial exchanges, the speed of information, the new culture of information and communication technologies, and the expansive democracy we are living, with that uncontainable and growing social participation, have favored the emergence of new paradigms to be considered in any innovative process, in any governmental transformation.

The new paradigms

- Freedom
- Diversity
- Plurality
- Human Rights
- Care of the Environment
- Education
- Training
- Creativity
- Information and Transparency
- Trade Liberalization
- Globalization (financial, trade and labor)
- Productivity
- Competition
- Technological Development
- Ethics
- Good Government

The citizens included have freedom, those excluded do not, as they are unable to exercise it. Freedom only makes sense when it is practiced

This list is obviously not in order of importance; in the new reality, paradigms complement one another and provide each other with feedback; by being paradigms they are key objectives of development, as well as essential requirements for the latter.

Proper application of these paradigms should result in societies that are better served, with better development opportunities, with a sense of legality, with trust in their governments and their strategies—in which citizens also participate—with higher levels of education in keeping with the demands of the modern world and with the certainty of being heard and playing a participatory role.

1. Freedom

There is no full democracy without freedom, there is no human coexistence of respect and tolerance without freedom, there is no human development without freedom, there is no economic development without freedom, there is no consumption without freedom and without freedom, no possible choice. In poverty there is no freedom.

In the new civilization freedom is an unquestionable and indispensable paradigm. Only in freedom will nations be able to progress more rapidly along the paths of justice and well-being. Authoritarian models have been *totalitarianly* knocked down—by society. And that freedom, which increasing numbers of citizens are aware of, requires encouragement, understanding and appreciation. In the freedom of individuals lies their strength, multiplied in their group, in their community, in their nation. Free individuals move forward with greater clarity and determination; they always pose a threat to authoritarianism because they want the right to choose—from a government to a brand of shoes—and they know they have it.

> But freedom needs encouragement; it needs to develop in a climate in which it will be useful to the individual and to society, for what is the use of having freedom of choice if there is not much to choose from, if there are no options? Freedom can only come to fruition under the best conditions for development. Therein lies the paradox: freedom is essential to development, but without development it is extrinsically constrained.

In a climate of Freedom, Diversity and Plurality are intimately linked, and their practice enriches the notion of freedom and democratic life. Without plurality there cannot be an effective democracy

Freedom must also be fostered by the State; the government has to create the conditions for it to flower. It should implement policies of equality of opportunity in the sense of *inclusion*, as defined by Anthony Giddens, of the largest possible number of citizens, an *inclusion* that is ever growing. The citizens included have freedom, those excluded do not, as they are unable to exercise it. Freedom only makes sense when it is practiced.

2. Diversity

Today's societies the world over are increasingly complex. Migration flows, one of the features of the new civilization which will be compounded this century, redesign nations' profiles and demand new forms of coexistence.

The series of differences leads to points of agreement and develops their creative potential to the benefit of all. Acceptance of diversity, based on respect for differences, tolerance and solidarity, makes for a healthier environment, for it eliminates unjustified fears and enriches perception and knowledge of reality.

Minorities, the handicapped, senior citizens. All should play their part in an inclusive world, an inclusive environment.

Defending and respecting human rights constitute one of the pillars of democracy. And together with law enforcement they form an indissoluble whole

3. Plurality

A plurality of ideas enriches any nation culturally and ideologically. It creates better thinking tools for the operation and functioning of the State, and for internal and external relations society "pays attention" to the other's reasons. In the same way as for acceptance of Diversity, tolerance plays an essential role by allowing and respecting others' opinions and by living the climate of freedom in which they are expressed.

In a climate of Freedom, Diversity and Plurality are intimately linked, and their practice enriches the notion of freedom and democratic life. Without plurality there cannot be an effective democracy.

...what defines a humanist government is its conviction that respect for the individual is a supreme value that should be at the center of any public policy

4. Human Rights

Respect for and defense of human rights have been strengthened as a singular paradigm of the new civilization. Furthered with special emphasis in the seventies by US President James Carter, oversight of their application has gone beyond all borders and has fostered far-reaching international awareness against authoritarianism, abuse of power and tyranny.

Defending and respecting human rights constitute one of the pillars of democracy. And together with law enforcement they form an indissoluble whole.

There is no longer any cause for discussion as to whether or not the path to an efficient system of justice includes respect for human rights. Governments have the responsibility to give expeditious, timely attention to the complaints, conciliation proposals and recommendations issued by Public Agencies for the Protection and Defense of Human Rights when these are accepted and well-founded. Similarly, they should promote among public officials a sense of respect, protection and promotion of human rights, both for those allegedly responsible for crimes and for the victims and offended parties.

If the government's responsibility in this task is fundamental, the vigilant participation of an active society is of even greater importance. Defending and promoting human rights today is one of civil society's keenest, most admirable and most respectable responsibilities; therefore, genuinely democratic governments are proud of it and spur it on with all the means at their disposal, since what defines a humanist government is its conviction that respect for the individual is a supreme value that should be at the center of any public policy.

5. Care of the Environment

Care o f the environment is an unquestionable paradigm of sustainable development. We only have one planet; we must care for it for ourselves and for the new generations. This also involves caring for resources, from forests to water.

> Care or deterioration of the environment affects all individuals equally; we are all subject to the impacts of climate change, water shortages or the consequences of deforestation.
>
> The challenge facing governments is to ensure that the impact of human activities on the environment, in using natural resources, does not exceed nature's capacity to absorb the pollutants emitted and regenerate itself.

The true creator brings something really new to daily life, which turned out to be almost indispensable to his environment and his culture

Today we all share the ideas—urgencies—of halting and reversing the pollution of life-sustaining systems, that is, water, air and soil; halting and reversing the loss of natural capital; conserving ecosystems and biodiversity, and encouraging direct, committed participation by civil society in all these enormous and noble tasks.

The new environmental policy encourages society to recognize the value and importance of natural resources so that they are used rationally and in such a way that society itself can participate in the formulation and execution of public policies.

6. Education

The best and perhaps the only path toward Inclusion is Education. Less and less opportunities are available for those who have no education in a world that calls for increasingly specialized skills.

Education is the only tool that reveals to human beings their capabilities and possibilities, that teaches them about the world they belong to and the best way of fitting into it. Lack of education leads to exclusion, not only in the labor sphere but also in the social milieu.

Hence, a government that prides itself in valuing human beings, making them the hub and the reason for its policies, should assume that investment in Education is an imperative, but in addition, an investment in human capital, the most important and vital capital of all.

Education now requires a key adjective: it must be "quality" education; the inertial notion of Education must be left behind, as well as most of its traditional methods. It must break away from traditional patterns and count on the optimal support of technology and telecommunications, which also requires new basic and advanced training for educators at all levels.

The new educational task also demands a change of mentality in parents, teachers and government institutions in charge of education, which turns out to be a gargantuan task that moves forward against the clock and is not easy to carry out. All in all, there is a need for changes in ways of thinking, reverting inertias and deeply-rooted, decades-long tendencies of traditional and conventional practices.

7. Training

In globalization nothing is static, knowledge least of all. Faced with the need for constant innovation in industry and government, training has become an ongoing need; training updates knowledge and the tools acquired are gradually increased. Only continuous training at all levels makes it possible to adapt to new organization, management and production methods.

Training needs range from workers in factories to top executives and government officials. Society must be in a constant process of learning, with far-reaching goals and a vision of the future. Only training, together with quality education, prevents backwardness, strengthens competitiveness and productivity, and enhances development.

8. Creativity

For a long time it was believed that creativity was the prerogative of artists; talking of "creation" always meant the fine arts, the performers, the "creators." Today, Creativity is a paradigm for innovation and the constant challenges of a changing world; it has manifold manifestations in work environments and systems; its area of expression and development lies both in science and in private enterprise and public management. The creative process is always that which makes it possible to reach something new, or better, based on a reference. Mihaly Csikszentmihaly, undoubtedly one of the most important theoreticians and researchers of Creativity and its processes, has a particularly significant way of expressing the creative process in the face of the challenges of the new civilization:

> "...creativity does not happen inside people's heads, but in the interaction between a person's thoughts and a sociocultural context. It is a systematic rather than an individual phenomenon."

This statement helps to understand why Creativity should be encouraged by governments, just as private initiative has encouraged it. The true creator brings something really new to daily life, which turns out to be almost indispensable to her environment and her culture. It is time, then, for the creativity required: new ways of seeing things in order to create new patterns of work, of coexistence, of service, of efficiency, of productivity, of... everything.

Creativity is a paradigm of the modern State and efficient government. Indispensable in the private sector, for its ultimate aim is being more competitive and satisfying the customer. Indispensable also in any social organization. Nurturing it and encouraging it is an imperative of development today.

Similarly, governments need to raise their institutions' productivity to make them more effective and more efficient, thus achieving better distribution of their resources, goods or services in benefit of the population

9. Information and Transparency

Providing apt and timely information is a requirement for the accountability of an honest and responsible government. Having such information available is a demand of society, and when governments favor this it gives rise to trust and certainty.

Information and transparency substantially reduce any leeway for corruption, but also make it more detectable when it occurs.

Just as corporations must be clear in their accountability to their shareholders, governments have to be so to theirs: their shareholders being each and every one of the members of their population. Citizens have a right to information in general, otherwise their freedom would be endangered, but in particular they have a right to public information, to know what the government they elected democratically is doing, how it is doing it, how much it is spending and on what.

10. Trade Liberalization

The times of closed, protectionist markets are over. Myths such as "import substitution" are over with. No country is capable of producing, with quality, everything required by their inhabitants who, in addition, demand the right to choose.

Trade Liberalization is the modern world's "give and take"

paradigm. It boosts domestic and foreign investment, makes it necessary to produce better quality goods, strengthens economies, favors inventiveness, innovation and creativity, but also requires governments to have clear rules, compels them to compete for investment, creates jobs, and demands new concepts of honesty and transparency in administrations.

11. Globalization

The trade, financial and labor Globalization is a complex and continuous process, yet uncurbed, although it takes on different speeds and rates depending on countries' level of development and even different population sectors in each of them. However, big business and the big corporations are globalized. It should be borne in mind that Globalization is not only exchange, but also presence; that is why the world economy is increasingly integrated and its integration should be spurred on.

There has been persistent talk about the damage caused by capital flows at a given time in a country, but it is also true that such flows can contribute to economic growth if they take place under clear rules and macroeconomic certainty.

12. Productivity

This is the paradigm of efficiency and quality. It is applicable to corporations and to federal, local and municipal governments. High productivity would be futile if it were not coupled with quality. Productivity means doing more with less; it involves the optimization of all available resources through effective systems in order to achieve efficiency and savings.

Productivity in corporations requires inventiveness and teamwork. Why should it not be applied to governments?

For there to be Productivity there also has to be a market; it

That capacity for competition among countries is attributable to the synergy generated by efficiency in the relations between government, private sector and society, which is capable of crossing borders

would be absurd to have high productivity and a restricted market, for in that case productivity would be very costly.

Similarly, governments need to raise their institutions' productivity to make them more effective and more efficient, thus achieving better distribution of their resources, goods or services in benefit of the population.

Productivity requires continuously-trained, innovative, creative personnel. To involve human beings in methods and systems of productivity is also to encourage their imagination, as well as appreciation and valuing of their work.

With the paradigms of the new civilization it should be understood that a quality job that relies on the imagination and knowledge of the person performing it, is an essential condition for it to be pleasant, so to speak, and not just a way of "earning one's living."

13. Competition

Greater encouragement of quality and options of freedom in consumption make creativity and productivity obligatory. A term that hardly had any meaning in the commercial and industrial world, Competition was taken for granted, but its prime importance in day-to-day life had not been appreciated; now, however, it also embraces the fields of public administration.

One of the main challenges facing humankind is poverty reduction. Poverty will not be able to diminish unless there is economic growth, and this requires both a vigorous, active private sector and a government that promotes it. Economic growth needs to take root in society and in the thrust of public policies. Society, government and enterprise need to work in harmony to achieve that growth.

And there is another important factor in competition which before seemed dispensable and which today has a new and real dimension: companies' social presence. It is not enough to offer good products, a company also has to have a good image: it also competes in that area, for enterprises, corporations, are monitored by society and approved of or disqualified accordingly.

In 1987 the American Council on Competitiveness defined Competitiveness as ""The degree to which a nation can, under free and fair market conditions, produce goods and services that meet fair tests in international markets while simultaneously maintaining or expanding the real income of its citizens." This definition, which obviously covers a macroeconomic concept, was adapted for its microeconomic expression by Thomas Mosgaller, President of the American Society for Quality (ASQ):

> The degree to which a firm can, under free and fair market conditions, produce goods and services that meet consumer tests in its chosen markets, while simultaneously maintaining or expanding the real income of its stakeholder owners.

Globalization offers benefits, but it also has its costs, and therefore among the priorities in steering through it with the greatest social benefit possible, technological development is as important as institution-building and the development of human capital

Both definitions can be adapted to government performance, which should offer services and attention to customers with a high level of quality, in such a way that both government officials and customers are satisfied. In this case, Competitiveness means efficiency. A product or service offered by the government can have quality and reach citizens through expeditious, efficient methods, which in other circumstances or milieus would be "competitive", and leave them satisfied. But also the institution that provides or offers them is highly valued by customers, it is rewarded with "appreciation." The members of the institution, like those of private enterprise, are remunerated by "public recognition." And somehow it is also legitimate to talk about "competition" among public institutions, simply because some provide better service quality than others; in the modern administration, institutions "compete" to be better: in their customer service, in their web pages, in the speed of their procedures, etc. All of that requires competition, productivity and quality. Furthermore, countries become competitive to the extent that they offer the global world better qualities, advantages, appropriate regulation, legality, etc. in attracting productive foreign investment. That capacity for competition among countries is attributable to the synergy generated by efficiency in the relations between government, private sector and society, which is capable of crossing borders.

14. Technological Development

Cornerstone of all competitiveness and human well-being. The countries with the most advanced technological development are the most prosperous at world level. It transcends the limits of the specific to make itself felt in day-to-day life.

Scientific and technological development is an important factor that contributes to sustained economic development. No country has become well established in modern growth without significantly increasing its national capacity to develop scientific research and create its own technological innovation.

It is of the utmost importance to grant tax incentives to research and technological development, supported by corporations. This policy has begun to reap its benefits, although obviously the most important ones will be appreciated in the medium and long terms. This has been a momentous political decision with a vision of the future. Even though it is not a new practice in the developed countries, it is beginning to permeate satisfactorily in countries with medium and low levels of development.

Globalization offers benefits, but it also has its costs, and therefore among the priorities in steering through it with the greatest social benefit possible, technological development is as important as institution-building and the development of human capital.

15. Ethics

In an article by Jannik Lindbaek, Ethics is understood as a social responsibility for coexistence by all sectors.

Lindbaek says that in the industrialized world, competition for the best people is very tough, and feeling that one is working for a company that pays attention to social values is rapidly becoming a powerful motivating force and an important factor in the struggle to feature among the best persons.

If this is true, we must assume that we can talk about natural persons and legal persons. One must be a good person in the community, but it is also important to be a good corporate person or a good government person. That can only be achieved with an ethic of commitment to others in order to have a positive influence on their development. An enterprise has the responsibility to practice an ethic in keeping with the social milieu in which it develops and with society's most elementary needs; it is not in vain, for example, that the model of the European Foundation for Quality Management (EFQM) includes Social Responsibility Results among its assessment criteria.

It is up to the government to practice ethics of responsibility, well-being, inclusion, facilitation of development, without corruption, patronage or favoritism and with information and transparency.

It is up to social groups to practice ethics of solidarity, inclusion, respect for differences, and tolerance.

And such ethics are spreading across the world at a fast pace in a much more conscious manner in practice, not as a conduct that was assumed to be obvious and even unnecessary.

16. Good Government

This singular paradigm has been left until the end because of its importance and value at all levels of human development and economic growth. Without Good Government the efforts and capabilities of society and private initiative are not put to good use.

Trends in Government Innovation

Every country that has embarked on government innovation or reinvention has had its priorities and its emphasis on diverse aspects.

Singapore, for example, has opted for administrative redesign in order to do more with the same money, which for the country means combining a Government that Costs Less with a Quality Government. This has led to government agencies and the Ministry of Finance seeing themselves as collaborators doing the best for the

Practices of government innovation, restructuring or reinventing governments have spread throughout the world: they happen both in the central government of Canada and in its provinces; in Germany, Korea, Japan, Spain and so on, but they have always had as a starter motor citizen demands which have largely arisen as a result of the new forms of democracy

country. Their fundamental premise in practice is always to maintain fiscal stability.

New Zealand, a country that has made astonishing progress in reinventing government in less than a decade, has linked budget design to performance rating and results while focusing on cost reduction, raising government productivity and transparency in the use of resources, in addition to providing citizens with information.

So that budget application is more useful and promotes efficiency in meeting objectives, New Zealand sets performance goals, earmarks resources according to priorities, invests in policy analysis to design the best implementations, and has rebuilt institutional capacity to translate those resources and implementations into the results citizens want.

France has a tradition of having endowed itself with a high-level public function, competent, attractive to the best and impartial, which, due to its professionalism, does not yield to private interests and pressure groups. Its strength has been a successful career civil service which, in the opinion of some theoreticians, has been declining in recent years.

It embarked on a modernization of government methods, and first of all, management of public spending by means of multi-annual financing, adopted in the year 2000, a practice also applied previously by Hungary.

Chile is undoubtedly a pioneering country in government innovation in Latin America. In 1997 it designed the Program "Service Quality and Citizen Participation," based on recognition of the fact that quality public management is an essential instrument for the country's development. Since then it has been assumed that "The existence of an effective State, heedful of the population's needs, is vital to long-term well-being and prosperity."

During the eighties Australia embarked on a process of government restructuring that continues to date, for it is assumed to be a constant task with ongoing innovations. The government restructuring covers the fields of institutions' own internal organization, the career civil service and administrative and operative practices in government entities. But it has also placed special importance on government information and its scrutiny by Parliament and citizens.

Practices of government innovation, restructuring or reinventing governments have spread throughout the world: they happen both in the central government of Canada and in its provinces; in Germany, Korea, Japan, Spain and so on, but they have always had as a starter motor citizen demands which have largely arisen as a result of the new forms of democracy.

In its document *Public Sector Modernization: Changing Organizational Structures*, of October 2003, the Organisation for Economic Co-operation and Development (OECD) asked itself ***Why do governments change their work structures?*** And it indicated eight substantive points as basic answers.

1. Most government re-organizations respond to immediate concerns, both internal and external. Internal reasons can be political or aimed at improving general management processes and culture for better implementation of public policies.
2. External pressures can be very varied, from trade issues to the need to confront terrorism, as has happened in many countries after September 11, 2001.
3. In some cases reorganization can be used as a substitute for making hard choices about management and priorities. It depends on the circumstances.

In the longer term, a number of underlying social trends influence the way governments organize how they work. These include:

4. **Diversification:** The move towards measuring and controlling output, rather than input and processes, increases the tendency towards organizational diversity.
5. **Specialization:** There is an increasing need for specialized skills as society and government become more complex, and as governments are required to provide more individualized services to citizens.
6. **Incentives:** There is a new tendency to apply to government organizations the thinking derived from economics on the way incentives of different kinds influence people's behavior. This has meant that attempts to change the public service culture increasingly include organizational change.

7. **Building of trust:** Governments are genuinely concerned about recovering and even building a renewed trust by citizens in institutions and decision-making; society's trust is an essential tool in applying organizational changes and implementing new policies.
8. **Accountability:** This is a growing need in governments before societies. This trend leads to a clearer control of results, over and above control of processes, and facilitates identification of those responsible for actions, beyond a mere generalization of "the bureaucracy."

Guido Bertucci, Director of the Division for Public Economics and Public Administration of the Department of Economic and Social Affairs of the UN, has defined four world trends, or four priority approaches, in accordance with worldwide diversity, in trends in government innovation and quality.

The first of these is ***Construction or reconstruction of the State***; construction is the path followed by African nations, especially those with prolonged internal and also international conflicts; and reconstruction, fairly successful over time, is the path chosen by various Eastern European countries in their difficult transition toward democratic regimes.

The second is ***Modernization of the State***, a challenge which in his view affects all countries and is related to "the adaptation and improvement of administrative structures, managerial capabilities, financial management and technological adequacy."

The third trend is ***Reconfiguration of the role of the State***. This trend is mainly determined by the changes that have arisen as a consequence of globalization. It is compelling a number of governments to rethink public policies, continually assess their performance in light of citizen demands and global requirements, and consider a reengineering of government processes and new ways to train public officials.

And finally the fourth is ***Revitalization of democracy***, a consequence of making democracy more meaningful and participatory, thus providing people with greater opportunities to participate in policy design.

As a whole, successful experiences of government innovation both in Europe and in the United States, although we could also include here processes in which substantive progress has been made in some Latin American countries, have substantially centered on the following points:

- Conceiving the State as a linking entity for stakeholders and partners from very diverse origins within the internal and external plurality and diversity.
- Administrative and government decentralization, which implies devolving more power to local governments and even to initiatives of organized society.
- Reconsidering and reassessing government programs and their budgets. Optimization of spending and its proper application is a demand not only of an economic nature, but also of democratic life.
- Promoting quality education and training at all levels.
- Broadening the capacity for dialogue with civil society with full respect for diversity and plurality.
- Restructuring internal methods and processes with a view to simplification.
- Assessing service quality.
- Making substantial changes in regulations to make them more accessible and understandable at all levels of the administration, particularly those that directly affect ordinary citizens.
- Encourage the creative and innovative capabilities of public servants. Any adjustments and changes undertaken will have a long learning curve and new adjustments will always be necessary in a rapidly changing world.

Quality is a universal concept that transcends economics, politics, relationships with family, friends, colleagues, nations and also qualitative considerations about ourselves. It is at the heart of what we are and what we do

The above premises are put into practice within a general framework of reform of the State which could be its readjustment, modernization or transformation. At the same time, in internal aspects, they are subject to various assessment and quality certification models.

Since the year 2000 the European Union has been using the Common Assessment Framework (CAF) to support the initial phases of development of the culture of quality. This instrument is based on the model of the EFQM which, as pointed out earlier, has an entirely entrepreneurial origin. The CAF model focuses on three basic aims:

To be effective it is necessary to develop in an atmosphere of democracy and freedom, for only thus can the needs of the social sectors be clearly known and the forms of response better identified

- Serving as an introductory tool for public officials in initial assessments.
- Serving as a bridge between the different models and methodologies used in public administration quality management in the different countries of the EU.
- Allowing the introduction of referential comparison studies between public-sector organizations.

To strengthen the application of CAF various prizes for innovation and quality have been created and its application has extended to the countries of Eastern Europe that recently acceded to the European Union.

In the United States the model is based especially on the Malcolm Baldridge Quality Award and on Osborne and Gabler's ideas of "reinvention", who believe that government should center on the good performance of the organization and on raising productivity through a more effective use of funds. This concept combines with the precepts of TQM, which is essentially related to change in organizations, where quality and customer satisfaction are the basic motives, and which when applied to government should seek greater efficiency by being more results-oriented.

Furthermore, international standards such as ISO 9000 have also been established, which focus on the function of quality and its maintenance. This standard represents the minimum of quality that any customer should expect. It focuses on procedures and processes and on its requirement of an infrastructure based on relevant documents. Its procedures have minimal complexity.

In applying ISO 9000 to governments, the expected results should include:

- Better service to citizens
- More transparent administration
- Lower service costs by means of efficient administration
- Sound communication and information systems
- Reinvigorated organization
- More actions centering on the good of the citizen

Trevor Smith, Chairman of the ISO TC176 Technical Committee and a top Kodak executive, has stated that *"Quality is a universal concept that transcends economics, politics, relationships with family, friends, colleagues, nations and also qualitative considerations about ourselves. It is at the heart of what we are and what we do"*. Viewed thus, quality is a need and a responsibility, but also a goal to be aspired to.

Government innovation can be set in motion unilaterally, but it would be difficult for it to attain positive results unless it obtains feedback from the other stakeholders and social sectors, for which purpose democratic communication is an irreplaceable factor

If we take as a basis the experiences of government innovation based on a sense of quality carried out in the European Union and the United States, and add to them the requirements and recommendations of standard ISO 9000, we can arrive at a set of basic action lines that determine Quality Government:

- Achieving effectiveness

Provide an appropriate, timely response to social needs and those of other productive stakeholders. The government must attain the greatest benefits for the different social sectors with the application of its policies.

- Achieving efficiency

Use available resources to the utmost, create new ones that may be necessary, at acceptable costs, in order to respond to the demands of the various social sectors, and have flexible methods and systems capable of continuously readapting to new needs.

- Satisfying the customer

The government should operate with standards of efficiency and effectiveness, with a high level of productivity, in applying its policies and supplying the goods and services it is responsible for, seeking always to leave the customer satisfied.

- Achieving honesty

Only an Honest and Transparent Government can work in favor of efficiency, effectiveness and quality. Corruption obstructs and deviates public policies and discourages society.

But these basic lines should be in synchrony with a set of components of the paradigms of what could be considered, as mentioned earlier, Expanding Democracy.

To be effective it is necessary to develop in an atmosphere of democracy and freedom, for only thus can the needs of the social sectors be clearly known and the forms of response better identified. Civil society, social organizations, the private sector, etc. require, demand, urge, and only a democratic government that respects freedoms is capable of listening and acting responsibly. An effective government is close to the people and considers the human person the origin and purpose of its work.

To be efficient, a government has to be responsible, creative and have the capacity to optimize its resources of all kinds (economic, human, technological, etc.), which also implies applying the paradigms of Productivity and Competition, and even Technological Development. The government has to be efficient to do what is best: timely responses, respect for citizens' rights and freedoms, obtaining resources, facilitating services, and encouraging the imagination, creativity and productivity of the social sectors.

Honesty is a fundamental paradigm which is of course linked to Ethics; without them there is corruption, inefficiency, lack of willpower, squandering of resources, etc.

When a government achieves the aforementioned basic lines of action, plus those its own reality indicates, it becomes a Quality Government in two ways. First of all, it provides its clients with quality services: citizens are satisfied with it and they trust it. Second is the quality of life and work within institutions, for achieving benefits outward implies having possibilities for innovation, recognition, incentives for creativity and son on, within.

Consequently, a Quality Government focuses particularly on results whose ultimate consequences are better quality of life for citizens and at the same time, the best means of using the resources of all social sectors.

To provide quality service in its own territory —and which is also recognized abroad— a government should itself have quality.

Chapter 3

Good Government Agenda in Mexico

It is worth beginning with a reflection by President Vicente Fox:

> Over the past 20 years, the idea and practice of governance have changed radically in the global context. The path of this evolution is clear and irreversible: distinctive forms of participatory democracy are replacing the previous model. Government leaders the world over are incorporating democratic ideals into the manner in which their governments serve citizens.

Today many countries are lagging behind as a result of governments that had no mobility, that were caught up in an unworkable model; coping with modernization processes and the demands of globalization is one of their most important challenges

Mexico remained mired in backwardness for many years. The efficiency and transparency of government practices gradually became stagnant. The existence of a one-party system curbed the natural movement leading to the implementation of substantive and in-depth improvements.

Today many countries are lagging behind as a result of governments that had no mobility, that were caught up in an unworkable model; coping with modernization processes and the demands of globalization is one of their most important challenges.

In Mexico the inertia is being broken. The government is making a dual effort. Without stopping daily tasks and attention to national urgencies, methods, structures and procedures are being changed so as to give citizens the responsive, efficient, Honest and Transparent Government they demand.

Now it is working with another model, under other premises,

although it should be understood that innovative coordinated work changes require the participation of both institutions and citizens.

An important movement has been undertaken which seeks to dismantle archaic, opaque systems in order to pave the way for a new paradigm of democratic government based on Innovation and Quality.

A different, participatory government is required, one that consults society on its needs and priorities in order to turn them into government policies and also that constantly submits itself to rigorous accountability, not only as regards the honest and transparent use of resources, but also the efficiency and quality with which they are applied

What Is Needed for Good Government?

In order for President Fox's Administration to fulfill its responsibility to respond to society's demands and expectations, it was necessary to have a Good Government capable of radically transforming traditional management systems.

This concept does not refer to a government whose transformation is based upon gradual improvement, but one that can bring about in-depth changes to make up for lost time and has sufficient response capacity to deal promptly with society's needs.

Despite this evident urgency for change, the challenge of shaping a Good Government is not a task that can be done by decree or by imitating a world trend, rather it demands conscientious hard work and requires, above all, motivating new attitudes and behaviors in both public servants and citizens.

A different, participatory government is required, one that consults society on its needs and priorities in order to turn them into government policies and also that constantly submits itself to rigorous accountability, not only as regards the honest and transparent use of resources, but also the efficiency and quality with which they are applied.

The change needs a strategic, competitive government that sets social priorities democratically and invests its resources efficiently; a responsive, flexible government capable of seizing opportunities, dealing with problems and adapting to circumstances quickly and effectively.

In short, today Mexico needs a world-class, innovative, total quality government that places the satisfaction of society's needs and expectations at the center of government affairs.

To achieve this, efforts are being made on two fronts contained in the Innovation and Quality Model. On one hand, the innovation that makes it possible to devise new ways of doing things, and on the other, the total quality that makes it possible to improve and optimize what has been done well and has shown itself to produce added value for society.

Through innovation, the aim is to replace bureaucratic systems with enterprising systems that transform public organizations into elements of improvement and development by means of a radical cultural change that favors the evolution of traditional approaches toward visionary, forward-looking approaches to find solutions to major national problems.

Changing the government's course of action, a task on which President Fox's Administration is set, will only be fully possible if we succeed in encouraging all public servants to work in a single direction, for which purpose it is necessary to leave behind lines of command based on control, which inhibit creativity and innovation, and pave the way for schemes that empower and foster teamwork.

A government of genuinely democratic origin has placed priority on the fight against corruption at all levels; on furthering the redesign of the Federal Public Administration, the improvement of processes and the quality of public actions; and on achieving society's participation in a setting of close coordination between the three levels of government, in order to build a new culture of public affairs. President Fox's Administration is fully aware that the fight against corruption is not just a question of laws, but of fostering attitudes, of shaping values, of respect for principles and of quality in education.

A government of genuinely democratic origin has placed priority on the fight against corruption at all levels; on furthering the redesign of the Federal Public Administration, the improvement of processes and the quality of public actions; and on achieving society's participation in a setting of close coordination between the three levels of government, in order to build a new culture of public affairs

Presidential Agenda for Good Government

There is a long-term outlook in the government that constantly creates new schemes. Today we have a "Presidential Agenda for Good Government" at the service of citizens.

In the area of Good Government, the current administration's work agenda has been based on the following action lines:

1. **An Honest and Transparent Government** to recover society's trust in its government.

2. **A Professional Government** that has the best men and women in public service, so as to guarantee that the public administration moves on to the next six-year term with the least disruption and maximum effectiveness, and assuring that, being politically neutral, it becomes a strategic factor in the country's competitiveness.

3. **A Quality Government** that meets, or even surpasses, citizens' expectations in the services provided to them.

4. **A Digital Government** to make it possible for citizens—from the comfort of their homes or offices, or from an e-Mexico Digital Community Center, favoring efficiency and the value of time—to obtain government information and have access to the services it provides.

5. **A Government with Regulatory Improvement** that guarantees that the citizenry and public servants carry out procedures and processes easily, securely, quickly and at a low cost.

6. **A Government that Costs Less** to reduce spending that does not add value and thus provide society with greater benefits.

1. An Honest and Transparent Government

Undoubtedly one of the population's most deeply-felt demands in achieving democratic change was the fight against corruption. Mexicans were sick and tired of promises and more promises in that regard while seeing how one six-year term after another, corruption continued to reign in the country, to the extent—and we have to acknowledge it shamefully—that government corruption became one of Mexico's distinctive features in the world.

Blocking corruption's path is not an easy task, nor can it be done quickly; sometimes, where some doors are closed, small windows open; neither are laws, rules or regulations sufficient; the most important thing is having public officials with a new mentality of service, with a new vision of their commitment and responsibility to society, with a sense of professional pride in the job they perform and the privilege it means to work in the Government. Thus, it is necessary to achieve changes in mentality and have officials with an ethic of respect, honesty and commitment.

President Fox has evidenced his determination to build a better government that responds to society's needs. There is still a long way to go. At times the result of the task is not appreciated in many areas because the work is carried out from the foundations, but with impetus, in order to make this an exemplary administration governed by a strict code of ethics and conduct.

At times the result of the task is not appreciated in many areas because the work is carried out from the foundations, but with impetus, in order to make this an exemplary administration governed by a strict code of ethics and conduct

The Fight against Corruption

A corrupt society, with corrupt governments, cannot progress. Corruption provokes mistrust in citizens and in investors. The fight against corruption is therefore a priority item on President Fox's Good Government Agenda.

Maintaining trust in the government and in the public sector's decision-making is a crucial aspect for investors' confidence and economic growth. However, as the public sector works more and more closely with businesspeople, many forms of conflict of interest can arise among officials with regard to their private interests and their public responsibilities, which means that special attention is required in these processes and situations so as to avoid corruption. It is no coincidence that the Organisation for Economic Co-operation and Development (OECD) has published a document containing a series of recommendations to prevent this type of situations in the governments of its member countries.

On tackling corruption, ineffectiveness and lack of quality in public management, it is necessary to attack problems at the root and be clear as to what provokes this corruption. The current government is carrying out an ongoing analysis of the most frequent types of conduct

It should be emphasized that on December 1, 2000, during the event held in the National Auditorium, President Fox announced the establishment of a Code of Ethics for all public officials, which was assumed that very day by the members of the Cabinet and the extended Cabinet

This was an unprecedented act in Mexico's public administration. To combat corruption the first thing that is needed is honest officials and public servants at all levels who share one same set of moral values of commitment and service to society

that lead to infringement of the legal order within institutions. It was found that there was a complex set of regulations, lack of staff training, systems and procedures lacking in standards of both quality and effectiveness. It was also found that deeply-rooted customs and impunity encourage the proliferation of corruption and that the absence of transparent, truthful information provided to society prevents citizens from demanding their rights.

Improved public management and the honest and effective performance of those who work in it require systemic, consistent efforts by the population and its authorities, ranging from education in the family and in the early school years, to recognition and reward for those who devote their lives to community service, including hiring, selection and development of personnel, as well as administrative and process simplification and the active and continuous participation of society.

Due precisely to the above and in view of the fact that in the year 2000 the demand to eliminate corruption in the Federal Government became generalized among the citizenry, a systematic program was implemented in this regard for the first time which integrally combined the efforts of the Federal Public Administration's institutions.

It should be emphasized that on December 1, 2000, during the event held in the National Auditorium, President Fox announced the establishment of a Code of Ethics for all public officials, which was assumed that very day by the members of the Cabinet and the extended Cabinet.

This was an unprecedented act in Mexico's public administration. To combat corruption the first thing that is needed is honest officials and public servants at all levels who share one same set of moral values of commitment and service to society.

Code of Ethics

Research on successful governments has shown that they have conducted themselves in line with strict codes of public ethics and moral values. Absence of corruption (impunity) has been an evident sign in the eyes of the citizens. This includes top officials in government, for they have avoided succumbing to the temptations of power.

In Mexican society, the demand for honest officials, for doing away with government corruption and impunity was a constant for many years which was highlighted in the presidential campaign prior to the 2000 elections.

As has already been pointed out, on the very day he took office President Vicente Fox made the members of his Cabinet and his closest collaborators commit themselves to a Code of Ethics; it is important to repeat that never before had anything similar ever taken place with an administration. The Code of Ethics calls for:

- **Seeking the common good.** Public service is the patrimony of all Mexicans, and it is only justified and legitimized when the common good is sought over and above private interests.
- **Integrity of public officials.** Actions and words should be honest and worthy of credibility, always fostering a culture of trust and truth.
- **Honesty.** A public post is not for obtaining personal gains; it is not ethical to accept privileges from individuals or organizations that imply failing to fulfill responsibilities for the common good.
- **Impartiality.** Officials should not unduly privilege individuals or organizations.
- **Justice.** Every official should set an example of abiding by and observing the law.
- **Transparency.** Society has the right to know government information with no other limit than the public interest and individuals' right of privacy as established by law.
- **Accountability.** Participating in the continuous improvement of government administration, holding as fundamental principles the optimization of resources and accountability.
- **Cultural and environmental setting.** Putting into practice a clear will of understanding, respect and defense of the country's cultural and environmental setting.
- **Generosity.** Acting always with special sensitivity, commitment and concern for children, senior citizens, our ethnic groups and in general all those who have least.
- **Leadership.** Each official should promote and support these commitments with his or her personal example.

On April 22, 2002 the National Program for the Fight against Corruption and Promotion of Transparency and Administrative Development was published in the Official Gazette of the Federation and set in motion

The Program is a clear manifestation of the unwavering commitment to preventing acts of corruption by means of an ethic of service and transparent and simple programs, systems and procedures as well as properly qualified personnel

A government that does not base its actions on higher, universal values shared by the majority of public servants is doomed not to transcend.

On December 4, 2000, just three days after he took office, President Fox issued the decision on the creation of the Inter-Ministerial Commission for Transparency and the Fight against Corruption (CITCC). It is most important to stress that this decision was the first one issued by President Fox, which pointed up his determination and commitment in the fight against corruption.

This Commission, of a permanent nature, and in whose sessions the President of the Republic always participates, has made public twenty decisions:

1. Implementation of a program of recognition of integrity for public servants.
2. Dissemination of public information on the Internet, in anticipation of the Law on Transparency and Access to Public Government Information.
3. Implementation of a program of internal regulatory improvement.
4. Implementation of the Simulated Customer strategy.
5. Drafting and dissemination of a code of conduct.
6. Implementation of a training program in values.
7. Implementation of rigorous personnel selection mechanisms.
8. Incorporation of a set of values in the personnel selection system.
9. Review of salaries in critical areas.
10. Dissemination of the National Program for the Fight Against Corruption and Promotion of Transparency and Administrative Development (PNCTDA) results.
11. Dissemination of prior bidding conditions.
12. External participation in the review of prior bidding conditions.
13. Carrying out bidding processes electronically.
14. Assessment of users of critical processes.
15. Fulfillment of commitments for transparency.
16. Improvement of citizen service and attention standards.
17. Carrying out of procedures and services electronically.

18. Creation of the Subcommittee on Access to Public Government Information.
19. Creation of the Subcommittee on Improvement of Indices of Perception of Corruption and Good Government.
20. Implement the necessary measures to address recommendations of the "Convention on Combating Bribery of Foreign Public Officials" sponsored by the OECD.

By the year 2003, 155 Federal Government institutions had Programs for Transparency and the Fight against Corruption; in them, more than 3,000 actions of improvement are applied to 292 processes and 550 areas defined as critical, with an impact on more than 770 possible types of irregular conduct

Furthermore, on April 22, 2002 the National Program for the Fight against Corruption and Promotion of Transparency and Administrative Development was published in the Official Gazette of the Federation and set in motion.

The Program is a clear manifestation of the unwavering commitment to preventing acts of corruption by means of an ethic of service and transparent and simple programs, systems and procedures as well as properly qualified personnel. But it also underscores the government's full responsibility to punish illicit acts that should not be tolerated, but always within the legal framework governing the authority's role. A reliable and transparent Federal Public Administration is built by applying the law and sanctioning guilty parties.

By the year 2003, 155 Federal Government institutions had Programs for Transparency and the Fight against Corruption; in them, more than 3,000 actions of improvement are applied to 292 processes and 550 areas defined as critical, with an impact on more than 770 possible types of irregular conduct.

By the year 2004, 161 Federal Government institutions had Programs for Transparency and the Fight against Corruption; in them, more than 4,000 actions of improvement are applied to 378 processes and 655 areas defined as critical, with an impact on more than 940 possible types of irregular conduct.

Furthermore, 75 percent progress has been achieved in compliance with the decisions issued on the matter by the Inter-Ministerial Commission for Transparency and the Fight against Corruption.

As of 2003, assessment of the Operative Programs of Transparency and the Fight against Corruption is carried out through the Transparency Follow-up Indicator (IST), which comprehensively evaluates the efforts made by institutions in their transparency and anti-corruption tasks. This indicator has made it possible to establish presidential goals for the Honest and Transparent Government action line.

Efforts in this action line have concentrated on:

1. Improving processes and public services.
2. Training public servants.
3. Establishing better control systems.
4. Applying sanctions for irregular conduct.
5. Providing public management with quality and transparency.
6. Reaching agreements with society and promoting a new social culture of combating corruption.

Social Actions for Combating Corruption

Initially, corruption has been combated by measuring it. Thus, the studies by Transparencia Mexicana: "National Survey on Corruption and Good Government 2001" and ITSM: "Government-Corporate Corruption in Mexico. Perspective of the Private Sector" were carried out.

Thirty-two collaboration agreements were signed with organizations of society to further actions in favor of transparency, and very varied mass communication actions are being carried out, including short films. Also, in the area of instilling values, the subject Ethics, Social Responsibility and Transparency, which is taught at various universities, was prepared with the National Association of Universities and Institutes of Higher Education (ANUIES), the Ministry of Public Education (SEP) and experts in the matter.

The risks of corruption have been reduced and the transparency of information and public management have improved. It should be highlighted that among the results of the operative programs for Transparency and the Fight against Corruption (POTCC), from 117 participating institutions in 2001, in 2004 the total reached 161.

With regard to the establishment of liabilities, in 2004 more than 3,700 administrative sanctions were applied to 2,944 public servants, figures 58.1 and 59.3 percent lower than in 2002.

Simulated Customer Program

By means of this strategy, in the 2001–2003 triennium the Ministry of Public Administration carried out 2,360 verifications in the offices and entities of the Federal Public Administration. By 2003 it had effected 929 actions of verification of procedures and services of greatest impact on the population.

During the first three years of the administration 76 special simulated customer operations were carried out in which 87 administrative suits were filed, involving 47 public servants in administrative proceedings.

Citizens' demand for access to information and transparency in the management of public affairs and the political will to satisfy it evidenced by President Fox's administration created favorable conditions for activating accountability mechanisms that are more effective than elections

Federal Law on Transparency and Access to Public Government Information (LFTAIPG)

In order to allow corruption no leeway, it is essential for citizens to know in detail what the government is doing, how it is applying public funds, and also who its members are in all the agencies and who has the capacity for decision or management. Undoubtedly one of the best ways of guaranteeing accountability and honesty is precisely the free flow of information.

> President Fox assumed a fundamental premise in democracy: Making public what essentially is public.

Transparency and access to information are two mechanisms that promote accountability, and both have a direct bearing on the "good government" of the democratic system, for they contribute to ensuring that a multiplicity of stakeholders—chiefly non-governmental organizations, civil society, academia and even the Branches of Government—reduce the costs associated with supervising and overseeing the exercise of power. Likewise, transparency and access to public government information favor the creation of communication channels between State institutions and society, which enable citizens to carry out a critical, well-informed and periodic scrutiny of the exercise of government. Citizens' demand for access to information and transparency in the management

The right of access to information, guaranteed by means of this legislation, contributes to Mexico's progress in the consolidation of a more democratic government, for it enables citizens at all times to avail themselves of public information in possession of the government

of public affairs and the political will to satisfy it evidenced by President Fox's administration created favorable conditions for activating accountability mechanisms that are more effective than elections. And they are more effective because at any time—not every three or six years—citizens can carry out a critical scrutiny of the performance of elected representatives and appointed authorities. This type of accountability is indispensable in a government that seeks to consolidate democracy as a form of government, since it enables the citizenry to analyze government actions and put a stop to any possible abuse of power.

> Today all citizens have a weapon in the fight against corruption and impunity and a means to ensure that government institutions comply with the provisions of the new Federal Law on Transparency and Access to Public Government Information, a long-standing citizen wish, which seeks to recover citizens' trust in their government, among other things, through transparency in information on social programs and on application of public spending.

The LFTAIPG was unanimously approved by the Congress of the Union and enacted on June 12, 2002. As a result, it is now obligatory to make available public information on budgets, goals, officials' salaries, acquisitions and contracting of services. The information available is also a means of rendering accounts in an ongoing manner.

Twenty-five years had to elapse before the right to information set forth in Articles 6 and 7 of the Constitution became law. These Articles recognize, respectively, the right to obtain government information and the "right of petition" which empowers any Mexican citizen to make consultations relative to government activities.

It should be recalled that all previous attempts to have a law on access to information were in vain in a game in which the government blamed the media and some of these, as its allies, opposed such rules, arguing that they would restrict freedom of speech. A game of collusion that served only government aims to avoid transparency in public information.

Faced with the absence of applicable regulations on the matter, access to information was a gracious concession by the authority, subject to the interests of public officials.

> This is the first time that a law of this nature occurs in our country and it implies a change of paradigm by moving from a situation of "State secrets" to total transparency. This is a major step forward; we know that the countries with the highest rates of corruption are those that do not have a Law on Access to Information.

With the enactment of the LFTAIPG, Mexico has undertaken a process of change in the relations between government and citizens and has progressed toward a new way of exercising the public function, with open doors and facing society.

The right of access to information, guaranteed by means of this legislation, contributes to Mexico's progress in the consolidation of a more democratic government, for it enables citizens at all times to avail themselves of public information in possession of the government. This has a bearing on a substantive reduction of asymmetries in information between representatives and those represented, as a result of which the latter have more elements with which to favor government accountability.

The LFTAIPG is a valuable, well-conceived, well-articulated piece of legislation, unequivocal in definitions and objectives to guarantee the right of individuals to obtain information in the possession of the government

The LFTAIPG guarantees the right of access to information and protection of personal data in possession of the Executive, Legislative and Judicial Branches, as well as of the autonomous constitutional agencies —Federal Electoral Institute (IFE), National Human Rights Commission (CNDH), Bank of Mexico (BANXICO)—, under three fundamental principles:

1. The information possessed by federal powers and agencies is public and should be accessible to society unless, in the terms of the Law itself, it is demonstrated clearly and in a duly substantiated manner that its disclosure can endanger matters of general interest for the country, such as national security, public security and national defense.
2. The right of access to information is universal, which means that

any person, without any distinction whatsoever, may request it without the need to prove any legal interest or explain the reasons or purposes for his/her request.

3. The personal data in the possession of public institutions are confidential and must not, therefore, be disclosed or used for purposes other than those for which they were received or required, in such a way that the right to privacy and private life is guaranteed, and at the same time their proprietors should have access to them whenever they request it.

The LFTAIPG is a valuable, well-conceived, well-articulated piece of legislation, unequivocal in definitions and objectives to guarantee the right of individuals to obtain information in the possession of the government. It establishes that all government information is of a public nature (Article 2) and instructs all government agencies and entities to favor the "principle of publicity" (Article 6) above reserve.[1] It grants individuals the right to request information that has not yet been made public by means of simple, expeditious procedures (Article 40). It also grants any person the right to appeal against an entity's decision to deny information (Article 49), and also grants the right to take the entity to court if the appeal for review that has been filed is rejected.

---

[1] In accordance with Article 13 of the LFTAIPG, certain *information* in the possession of the government may be considered "reserved"; that is, certain information may be temporarily subject to exceptions of access and disclosure if and only if its dissemination could:

I) Compromise national security, public security or national defense;

II) Impair the conduct of international negotiations or relations, including information of a confidential nature that other States or international agencies transmit to the Mexican State;

III) Harm the country's financial, economic or monetary stability;

IV) Endanger the life, safety or health of any person; or

V) Cause serious damage to activities of verification of compliance with laws, prevention or pursuit of crimes, administration of justice, tax collection, immigration control operations, procedural strategies in judicial or administrative proceedings while the decisions are not final.

Federal Institute for Access to Public Information (IFAI)

The mere existence of legislation in the area of access to public government information, however, does not guarantee the effective practice of citizens' right of access to information. In some countries the legislation does not provide mechanisms that reinforce access to information; other governments create obstacles or take advantage of legal gaps to resist disseminating the information in their possession.

For these reasons and in order to advance successfully in the execution of the right of access to information, some legislation provides for the creation of autonomous institutions in charge of overseeing observance of the legislation of access to information in possession of the government.

In Article 33, the LFTAIPG provides for the creation of the IFAI, which began to operate officially on June 12, 2003. The IFAI is in charge of observing and enforcing the LFTAIPG in the sphere of the Federal Executive Branch and is the agency in charge of promoting and disseminating the exercise of the right of access to information and of settling any refusal by the authorities to respond to requests for access to information. Similarly, the IFAI has the mandate of safeguarding the confidentiality of personal data in possession of agencies and entities.

The IFAI is an organ of the federal public administration that is not sectorized, which means that it is not subordinate to any state ministry. It has operative autonomy, which enables it to decide on its internal organization and operating rules; it has budgetary autonomy, which allows it to define its financial needs and provides it with sufficient flexibility for internal allocation and application of its resources under the regulatory control of the Federal Public Administration. And finally, it has autonomy of decision, which guarantees independence in its resolutions and decisions.

Functions of IFAI

- The functions of IFAI can be classified into four types:
  1. The dispute resolution and regulatory functions are essential to guaranteeing access to public government information and protecting personal data, by means of the settlement of denials of access to information, interpretation of the law and issuance of guidelines.
  2. The function of oversight and coordination is essential to furthering advances in the Federal Government's transparency.
  3. The function of promotion is fundamental for fostering and disseminating the benefits of the right of access to information and advancing a culture of transparency and accountability.
  4. The operative and administrative functions are necessary for ensuring all the above.

The IFAI is in charge of promoting a genuine cultural transformation in the conception and practice of public service; it involves submitting government activities and public servants' performance to daily scrutiny by society; it demands publicizing and instilling in the entire population the right of access to information and effectively promoting its exercise, as well as the right to people's privacy and private life by protecting their personal data.

As of the establishment of the IFAI, any individual interested in requesting information in the possession of the Federal Government can apply for it by means of a letter or on the forms approved by the Institute. Nevertheless, here we would like to underscore the form associated with Digital Government, which facilitates and broadens the possibilities of such a request, since it can be made from any part of the country and also from abroad, by means of the System of Requests for Information (SISI), which can be accessed through the Internet at: *www.informacionpublica.gob.mx*

This mechanism for access to information in the possession of the government is an innovation at international level, as few countries have such an accessible means for citizens to request public government information through the Internet. The IFAI has advised officials from Canada, Germany, Great Britain, the Czech Republic and Peru, among other countries, interested in adopting systems of access to information similar to the SISI. The electronic revolution has affected access to information and has turned the government into a disseminator of information, thus vindicating the values that now support the provisions of open government. The IFAI is immersed in that current and facilitates citizens' access to information in possession of the government through remote means of communication, as occurs with the SISI.

According to SISI statistics, between June 12, 2003, and August 12, 2004, agencies and public entities received 47,186 requests for information, which meant, on average, receiving almost 3,150 per month.

Of the total number of requests, 92.3 percent were made electronically, a reflection of the simplicity of the System, which makes it possible to submit requests from any computer terminal and at any time of day, whereas the remaining 7.7 percent were manual requests.

Moreover, 87 percent of the requests for information received were replied to, and three in every 100 have resulted in appeals for review or proceedings of verification of lack of response.

Total of requests and replies processed, 2003-2004[1]

Item	2003	2004	Cumulative to 2004	Share of total requests (%)
Total requests	24,729	22,457	47,186	100.0
Electronic	22,898	20,652	43,550	92.3
Manual	1,831	1,805	3,636	7.7
Total replies	21,530	19,514	41,044	87.0
Electronic	20,051	18,171	38,222	81.0
Manual	1,479	1,343	2,822	6.0
Appeals for review presented to the IFAI	636	791	1,427	3.0

[1] For 2003, figures from June 12 to December 31. For 2004, figures to August 12.
Source: Federal Institute for Access to Public Information.

As the OECD has pointed out, the professional service in the public sector is facing new challenges in the world as a whole stemming from new tasks, changes in the labor market and in administrative practices, from new, different political pressures, and from new risks arising from emerging power interests and changing values in our societies

2. A Professional Government

The second line of action of the Presidential Agenda concerns the professionalization of the public sector, in response to the fact that previously there was no system of comprehensive development of functionaries, which was evidenced in the lack of strategic personnel planning, little training and not focused on objectives, lack of detection of needs, absence of vocation for service, failure to act according to values in broad sectors and lack of a sound system of compensation and incentives for growth. The exercise of authority was characterized by absence of information, consultation and participation, which frequently gave rise to frustration.

This action line known as Professional Government seeks to attract and retain the most motivated, well-trained personnel, committed to society.

> Recommendation 2.3 of the Final Declaration of the Fifth Global Forum on Innovation and Quality in Government, points out that: "State capacity to respond to and manage change is essential to meeting the challenges of the 21st century and to improving quality of life for citizens. To undertake these efforts, governments need a professional civil service where employees and managers are recruited on merit, are trained for the jobs they carry out, are evaluated on programme results and promoted and paid for performance. It is important that recruitment is transparent and open to all sectors of society. Evaluating competencies necessary for 21st century governments is crucial. Governments with an established civil service must engage in efforts to reform their rules and regulations to make them responsive to the needs of citizens and competitive with private sector jobs. It is important to benchmark with the private sector about lessons learned in human resource management."

As the OECD has pointed out, the professional service in the public sector is facing new challenges in the world as a whole stemming from new tasks, changes in the labor market and in administrative practices, from new, different political pressures, and from new risks arising from emerging power interests and changing values in our societies. All this requires an administration capable of combining strong determination in very well-defined objectives, promoting at the same time the values that interest society as well as trust in public institutions. There is a need for policies and provisions to strengthen the professional level of the civil service while promoting its readaptation to the new realities.

To count on a Professional Government, capable officials are needed. Service to citizens requires public servants who are better trained in their areas of competence, in their professional lives, and with a vocation for service

Professionalizing a government is no easy task. Rather it is a complex one for at least two reasons. One involves important techniques because various aspects of personnel management are still insufficient, due precisely to lack of solid experience in the matter. And the other implies a genuine cultural change. Entry into public service is normally due to recommendations, commitments or chance. In no case are objective, proven and effective personnel selection methods applied. Good performance of the duties entrusted to a public servant was not, for many years, the decisive factor for occupying a post with greater responsibility. The reverse also occurred: failure to comply with duties was not a reason for dismissal from the post.

To count on a Professional Government, capable officials are needed. Service to citizens requires public servants who are better trained in their areas of competence, in their professional lives, and with a vocation for service so as to provide citizens with the best attention. In this way it will be guaranteed that the public administration's professionalism goes beyond six-year terms and becomes a strategic factor in the country's competitiveness.

Therefore, entry into the federal public administration by means of public, open competitive examination, officials' tenure and labor development according to their merits and equality of opportunities, ongoing performance assessment, appropriate management of information, training by electronic means and officials' integral development, are central characteristics for a Professional Government that effectively meets citizens' demands.

The actions undertaken to achieve a Professional Government in our country have focused on implementing a professional career civil service; on the creation of *@Campus Mexico* for the training of public servants through education by electronic means, making it possible for them to develop the capabilities required to perform their duties; Technical Professionalization and Selection Committees were installed in the agencies, and the Sole Register of Public Servants was developed.

In order to implement the Professional Career Civil Service, the respective Law (LSPC) was passed, entering into force in 2002, the Professional Service and Human Resources Unit of the Federal Public Administration was created, the Consultative Council of the System was installed, the Technical Professionalization and Selection Committees were installed and the Sole Register of Public Servants (RUSP) was developed.

In this regard, we should recall what President Fox said:

> With the approval of the Law of the Professional Career Civil Service, the current government is leaving an important legacy for today's and tomorrow's public servants, who from now on will be hired, assessed and promoted on the basis of their merits, in equality of opportunities.
>
> If in the private sector the personnel is the most valuable element to be able to compete in a globalized world, much more should it be so in the public sector where the objective is to provide citizens with opportunities for growth and development.

In regard to the Technical Professionalization and Selection Committees in the agencies, in a first phase it was determined to set up the Committees in the 15 agencies subject to the LSPC, in their role as agency and sectoral coordinator.

As concerns the Sole Register of Public Servants, the database containing the human resources of 232 institutions that form part of the Sole Register of Public Servants was developed with basic data defined for the first phase. That is, a total of 284 institutions of the Federal Public Administration are already registered, 232 of them in the RUSP.

Here it is worth recalling some ideas of Tim Kemp, Director of the Human Resources Strategy of the Cabinet Office of Great Britain:

> No matter how much process re-engineering happens, no matter how far and fast technology changes, and no matter how many worldwide conferences we convene to discuss how to bring about change, if people in their day to day jobs don't see things happening differently tomorrow and the next day, then nothing will really have altered.

Those in charge of bringing about change should be capable of developing a future vision for the country; transmitting energy and enthusiasm to their personnel in the daily effort to attain that vision; and they should have the necessary strength and resistance to lead the change toward its next level and so on successively.

The Ibero-American Charter of Public Administration, approved in 2003 and endorsed by the Thirteenth Ibero-American Summit, establishes in its Preamble that:

> To attain a better State, an indispensable instrument for countries' development, the professionalization of the public administration is a necessary condition. Understood as such is the guarantee that public servants possess a series of qualities such as merit, capability, vocation for service, effectiveness in the performance of their duty, responsibility, honesty and abidance by the principles and values of democracy [...]
>
> Diverse studies carried out by international agencies show evidence of a positive relationship between the existence of public administration or civil service systems invested with such qualities and citizens' levels of trust in the public administration, government effectiveness and the fight against corruption, and countries' capacity for sustainable economic growth. Moreover, a professional Administration that embraces such systems contributes to countries' institution-building and to the soundness of the democratic system.

3. A Quality Government

Excellence and quality are essentially aimed at citizens and customers; any effort in this regard will meet with failure if it ultimately neglects the human factor of the beneficiary

The Presidential Agenda's third action line is to achieve a Quality Government irrespective of who occupies the Presidency of the Republic.

Here we quote Thomas Mosgaller, President of the American Society for Quality (ASQ):

> Quality is typically understood from two distinct perspectives: quality facing the customer (sometimes this is viewed as merely service quality) that represents the external activities involved to meet constituent needs (this includes all stakeholders such as customers, suppliers, communities and governments) and quality that assures internal performance (managing by process the performance of an organization's quality management system). These elements must be combined within the context of the macro- and micro-economic focus of government in order to establish the proper framework for defining quality.

Since the beginning of his mandate, President Fox pledged to incorporate the concepts and practices of the culture of ***Total Quality*** into government tasks. This means, first of all, having an efficient and effective government that has a quality management model at a reliable level of maturity; secondly, that it should be reliable in its policies, processes and services, endorsed by certification of its quality management systems in all its administrative units with the capacity for self-management, and thirdly, that it should be a government with tangible, improved results that continuously assesses resource management and the impact of its actions and projects.

In recent years, especially as of the nineties, as we saw earlier, a dual movement took place in governments: one aimed at entities' internal excellence and the other at systems that assure quality in benefit of citizens and customers.

Excellence in organizations as defined by Alain de Dommartin, CEO of the European Foundation for Quality Management, could well be adapted to public management:

> A management scheme that mixes concepts of public and corporate administration, that embraces relevant management practices and helps *agencies to customize their management and service* models, defining how to achieve success.

Excellence and quality are essentially aimed at citizens and customers; any effort in this regard will meet with failure if it ultimately neglects the human factor of the beneficiary.

At the same time, agencies' internal excellence fosters the creativity, responsibility and vocation for service of officials at all levels.

To achieve a Quality Government, progress has been made in the establishment of a culture of quality in the delivery of public services by introducing the INTRAGOB Model, which is a management system aimed at addressing three priority aspects: service quality, the integrity of public servants and society's perception of the reliability and effectiveness of the Federal Public Administration.

In the INTRAGOB Quality Model, eight basic lines have been defined along which the different agencies and entities of the Federal Public Administration should advance to acquire the degree of maturity in the quality process. These lines are: customer satisfaction; leadership; officials' development and management of intellectual capital; management of information and technology; planning, management and improvement of processes, and impact and results.

For the operation of the model in the first three years of this administration, the following have been implemented:

The revolution in information and communication technologies has paved the way for a society that organizes itself and works online, transforming its institutions and all sectors of the economy

- A network in which 19 agencies and 30 entities of the Federal Public Administration participate.
- The establishment of an Executive Committee for Quality in 92 percent of the agencies and 65 percent of the entities of the Federal Public Administration.

Chapters 4 and 5 fully explain both the Strategic Model for Government Innovation and Quality and the INTRAGOB Model.

To boost improvement processes within the public administration, the INTRAGOB Prize for Quality, in recognition of best practices in total

Creating trust between government and citizens is essential to achieving effective governance. Information and communication technologies help to create this trust because they incorporate citizens into public administration and have a direct bearing on the shaping of an Honest and Transparent Government by providing more effective communication channels to carry out operations with the government

quality, and the INNOVA Recognition Award and INNOVA Prize for best practices in innovation, were instituted.

Chapter 6 talks about the awards and recognitions.

Confidence has also been gained in the delivery of public services, increasing the certification of work areas with international standards (ISO 9000) by 98 percent. That is to say, whereas in the year 2000 there were 429 work areas certified, in 2001 the figure rose to 541, in 2002 it increased to 650, in 2003 there were 850 and 1,273 areas certified in 2004.

Work Centers Certified with ISO 9000 in the Federal Public Administration, 2000–2004

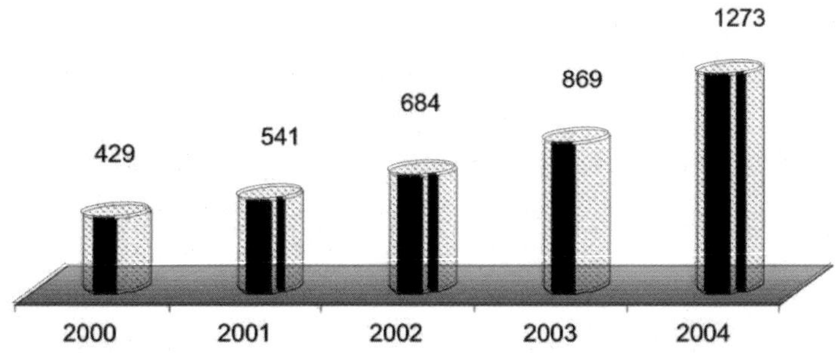

4. A Digital Government

President Vicente Fox has stated that:

> This century should be considered the century of intellectual capital and innovation. In a globalized world in which it would seem that distances and times have shortened, no one can be unaware of the challenges and opportunities offered us by the use of information and communication technologies in responding more effectively to citizens' needs.

Therefore, the Presidential Agenda's fourth line of action seeks to ensure that citizens have an efficient Digital Government that enables them to obtain public-sector information and access to the services it offers from the comfort of their homes or offices, or from a Digital Community Center of the e-Mexico National System. The revolution in information and communication technologies has paved the way for a society that organizes itself and works online, transforming its institutions and all sectors of the economy. This means of communication will increase mobility, for neither processes nor persons will be tied to a particular place. Traditional channels are already insufficient, cities are increasingly larger and people have less time. It is therefore necessary for citizens to be able to obtain information, access services and carry out procedures from any place, at any time, every day, that is, "wherever and whenever."

President Fox's Administration is helping to make the processes citizens have to face simpler, instead of making life complicated for them. The time it used to take to carry out government procedures, and their lack of integration, is another critical factor that had a negative impact on the government's response capacity and that justifiably irritated society. Access to the Internet is an excellent tool for keeping citizens in touch with their government.

To become a government on a par with the best in the world, federal government institutions should become digital and intelligent organizations. To that end, use has begun to be made of systems and technological applications that improve the management of knowledge and its components

The new information and communication technologies have paved the way for a society that organizes itself and works online, transforming its institutions and all sectors of the economy. Nevertheless, Digital Government, or e-Government—as the tendency of governments to take advantage of said technologies to transform public administration and offer citizens electronic services is known—requires incorporating broader goals such as the processes to *reform the administration* and furthering the information society.

The General Recommendations of the Fifth Global Forum on Government Innovation and Quality point out that:

The transition to electronic delivery of services enables governments to better quantify cost effectiveness of electronic service delivery, and hence more effective use of limited resources and improves accountability. E-government strategies also can improve commerce, democracy and transparency. With this in mind, states need to assess the potential for investing in e-government initiatives with a view to improving the cost effectiveness of the use of their increasingly stretched resources.

Creating trust between government and citizens is essential to achieving effective governance. Information and communication technologies help to create this trust because they incorporate citizens into public administration and have a direct bearing on the shaping of an Honest and Transparent Government by providing more effective communication channels to carry out operations with the government. These technologies eliminate discretionary authority because they inhibit dishonest practices and make it possible to carry out strict and transparent follow-up of government administration. By facilitating citizens' access to the information society, digital government not only improves the availability and quality of services but also increases their added value.

In Mexico, the electronic government strategy is carried out along the following strategic lines:

- Government Technological Infrastructure

In the digital era the basic requirement for effective communication and collaboration within the government is having an informatics and telecommunications network that incorporates all the agencies and their public officials through a government Intranet that makes up the "Network of networks of the Federal Public Administration." Currently 11 Federal Government agencies and entities are already interconnected. At the federal level, the government coordinates Internet connection projects with the aim of obtaining efficiencies and economies of scale. Likewise, it combines efforts for the management of government technological infrastructure, which includes hardware, software, systems, networks, Internet connectivity, databases, infrastructure for online training (e-*learning*), as is the case with the *@Campus Mexico* Portal, and specialized human resources. Finally, it shares methodological infrastructure and knowledge resources among public servants with the aim of improving their achievement and avoiding duplication.

- Management of knowledge and digital collaboration

To become a government on a par with the best in the world, federal government institutions should become digital and intelligent organizations. To that end, use has begun to be made of systems and technological applications that improve the management of knowledge and its components—learning, collaboration, assessment and decision-making—thus forming a channel for the delivery of government services to public servants, such as DECLARANET (Electronic System of Governmental Declarations of Assets) and NORMATECA (Electronic Regulations Library).

To facilitate agencies' assessment and decision-making, we promote the use of systems to assess government performance and institutional intelligence. These tools support the National System of Indicators and the Strategic System of Results. The use of online learning and project management tools is also fostered.

- Process Redesign with Information Technologies

To achieve government efficiency and effectiveness, we have developed information-technology systems that facilitate process redesign in public institutions' adjective tasks: Government Resource Planning (GRP) technology is implemented to ensure rapid integration of this type of systems; we foster the use of technological applications that support substantive and strategic tasks that create savings, economies of scale, cost reduction and better quality services. To achieve this, the technological tools necessary for the redesign of "*key macro-processes*" have been identified—and this continues to be done. We are also furthering the redesign of the process of acquisitions and procurement of goods and services by means of e-*Procurement* technology, with the aim of reducing costs, linking it to existing electronic government purchasing systems such as the Electronic Government Procurement System (COMPRANET).

- Electronic Services and Procedures (e-*Servicios*)

Citizens will be able to have electronic access to more than 834 electronic government services and procedures more comfortably and with greater satisfaction. To that end, processes were redesigned in federal government agencies and entities; technological interoperability standards were established and an intergovernmental technological platform was developed that allows the incorporation of all the information, services and procedures, following the web services technological model. This infrastructure includes digital signature solutions, security mechanisms and privacy safeguards and methods for logical data integration.

- Informatics policy and organization for Digital Government

This operates under a horizontal organizational structure based on a work network made up of those responsible for information technologies in federal government agencies. This *e-Government* Network or Digital Government, established by Presidential Decree and a Master Plan for Digital Government, furthers the guiding plans on the matter, defines internal policies on information technology and encourages them strategically with the government innovation goals. This network also promotes appropriate and responsive regulations and coordinates actions for the development of Digital Government in Mexico, in addition to supporting the career civil service in the areas of information technology by promoting the reformulation of government informatics; it creates models of inter-sectoral cooperation and collaboration with the other levels of government and other powers of the Union; it seeks financing funds for strategic projects and will promote alliances with international agencies such as the Organisation for Economic Co-operation and Development (OECD), Latin American Center for Administration for Development (CLAD), Institute for Connectivity in the Americas (ICA), Government Online International Network (GOL) and Asia Pacific Economic Cooperation Mechanism (APEC), as well as with leading countries in Digital Government, such as Canada, Singapore, the United States and the United Kingdom. Furthermore, it prepares methodologies to assess the economic and social impact of Digital Government, and designs policies in the area of acquisitions and procurement related to information technology, seeking the negotiation of corporate contracts for the purchase of hardware and licensing of software with the federal government's main suppliers to improve investments in this regard.

Online Government Procedures and Services, 2001–2004

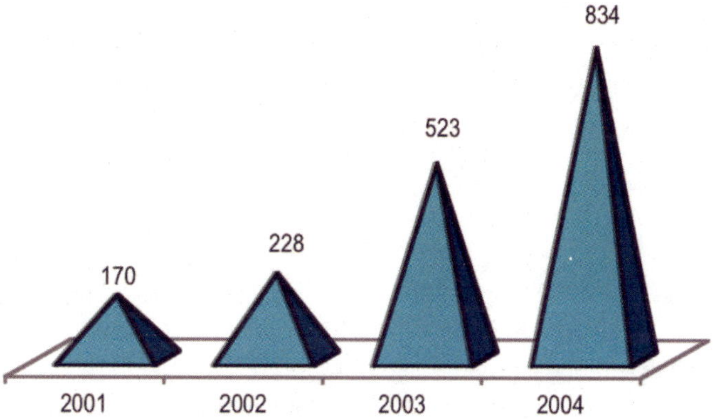

Source: Ministry of Public Administration.

Some examples of the progress made so far by the Digital Government or e-Government line of action are the following:

- Mexican Government Citizen Portal

At the Citizen Portal *(www.gob.mx)*, citizens are presented with a single site where all the most important services, procedures and information resources are offered. This portal is organized according to the following channels or topics, which were defined with citizens' needs in mind: education, health care, housing, family, transportation, employment, security, culture, tourism, democracy, migrants, business, foreigners, environment, rural sector and sports.

The Portal is designed so that citizens can participate in its improvement and so that they can freely express their opinions, criticisms and suggestions on the different fields of government affairs.

After having obtained the 2003 INNOVA Recognition Award and the 2003 Prize for Innovation and Quality in the Public Administration, and having been nominated by Yahoo! Mexico as the best on the Internet in Politics and Government, the Citizen Portal received the "2004 Stockholm Challenge" International Award in May 2004 in the Electronic Government category.

Chapter 6 enlarges on this Portal.

Along the same lines, through the e-Mexico National System, the Federal Government succeeded in linking up all the country's municipalities and the Federal District to the network through 3,200 Digital Community Centers (CCDs), which will expand to around 8,000 by the end of 2004, and which enables remote communities to have access to the Internet, as well as to the contents of *e-government, e-education, e-health* and *e-economy*.

- Electronic Government Procurement System (COMPRANET)

The System was created to handle all the purchases of the Mexican Federal Government, and by means of agreements and collaboration mechanisms which respect the autonomy and sovereignty of each level of government, it has been incorporated into acquisitions and public works in Federative Entities.

At present there are more than 2,800 Federal Public Administration suppliers authorized to carry out electronic bidding through the COMPRANET system, which helps to make government purchases and the contracting of public works more transparent.

In this regard it should be mentioned that the process of publishing tenders on the Internet has ISO 9000 certification.

The number of tenders by this means has grown exponentially, since whereas in 2001 a total of 608 were carried out, in 2003 there were 8,390, which means that 63.5 percent of the total amount awarded was carried out electronically.

In regard to the benefit from the electronic procedures and services with high impact for citizens, the following stand out:

- The Mexican Social Security Institute from your Company (ISDE)

This institution provides an option for presenting workers' affiliation movements easily and quickly, eliminating procedures and waiting time, which benefits almost 7.2 million workers.

- Electronic Clinical Record of the Social Security and Services Institute for Government Workers (ISSSTEMED)

The implementation of important tools for digital handling of images and telemedicine services in the Social Security and Services Institute for Government Workers (ISSSTE) benefits almost 110,000 patients with the creation of a Electronic Clinical Record, which processes and stores more than 2 million digital medical images by means of the most advanced processing system in Latin America.

- Foreign trade

To support foreign trade and foster foreign investment, online financial operations (letters of credit, fiduciary, treasury credit), Digital 50 and 250 SME Scheme, and commercial intelligence information are offered.

Electronic services enable the country's principal chains of production to become integrated around large corporations and public-sector agencies, benefiting 28,000 small and medium-sized enterprises.

The system of electronic procedures for exporters-importers seeks to provide swiftness and certainty to stakeholders in foreign trade.

- The CHAMBATEL and CHAMBANET programs

These programs link job applicants and employers with a modern tool for joining labor supply and demand. The CHAMBATEL program operates in 32 service centers in various cities in the country and has channeled 175,777 persons into a job and reached a placement rate of 7.3 percent of persons served.

- Taxes

Tax collection has become much more efficient and transparent with the use of technology. More than 54 percent of tax declarations and tax payments presented to the Tax Administration Service (SAT) is carried out through the Internet portal *(www.sat.gob.mx)*, which benefits over 10.5 million taxpayers with a flexible, efficient and secure process.

In summary, the electronic government applications created during the current administration for the Mexican Social Security Institute (IMSS) to become an electronic institution are the following: "IMSS is going to buy, IMSS bought"; IMSS from your company (ISDE) and Electronic Signature; e-health; Family Medicine Information System (SIFM) and Electronic Patient Medical Record; Institutional Resources Planning System; e-Government and Institutional Supply; and Executive Development Program; Comparison of e-Government practices vs. best practices at world level.

The UN also places Mexico fourth worldwide, surpassed only by the United States, Chile and Australia, in sophistication and maturity of online government services

Mexico stands as the country that registered the highest degree of progress in electronic government among the nations studied. In this area, our country has outpaced Belgium, Italy, Denmark, Hong Kong, Canada and Australia, among other countries at international level

Toward the Future

By the end of the current administration the aim is to consolidate the Electronic Government program by attaining the following objectives:

- One hundred percent of services and procedures with high citizen impact will be available to be delivered by electronic means.
- One hundred percent of public tenders will be carried out electronically; auctions will be effected through COMPRANET and minor purchases will be carried out in electronic format.
- For federal government purchases and procurements, implement an electronic market model (e-*Marketplace*) that makes it possible to increase the federal government's purchasing power, generating significant savings.
- Link the use of information and communication technologies to improve the government's competitiveness, making it possible to institutionalize a model of "paperless government" through electronic signature and digital certification to deliver services and carry out the most important internal processes.
- By the end of 2004, the Sole Register of Accredited Persons (RUPA) and the Electronic Payment of Charges (eSAT5) will be in full operation. The former will contain information on the incorporation and operation of companies and will prevent having to hand in the same documentation again when carrying out another procedure. The latter will simplify and facilitate payment of charges for the services provided by the Federal Government.
- Likewise, by the end of 2004, we will have developed the technological infrastructure to make it possible to operate uniformly, throughout the Federal Government, the advanced sole electronic signature. With this signature, private individuals will have a digital certificate, valid for carrying out procedures and services before any agency of the federal public administration, including the Tax Administration System (SAT).

At present work is also under way to link the Digital Government line of action to similar strategies in the states and municipalities through the establishment of the model of an integral government services center. This model is an accepted practice in the country's most important municipalities.

Government agencies tended to complicate everything due to the diversity of requirements, which gave rise to confusion and made people want to do things "under the table", which in turn encouraged bribes and corruption

Digital Mexico in the World

As a result of the actions carried out, our country's international placement with regard to e-Government has notably improved.

The 2003 UN World Public Sector Report, focusing particularly on *e-Government*, places Mexico in 30th position among almost 200 countries evaluated.

The UN also places Mexico fourth worldwide, surpassed only by the United States, Chile and Australia, in sophistication and maturity of online government services.

The report also recognizes that Mexico, particularly in the past two years, is one of the ten countries that has most effectively and rapidly progressed in its Electronic Government strategies in comparison to several of the most industrialized nations, and is one of the five countries with developing economies that has made substantial efforts to offer its citizens online transaction services.

It is a fact that Mexico stands in ninth place worldwide in e-Participation, that is, it has the possibility of allowing society to become involved in a dialogue with its government as a customer of its services, and also to participate in the political decision-making process.

Furthermore, in the study *e-Government Leadership: Engaging the Customer, 2002–2003* published by the consulting firm *Accenture*, Mexico stands as the country that registered the highest degree of progress in electronic government among the nations studied. In this area, our country has outpaced Belgium, Italy, Denmark, Hong Kong, Canada and Australia, among other countries at the international level.

As a consequence of observations made in audits, public servants reacted by drafting and issuing new rules and provisions to avoid making the same mistake again, leaving aside the need to simplify internal processes

5. A Government with Regulatory Improvement

Regulatory improvement is also a worldwide trend of the highest priority, especially when the aim is to make in-depth changes in all public-administration bodies. In 1995, the OECD prepared a list of the necessary requirements to carry out a reform in this regard.

This is a list of the questions that should be asked in regard to a rule or regulation:

- Has the problem been correctly defined?
- Is government action justified?
- Is the regulation the best that government action has in that aspect?
- Are there legal grounds for that regulation?
- What is the most appropriate level or levels of government for that action?
- Do the benefits of the regulation justify its cost?
- Is the distribution of benefits among society transparent?
- Is the regulation clear, consistent, understandable and of easy access for users?
- Have all the parties involved had the opportunity to express their opinions?
- How will the complement to the regulation be carried out?

To comply with the fifth line of action of the Presidential Agenda for Good Government, the actions focused on making federal government institutions more efficient by eliminating excessive regulations that did not produce added value and allotting more time and resources to attention to citizens and corporations.

Formerly, citizens who wanted, for instance, to set up a business suffered in doing so because of the number of procedures required. Often the population's most creative initiatives were held up at the "go to another window" stage. Government agencies tended to complicate everything due to the diversity of requirements, which gave rise to confusion and made people want to do things "under the table", which in turn encouraged bribes and corruption. Previously, excess regulations and lack of dissemination caused public officials' work to become paralyzed or to be concerned more with complying with the regulations than with providing citizens with quality services.

There was an interminable amount of pointless procedures, produced by a static regime without the obligation to respond clearly to society's demands, which made citizens feel subdued and impotent. At present the public administration as a whole is making significant efforts to respond with better results and greater productivity to the needs of citizens and companies. At the same time the aim is to promote mobility and flexibility in decision-making by public servants, who for many years experienced a deeply-rooted culture of centralization in decision-making under an over-regulated and highly coercive system which produced aversion to decision-making for fear of being sanctioned, especially in matters of budget or financial resource management.

As a consequence of observations made in audits, public servants reacted by drafting and issuing new rules and provisions to avoid making the same mistake again, leaving aside the need to simplify internal processes.

In response to this growing problem, the current government has affirmed its commitment, in various agreements and programs, to promoting regulatory improvement as an immediate need so as to reduce corruption rates, boost the transparency of the public administration, create a discipline of good government committed to society, raise the productivity of all federal government institutions and better serve society and its enterprises.

As a complement to the presidential initiatives, the Government with Regulatory Improvement action line incorporates the unwavering commitment of all the agencies, as well as of State-owned enterprises and entities, to implementing a program aimed at simplifying and modernizing their internal processes so that the procedures and services provided at all windows and service points for citizens and their companies are more efficient and timely.

The efforts made in the past to improve the regulations of the public administration were isolated; some of them produced good results, but they turned out to be insufficient. There are no precedents in Mexico of a generalized, standardized strategy of regulatory improvement such as the one being implemented at present, which has reported very good results as of the start of its implementation.

At the beginning of the third year of government, President Fox, aware of the need to establish competitive conditions for the start-up and operation of more enterprises in Mexico, pledged to provide the country with a regulatory framework for the development and promotion of productive activities that create more and better jobs. The private sector, under the coordination of the Entrepreneurial Coordinating Council, in response to an invitation from the Federal Government, submitted a list of 63 procedures that needed improvement. By September 2004, 48 of them had already been resolved.

Continuing with the task of providing citizens with better service, the Federal Government, through the Federal Commission on Regulatory Improvement (COFEMER) and the Ministry of Public Administration (SFP), initiated the improvement of procedures with the greatest impact on productive activities and on citizens. From this exercise, 240 procedures with this profile were identified, according to five weighted criteria: 1) frequency with which the procedure or service was carried out, 2) number of customers who carried it out, 3) customer recurrence, 4) revenues generated, and 5) number of complaints or reports of corruption. For 2004 they pledged to simplify 156 procedures and services with high citizen impact, as well as 4 social benefit programs, in 38 public institutions.

> Currently more than 10,000 provisions are included in the original inventory of regulations produced within the agencies and entities; at the end of the third year of President Fox's administration, only about 5,300 of them had been validated, that is, there has been a regulatory improvement of 50 percent, promoted in 32 institutions.

Under this heading it may be said that for the first time, public servants know the current regulations and have them at hand, which enables them to have certainty and security in their administrative management, focusing their efforts on serving citizens more quickly. Nowadays, citizens and companies have immediate access to 100 percent of applicable federal provisions.

- Internal Regulatory Improvement Committees (COMERI)

To achieve a regulatory framework adapted to the needs of issuers and customers alike, and to avoid the unfettered growth of new regulations, the COMERI were created, which promote a scheme that seeks an intelligent set of regulations that avoids an overburdening of requirements within institutions and is quick and simple in its interpretation and observation by users.

These high-level Committees are promoted by State Ministers, who appoint their personnel with the highest administrative authority so that they, in turn, convene the issuers and internal users who, with the support of the legal and comptroller's areas, assess and decide on all the provisions to be issued. These provisions should ensure the promotion of internal regulatory improvements that foster dynamism and flexibility in decision-making and are geared to substantive tasks from the viewpoint of service, efficiency and control.

- The Councils and the Boards

In addition, other tools have been created with the aim of improving federal regulations through Councils of Chief Administrative Officers and Under Ministers, and the *Regulatory Simplification Boards*. These are made up of high-level representations in institutions' decision-making, and adopt a user-issuer methodology aimed at identifying aspects of federal and legislative provisions that are obstacles to institutions' productivity. Their objective is to propose to issuers the adjustments that give greater flexibility to operations but, of course, without losing control, which is also a requirement of society.

The results obtained in 2003 showed a 23 percent reduction in federal provisions issued for observance by all the federal public administration's institutions. This is largely due to the creation of the Federal Regulations Library and the Regulatory Simplification Boards.

Interesting challenges can be glimpsed in the short and medium terms, aimed at continuing to simplify regulations, standardize criteria, make forms and reports uniform, improve processes for dealing with institutions' substantive needs, and thereby head toward fair regulations appropriate for the needs of order and control.

- The Regulations Libraries (NORMATECA)

The Ministries of Public Administration and Finance and Public Credit, also known as globalizing agencies, issue 80 percent of the regulations governing the operation and functioning of the Federal Public Administration. The rest of the regulations are issued by each sector; the ones issued by the Legislature are supreme in governing the operation and functioning of all Federal Government institutions.

The point of departure for regulatory improvement was instituting a system that disseminates all the regulations issued by the agencies and entities. This system, called the Federal Regulations Library, consists of a web page with a powerful search engine that contains the entirety of the federal regulatory provisions of compulsory observance for the operation and functioning of institutions, classified by topic and legal rank. At the same time, public servants who use the Regulations Library are guaranteed publication of the regulations coming directly from their issuers.

With the aim of strengthening the functioning of the Regulations Library, an "Agreement on dissemination and transparency of the regulatory framework for the federal public administration" was issued, which commits all the agencies and entities involved to maintaining the content current and up to date. These advances, which give legal certainty to public servants and increase institutions' productivity, are undoubtedly reflected in benefits for society.

But the dissemination of federal regulations is insufficient to guarantee correct operation, because the public servant cannot have the same access to and knowledge of the regulations issued within institutions. Therefore the strategy followed by this administration has been to promote also the implementation of Internal Regulations Libraries in each institution, with an operation similar to the federal one, but with the regulations applicable within each one.

System of Rapid Start-up of Enterprises (SARE)

System of Rapid Start-up of Enterprises (SARE), 2002–2004

Municipalities with SARE	Date of Installation	Enterprises Benefited	Investment (millions of pesos)	Jobs Created
Puebla	May 8, 2002	4 776	53.3	12 294
Los Cabos	October 16, 2002	864	81.5	1 404
Aguascalientes	April 10, 2003	958	41.1	1 493
Guadalajara	May 28, 2003	8 556	366.3	13 212
Zapopan	May 28, 2003	985	n.a.	5 091
Tijuana	June 2, 2003	107	1.5	116
Mexicali	June 2, 2003	37	1.9	71
Leon	July 1, 2003	203	28.8	608
Tlalnepantla	September 8, 2003	2 774	745.2	14 319
Tehuacan	October 1, 2003	200	4.2	484
Oaxaca	December 8, 2003	543	16.3	608
Benito Juarez (Cancun)	December 12, 2003	4	0.3	7
Torreon	January 7, 2004	861	65.7	1 761
Pachuca	January 15, 2004	90	23.5	205
Othon P. Blanco Chetumal	February 2, 2004	166	3.4	131
Apizaco	February 4, 2004	208	4.4	274
Coatzacoalcos	March 15, 2004	7	0.4	42
Culiacan	March 24, 2004	29	86.9	270
Mazatlan	March 24, 2004	37	18.6	134
Navolato	March 24, 2004	6	76.4	58
Merida	April 14, 2004	7	1.3	19
Celaya	July 2, 2004	0	0	0
Ensenada	July 9, 2004	0	0	0
Tapachula	August 12, 2004	0	0	0
Campeche	August 20, 2004	0	0	0
Queretaro	August 24, 2004	0	0	0
Total		**21 418**	**1 620.9**	**52 601**

n. a.: Not available

Source: Federal Commission on Regulatory Improvement with information supplied by the municipalities. Ministry of Economy.

In March 2002 the System of Rapid Start-up of Enterprises was created, aimed at facilitating the launching of new enterprises in a maximum of 72 hours. This involves joint efforts between the Federal Government, the states and the municipalities. By August 2004, this system was operating in 26 economically important municipalities, and by the end of the year others will have joined the effort.

Federal Register of Procedures and Services (RFTS)

In May 2003 the Federal Register of Procedures and Services was set up, which includes all procedures (except those concerning taxes). All the procedures carried out by the federal public administration are recorded in it transparently and publicly, since by law those that have not been registered should not be applied. Likewise, thanks to this register, the authority must respond within the time-frames indicated and it cannot request documents other than those stated in the RFTS.

Regulatory Moratorium

In keeping with the actions to foster competitiveness and in order to curb regulatory inflation, on May 12, 2004 the Executive Order Decision establishing a regulatory moratorium entered into effect and will be in force until April 29, 2005.

By means of this decision, the Federal Executive instructed agencies and state-controlled enterprises to suspend the issuing of regulations, as well as the generation of procedures with costs for individuals. The moratorium applies to all Federal Government regulations and is particularly important in furthering productive investment.

The objective of the decision is to complement the actions carried out by the Federal Executive, such as identification and registration of federal procedures, assessment of the costs of compliance for individuals, public consultation and opinion of regulatory projects, as well as the simplification of procedures with a high impact on economic activity; all this, in order to respond to the concerns of the business sector regarding the volume and quality of regulations.

In this regard, the moratorium forms part of the agenda of actions aimed at strengthening Mexico's competitive position.

Throughout the period during which this measure will be in force, the agencies, in collaboration with COFEMER, will establish work programs to reorder, reevaluate and weed out the regulatory provisions issued and applied by the Federal Government.

A fundamental challenge for a government that responds in its origins and its objectives to a democratic conception, is that society should have greater trust and credibility day by day in the Public Administration.

This challenge, however, is the responsibility of the whole country. Only with full, ongoing participation by citizens will the government become more aware and have greater knowledge of Mexicans' needs; only thus will it be possible to consolidate a government with a human face. The commitment of Vicente Fox's Administration to the Presidential Agenda is of an urgent nature, with the aim of ensuring that at the end of his administration there will be a legacy with regard to Good Government.

> An efficient government is concomitant with the exercise of democracy; its premise is service to citizens and its quality with honesty and transparency.

The effectiveness of public service is intimately linked with democratic execution; the government should serve people, facilitate their procedures, respond to their petitions and improve their quality of life. This requires the integral functioning of a government focusing on citizens. The current government has also invited state and municipal governments throughout the country to join this change of mentality, this new way of doing things, calling upon *all* without discrimination, at whatever level of government, to join this cause and accept the challenge involved.

Considering, regardless of the country in question, that no government has sufficient resources to satisfy everything that citizens demand, it is essential for governments to adopt the necessary measures to enable them to do more with the same money

6. A Government that Costs Less

I. Introduction

The central mission of any government should be to improve its citizens' living standards and quality of life, thus favoring harmonious, sustainable development. A government that fails to understand this is irremediably doomed to failure. Considering, regardless of the country in question, that no government has sufficient resources to satisfy everything that citizens demand, it is essential for governments to adopt the necessary measures to enable them to do more with the same money. It is not merely a question of "spending less", but rather of combining a stringent government with a Quality Government that offers greater benefits to society, with special emphasis on giving back to citizens more added value for each peso they pay in taxes.

Over the past thirty years, various factors have radically transformed governments' vision and course of action and their approach to the application of public expenditure; a wide range of countries with different situations and varied results have worked to reexamine their fiscal balance, reduce government spending and win the battle against the growth of bureaucracies. The challenge is not limited only to efforts to reduce the deficit.

Throughout this time we have observed that the countries that undertook the task of reducing government spending did so in different ways, depending on their view of what the government's role in society should be.

For some, "less government means better government", and therefore the governments that cost less are governments that supposedly do less and depend more on market forces. This conception leads to accelerated deregulation and to the transfer of public-sector assets and instruments into the hands of private interests, with very mixed results.

For others, government is a "necessary evil and by nature inefficient", and therefore if left to their own devices, government institutions squander valuable resources and turn into obese creatures. Therefore, the task of reducing the cost of government consists of squeezing out inefficiencies under a "managerial" approach of performance assessment and improved productivity.

> Finally, there is another stance that maintains that the government is, in fact, an essential instrument for achieving a necessary balance between market forces, social needs and collective interests. In this case, reducing government spending means clearly defining the spheres of public and private affairs and hence, determining the role the government should play. From these definitions, the different ways of reappraising the size of the government apparatus can be inferred.

For President Fox's administration, a government should cost less with the aim of allocating more budget resources to dealing with social priorities; therefore, the objectives set for this line of action of the Presidential Agenda for Good Government are:

a. Reducing bureaucratic spending that does not add value to citizens.
b. Increasing investment spending on social infrastructure and programs of major benefit to the population.
c. Attaining the above two objectives within a framework of macroeconomic stability and financial balance.

a. REDUCING BUREAUCRATIC SPENDING THAT DOES NOT ADD VALUE TO CITIZENS

Its approach is based on the release of funds from the operating costs of government institutions, whether to broaden the scope and coverage of diverse programs that have proved their effectiveness and are highly valued by society, or for the implementation of new projects and programs that address the growing demands and needs of an increasingly well-informed society that is more demanding of its government.

With this in mind, various initiatives have been implemented to replace traditional public-management schemes with the most advanced administrative and technological systems. As a result of these initiatives, during these four years of government, effective savings of more than

55 billion pesos have been quantified and over 165,000 posts oriented to administrative tasks have been eliminated from the federal payroll.

To place the scope of these achievements in its proper dimension, suffice it to imagine that with all the measures carried out in 2004, in response to the mandate contained in Article 30 of the Expenditures Budget of the Federation, which involved an enormous effort on the part of the 258 institutions of the Federal Public Administration, savings were made for a total of 4.5995 billion pesos and there was a reduction of 12,759 posts.

> Among the series of measures regarding divestiture, rationality and budget stringency implemented within the government to comply with this mandate, the following, among others, stand out:

- Not granting salary increases to public officials in mid- and top-level management.
- Eliminating private secretariats in units, coordination offices and general directorates.
- Adjusting the structure of government agencies to three under-ministries, aside from exceptional cases that may be justified.
- Maintaining a ratio of three deputy general directors per unit, coordination office or general directorate.
- Setting standard rates for the use of cellular telephones, per diems, traveling expenses and meals that are strictly necessary for public servants in the performance of their duties.
- Carefully planning the contracting of studies and advisory services.
- Reducing administrative costs by 15 percent in offices of chief administrative officers and equivalent, in press and liaison offices, in representations abroad and similar, state delegations and representations, and in advisory and support offices.

This is one of the most difficult battles to win in terms of public opinion, especially when for so many years the use of public resources was managed in absolute opacity and absence of transparency mechanisms and accountability.

Winning it is difficult when there are still areas of opportunity in different federal government agencies and entities which have not fully assumed the commitment to conduct themselves with strict budget stringency and efficiency measures, and which in view of the pressing economic situation being experienced by many citizens, the levels of spending necessary for the good performance of government tasks can even be offensive.

Many success stories could be told about the radical transformations that have taken place in government institutions. Here we mention only one of them, which has been characterized by the implementation of a sound and consistent strategy over these four years which has made it possible to attain very important achievements. Below we present a summary of the experience of the Ministry of the Interior (SEGOB).

The Case of the Ministry of the Interior (SEGOB)

Responsibilities

SEGOB is the institution in charge of the country's domestic policy and of the integrity, stability and continuation of the Mexican State. It carries out intelligence activities in the field of national security and is responsible for coordinating and directing relations between the Executive Branch and the Legislative and Judicial Branches, as well as establishing and fostering relations between the Federation, the states and the municipalities.

In addition, it is in charge of linkage with social, political and religious groups, strengthening the rule of law, promoting the defense of human rights, directing population policy, managing the population register, coordinating civil protection and disaster prevention systems, and following up on policies on migration and refugee assistance.

This Ministry is also responsible for exercising the State's guiding functions with regard to radio and television, safeguarding the nation's historical, bibliographical, newspaper and periodical archives, managing and publishing the Official Gazette of the Federation, and supervising public games and drawings in the country.

Situation Encountered in 2000

At the outset of this administration, the Ministry of the Interior was faced with important challenges in view of the new role it was to play at this new stage in the country's democratic life. Bearing in mind that six different Chief Administrative Officers had been in charge of the administration of the Ministry in the previous six years, the situation we encountered was logical and included the following aspects:

- Nonintegrated, uncoordinated processes, many of them carried out manually, which was reflected in the lack of accurate, timely and relevant information.
- Significant lack of connectivity, since there were no interconnected servers or switchboards.
- Decentralized operations: each area was responsible for making its own payments, for which there was a revolving fund of 14 million pesos distributed in 39 checkbooks available for that purpose, and each area had its own warehouse, amounting to 39 in total.
- There were 642 pending audit observations, of which 330 were for the Office of the Chief Administrative Officer.
- Liabilities from past fiscal years.
- Buildings with wasted space and no preventive maintenance, which resulted in frequent power cuts, malfunctions, poor safety measures, telephone problems, disorder and lack of cleaning.
- Utility automobiles assigned, against regulations, to directors and deputy directors.
- Superfluous functions and staff, as well as duplications in programs and structures.

- Lack of timing and delay in administrative procedures; for example, new employees did not receive their first paycheck until three months after they started working.
- More than 1,377 people being paid under a fee system.

Approach and Action Plan

Like many of the government institutions that were in a similar situation, the Ministry of the Interior faced a major challenge: cleaning up the past, dealing with the present and building the future. To achieve these objectives, it adopted a transformation model that included the seven basic elements of all organizations: strategy, structure, systems, profile, spheres of competence, culture and style. A five-year action plan was prepared on the basis of this model, divided into three stages:

- Clean-up and basic operation to organize the operation and support the substantive areas (2000–2002).
- Transformation to define and align the elements needed to create a flexible and effective organization (2002–2004).
- Consolidation to conclude the projects initiated and establish an impeccable operation (2004–2006).

Control and Transformation Measures

Among the measures adopted to fulfill the objectives set forth in each of the stages, the following should be mentioned:

Centralization. The dispersion of expenses among the units was remedied and was one of the main measures that helped to reduce spending; in this regard, 80 expenditure items were centralized, a sole program for furniture and equipment procurement was established, and payment to suppliers was centralized.

Control. For non-centralized items, quota ceilings were

established and mechanisms to review expenditures and supporting documentation were defined.

Suppliers. A detailed selection of suppliers was made and existing contracts were renegotiated, achieving significant improvements in purchasing conditions; for example, reductions of up to 45 percent in leasing prices were obtained.

Transformation of Processes. All the processes of the Office of the Chief Administrative Officer were redesigned with the adoption of better management practices and the incorporation of technology as a powerful tool through the implementation of the SAP model for financial resources and materials and the *Meta4* model for human resources.

Redistribution and improvement of spaces. The measures taken to make more rational use of physical spaces included:

- Definition and application of standards for office space by type of post.
- Remodeling of buildings to provide staff with safer, more decent workplaces.
- Vacating of rented properties and return of buildings not in use to the National Assets Appraisal Commission (CABIN).

Progress and Results

Almost four years after the beginning of this transformation process, the Ministry of the Interior is showing significant progress in its operation and administration. Many challenges are yet to be met, but the foundations for consolidating an "impeccable" operation in 2006, as established in its transformation model, have unquestionably been laid. Some of the main advances include the following:

- In 2003 the Ministry managed to reduce annual current expenditures by 1 billion pesos in real terms, in comparison with the year

2000. In this regard, it accumulated savings of 2.52 billion pesos in three years.

- In the field of expenditure on personnel services, the total staff decreased by 20 percent and the staff of the Office of the Chief Administrative Officer by 41 percent. As a result, spending in this area was reduced by 12 percent in real terms.
- In the project for spaces, 32,000m^2 of offices have been modernized, 33,000m^2 in buildings not being used have been returned to CABIN and 10,300 m^2 of rented space have been cancelled.
- In relation to measures taken to correct matters of the past, more than 200 million pesos were paid for regularization, payment of liabilities and contingencies of previous years, and more than 500 pending observations were settled.
- The Ministry acquired 2,750 personal computers; a metropolitan data network connected to 17 Ministry buildings was installed; the number of computers connected to the network was increased 300 percent; central processing, storage and backup capacity was expanded; and a logical security plan was implemented.
- With economies generated in the field of personnel services through the implementation of various measures, such as the freezing of job openings and the elimination of jobs in non-substantive areas, progress was made in solving long-standing problems that hindered the operation of the Ministry, caused deficient service to citizens and encouraged corrupt practices and lack of transparency. Re-equalization of wages was effected on the basis of the performance of the 1,890 lower-income posts, the regularization of 258 temporary posts and the conversion to federal posts of 100 fee contracts for public servants at Games and Drawings; additionally, the Fourth Chamber of the Federal Conciliation and Arbitration Tribunal was established.
- Special emphasis was placed on training Ministry staff in the topics of ethics and public service, with more than 200,000 man-hours spent in support of cultural change in the institution.

Important Change-Related Figures

As we can see in the case of the Ministry of the Interior, government institutions have been carrying out various actions revolving around the lines we have established to advance in reducing the government's operating expenditures. A list of some of the courses of action implemented to attain this objective appears below:

Item	Unit	Variation 2000–2004 %
Current expenditures (millions of pesos)	(1,000)	-25%
Number of staff	(2,900)	-20%
Number of automobiles	(705)	-53%
Administrative expenditures (millions of pesos)	(121)	-29%
Number of observations	(500)	-55%
Number of PCs	1,454	54%
Number of PCs connected to the network	1,824	203%
Visits to the Internet (millions)	2.9	886%

- Orderly use of physical spaces and cancellation of leases.
- Freezing and cancellation of jobs in non-substantive areas. Implementation of the Voluntary Severance Program.
- Process redesign through the use of technology.
- Elimination of duplication in programs and structures.
- Elimination of discretionary payments to public servants and containment of the earnings of middle- and upper-level management.
- Reduction and standardization of rates for expenses such as travel, fuel, cell phones, food, etc.
- Reduction of government procurement costs for goods and services.
- Centralization of warehouses.
- Elimination of the administrative sections of units, coordination offices and general directorates.
- Outsourcing services.

With measures such as these and the creativity and commitment of all public servants, we will continue advancing towards a more austere administration and transparency in the use of resources.

b. INCREASE INVESTMENT SPENDING ON SOCIAL INFRASTRUCTURE AND PROGRAMS OF MAJOR BENEFIT TO THE POPULATION

It should be recognized that the resources available to governments are limited and insufficient to meet all of the population's needs and, in many cases, such as Mexico, their budgets encounter pressures which, year by year, significantly reduce their leeway for maneuver. Among these pressures is the exponential increase in the cost of pensions and the trend of increasing outlays to meet the payment obligations of the Deferred Budget Impact Projects (PIDIREGAS). Various alternatives that could enable them to obtain greater resources to increase social spending include:

- More borrowing by expanding the public deficit
  With a long-term outlook and in response to an adverse international situation, far from falling into the temptation of contracting greater indebtedness to meet the enormous expectations with which the administration of President Fox took over the government in December 2000, a responsible economic policy has been maintained that has enabled the fiscal deficit to be reduced from 1 percent as a proportion of GDP in 2000 to 0.3 percent in 2004, with the aim of attaining financial balance in 2006, as established in the National Development Financing Program. This means that, far from gaining greater resources in this manner, the resources available have decreased by nearly 50 billion pesos.

  This measure can only be appreciated in the sense of being an all-out effort to achieve macroeconomic stability to ward off the specter of recurring crises and provide certainty and a solid base for sustained and sustainable growth over the long term.

- An increase in available resources through greater collection
  Economic stability is the result of a responsible fiscal policy

that strengthens public revenues and prevents squandering. In view of Congress's refusal to approve a fiscal reform that would allow greater equity in the payment of taxes by all citizens and give the government a larger amount of resources for social spending, the only alternative for increasing government resources by this means was limited to gradual improvement in tax collection.

In 2004, the taxpayer register has grown 30 percent in relation to the year 2000 and many of those who did not pay taxes now contribute to the works being carried out by the three levels of government in benefit of all Mexicans. By the end of 2004, tax collection will have increased by one percentage point of GDP in relation to the year 2000, and will amount to 11.6 percent. This means that as a result of the Federal Government's greater collection efficiency, it will be possible to have more than 70 billion pesos a year available to address the needs of the population.

- Freeing up resources from operating expenses
  In previous paragraphs, this section has already been dealt with in general terms. However, the above-mentioned figure of 55 billion pesos saved during these four years only takes into account the items that have been fully identified. There are many other areas, however, in which savings cannot be listed because they are directly redirected within the agencies that generate them. The following is one example:

The Case of the National Commission on Free Textbooks (CONALITEG)

From March 1, 2001 to May 31, 2004, CONALITEG made savings of 1.14 billion pesos, of which 671 million pesos were used to buy 81.2 million books for the 150,000 school libraries and 850,000 classroom libraries; the remaining 468 million pesos were freed as net resources for the Federal Treasury.

It should be noted that the average cost of the books for primary school dropped to unprecedented levels at 4.17 pesos, when it was 9.42 pesos in the year 2000; similarly, the cost of the books for secondary school was 19.21 pesos compared with 34.87 pesos in 2001, which has made it possible to do more with less in benefit of Mexican children. With a staff 20 percent smaller, book production has increased by 40 percent. This is "doing more with less."

- Seeking more resources for investment
  Governments should make efforts to increase the scarce resources they have and find alternative sources of financing. An outstanding activity carried out by various funds and trusts, such as the Infrastructure Investment Fund (FINFRA), is using public contributions to trigger larger amounts of investment with state and private resources.

- Public-private investment schemes (SDP)
  The SDP are a type of public-private participation in which the private sector provides the government with support services so that the latter, in turn, provides a public service. In this type of scheme, the capacities, strengths and resources of both sectors are shared in order to provide the population with quality services, combining the State's social responsibility with the private sector's financial, managerial and technological capacity.

  The main advantages of this type of scheme are the following:

- The best capacities and skills of the public and private sectors are obtained for the provision of public services.
- Optimum levels of quality in public services are maintained in the long term.
- The potential of public-sector resources can be used to greater advantage and dedicated to other social needs.
- Private resources and knowledge are used to provide services in a timely manner.

- Delays and extra costs that commonly afflict the development of public projects are reduced or eliminated.

  A panorama of budget constraints such as that faced by the Federal Government makes it necessary to take advantage of this scheme; consequently, efforts are now being made to design these investment mechanisms for hospitals, universities and highways.

- Doing away with criminal practices that harm public assets
  It will never be easy to break away from long-standing practices and from the strong interests that have been created around different economic aspects. However, in President Fox's administration, we have struggled to eradicate corrupt practices that harm the assets of all Mexicans.

  An important case that has come to the public's attention in recent months is the one related to the theft of fuel from Petroleos Mexicanos (PEMEX). Thanks to the raids carried out, more than 4 billion pesos have been recovered.

  The Federal Electricity Commission (CFE), with the implementation of its program on non-technical losses caused by illicit use, recovered a total of 1.1 billion pesos in earnings in 2002 and 2003, and is expected to recover an estimated 600 million pesos in 2004. This program also represents the recovery of 731 million kilowatt-hours for 2004, equivalent to a reduction of 0.21 percent in the rate of distribution losses.

- Generation of additional revenue
  Throughout these four years, we have implemented various mechanisms that have allowed the generation of additional revenue and strengthened the investment programs of federal government agencies and entities. Some of these mechanisms are set forth below:

  Updating of federal government rates
  To provide incentives in government agencies and entities for generating additional revenue, in 2003 it was established that

revenues not included in the Revenue Law, classified as "surplus," could be used within the agencies that generate them. This measure encouraged either the updating of public service rates that had not been modified for a year or the establishing of quotas for services that were being provided free of charge.

Sale of unproductive assets and obsolete inventory stock
The transformation processes and the application of different measures implemented in federal government agencies and entities to make budgets more rational free up assets whose sale generates additional resources that are used for priority projects and programs.

Reduction of the past-due loan portfolio and improvement in collection and inspection mechanisms
Institutions such as the Mexican Social Security Institute (IMSS), the National Institute of the Workers' Housing Fund (INFONAVIT), the Federal Electricity Commission (CFE), the National Water Commission (CNA) and the Tax Administration Service (SAT), whose revenues depend on the recovery of quotas, payment of taxes or collection for basic services view this topic as an important alternative for increasing their revenues. This topic will be explained in the case that follows.

The INFONAVIT case is briefly described below and includes references to many of the measures presented.

The Case of the National Institute of the Workers' Housing Fund (INFONAVIT)

Financing Sources

INFONAVIT's main sources of financing are the mandatory employer contributions in favor of workers and the amortization of loans granted.

Total Revenue 2000–2003

Both portfolio collection and employer contributions improved during this period. Whereas in 2000, INFONAVIT reported total revenues of 38.24 billion pesos, it is expected that in 2004, revenues will surpass 71 billion pesos, an 86 percent increase.

Revenue through inspection also showed an increase due to improved procedures. Actions that have resulted in improved collection of employer contributions are: the creation of the General Sub-directorate of Fiscal Collection, the implementation of control systems that provide strict and timely follow-up on compliance with employer obligations, and the use of alternative channels, through Internet, which make it possible to consult, clarify and comply with employers' obligations with regard to housing.

Total Revenue

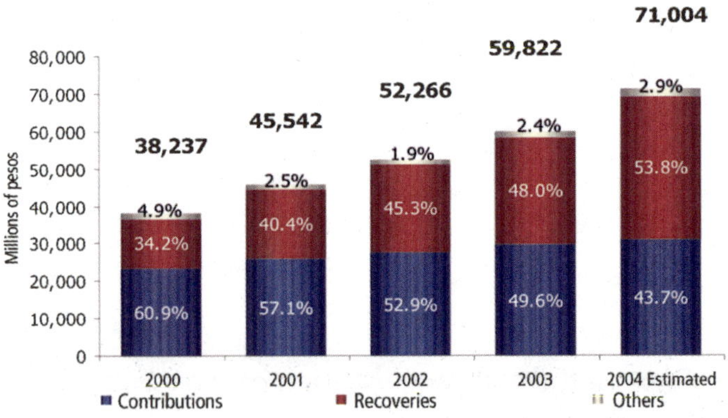

The proportion representing revenue from portfolio recovery in comparison with total revenue has risen: in 2000 it was 34.2 percent, and in 2003, 48 percent. Currently, revenue from credit recovery is higher than the revenue from employer contributions. The actions that helped to increase portfolio collections are: the creation of the General Subdirectorate of Portfolio Administration, the intensive borrower regularization program, the use of cutting-edge technology for portfolio management and collection, and the contracting of external collection firms, all of which have contributed to the improved results. The overdue portfolio index dropped from 21.4 percent in 2000 to 9.5 percent in 2003, and reserves have been created for credit risks which in 2000 were 78.8 percent of the overdue portfolio, and in 2003, 146.9 percent.

Income from Oversight

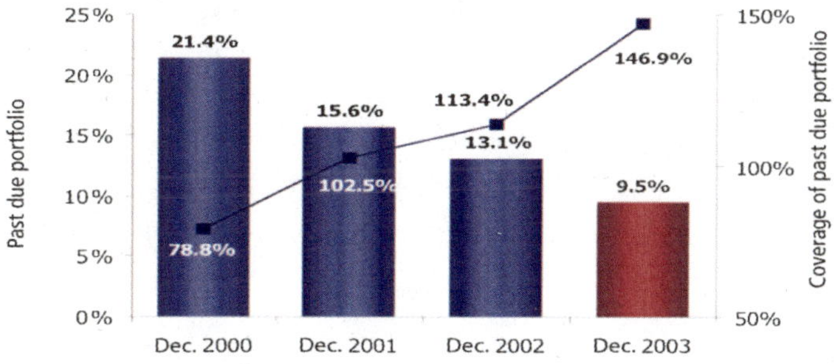

Alternative Financing Sources

In March 2004, INFONAVIT issued Low-Cost Housing Stock Market Certificates (CEDEVIS) for approximately 750 million pesos. It was the first time that INFONAVIT gained access to financial markets to channel funds into financing for housing. With the advance receipt of future credit flows, INFONAVIT expedites the rotation of its assets and enters a virtuous circle that allows it to strengthen its capacity for extending credit without contracting debt or committing its assets or altering the conditions for payment, terms and rate originally established with the borrower. With the issue of CEDEVIS, funds can be generated transparently, without limiting the Institute's financial and administrative autonomy. It is expected that two more transactions will be carried out in 2004 which will provide the Institute with an additional 4 billion pesos.

Design and Implementation of New Mortgage Products

For INFONAVIT beneficiaries with an income ranging from 7.1 to 11 times the minimum wage, TMW, a "Joint financing" program was designed to complement the funds from an INFONAVIT credit with those of another loan granted by a bank or a limited-purpose financial company, SOFOL. Under this system, the amount INFONAVIT will disburse includes the balance of the housing sub-account plus a credit equivalent to the current value of future employer contributions.

For workers who receive more than 11 TMW, the "INFONAVIT Support" program is used with loans granted by a financial entity other than INFONAVIT for the purchase of housing valued at less than 860,000 pesos. The balance of the housing sub-account remains in guarantee so that in the event of a job loss, the amortization is covered, while subsequent employer contributions of 5 percent of the integrated wage of the worker is allocated to amortize the loan; this results in a reduced amortization term.

Both "Joint financing" and "INFONAVIT Support" provide for the participation of private capital in financing for housing, boost the funds and broaden the Institute's capacity to grant more loans.

Certainty and Long-Term View in the Housing Sector

INFONAVIT has implemented a five-year Financial Plan, which is a planning tool for the medium and long terms. It also maintains fluid, ongoing communication with various agents which, in addition to an extensive network of specialized external suppliers, has increased its operating capacity and helped to create an environment of stability and certainty in the housing sector. The recent placements in the Mexican Stock Exchange have been from companies pertaining to this sector.

INFONAVIT has granted a million loans in less than four years. Since the beginning of this administration, 17 percent more loans have been granted than in the whole of the previous administration. One-third of the loans extended in the Institute's history were formalized between December 2000 and August 2004.

- Greater benefits to society:
  Without measures of this type it would not be possible to explain the growth of public investment and the higher budgets for programs that have the greatest impact on society. Below are some of the benefits that society has received from this type of measures:

  More specifically, the following should be mentioned:
- Public investment is the highest in the last 20 years
- 70 percent of the main highways have been modernized
- In 2004, public and private investment pledged for highway construction was equivalent to all the investment of the previous administration (55.95 billion pesos)
- Installation of 2,300 e-Mexico community centers
- Incorporation of 262,000 new hectares of afforestation
- New programs for social assistance and the fight against poverty, such as fortified Liconsa milk, which has succeeded in reverting anemia in 280,000 children
- The micro-regions strategy which is providing social infrastructure to the most marginalized localities in 1,340 municipalities
- The Habitat program, which operates in 170 cities, is designed to address urban poverty

- The number of families incorporated into the *Oportunidades* program has increased from 2.6 to 5 million families, benefiting more than 25 million people
- Support for 20,000 quality schools
- Start-up of the *Enciclomedia* project
- One million families affiliated to the People's Insurance
- Installation of 750,000 classroom libraries
- Increase in the number of SMEs attended by NAFIN, from 15,000 in 2000 to 450,000 in 2004

2000/2004 Budget Increases in Real Terms for Headings with the Highest Social Impact

Poverty	45.2%
Education	8.8%
Health care	14.3%
Agriculture	33.8%
Security	24.3%
Transfers to the states	17.0%

With a long-range vision and facing an adverse international situation, President Fox's administration has maintained a responsible fiscal policy which strengthens public revenue and avoids squandering, thus consolidating macroeconomic stability. This provides economic agents with a framework of greater certainty and trust that facilitates decision-making. This is essential for promoting investment and economic growth and generating jobs.

Mexico has firm bases for consolidating growth and taking advantage of the new surge in the world economy. Today, inflation, interest rates and the country risk are at the lowest levels in recent decades; on the other hand, our international reserves are becoming stronger, reaching record levels in 2004 of more than US$57 billion.

Mexico has firm bases for consolidating growth and taking advantage of the new surge in the world economy. Today, inflation, interest rates and the country risk are at the lowest levels in recent decades; on the other hand, our international reserves are becoming stronger, reaching record levels in 2004 of more than US$57 billion

7. International Standing

The efforts made by President Fox's administration in the area of Good Government are beginning to have international standing. For example, the Chairman of Transparency International, Peter Eigen said: *"Mexico has undertaken major reforms in favour of transparency and against corruption. Most of them are acknowledged by the international community and should provide inspiration to the countries of Latin America and other regions of the world. But they are just the beginning of a long-term effort."*

Similarly, the UN Secretary-General, Kofi Annan, stated: *"Mexico, the host of this forum [he is referring to the Fifth Global Forum on Reinventing Government, held on November 3 to 6, 2003 in Mexico City], is putting into practice a good government agenda that aims to do more with less resources."*

For his part, the Assistant Secretary-General for Economic and Social Affairs of the UN, Jose Antonio Ocampo, affirmed that *"Mexico stands in fourth place as regards the quality of the contents of government sites on the Internet, behind the United States, Chile and Canada."*

And in the Final Declaration of the Fifth Global Forum on Reinventing Government: Innovation and Quality in the Government of the 21st Century, the Mexico City Declaration, we can read the following:

> The participants of the Fifth Forum would like to express their sincere gratitude to President Vicente Fox Quesada for his leadership and commitment to implementing good government initiatives. The participants also cordially thank the government of Mexico for the successful organization of this major global event and commend the United Nations and international organizations for their invaluable support.

Chapter 4

Strategic Model for Government Innovation and Quality

In the first few days of his administration, President Fox instructed the head of the Office for Government Innovation to design the Strategic Model for innovation in the government. This project was submitted to him on January 20, 2001. President Fox approved it that same day with the order to publicize it widely and present it formally to the Extended Cabinet.

To build the Strategic Model for Government Innovation we started from a series of basic premises:

1. The best model is reality itself.
2. The proposed model is essentially a model of social innovation toward the interior of the Federal Public Administration.
3. Its vision focuses on recovering citizens' trust in the government, as well as on transforming it into a world-class competitive institution.
4. The intention is not to turn it into a straitjacket, much less into the last word.
5. It is a sound, structured guide that will be useful to us, like a map, in conducting the process of change.
6. We will have to submit it constantly to review, respecting the basic principles, as a consequence of our new learning and unlearning processes.

Quality Model

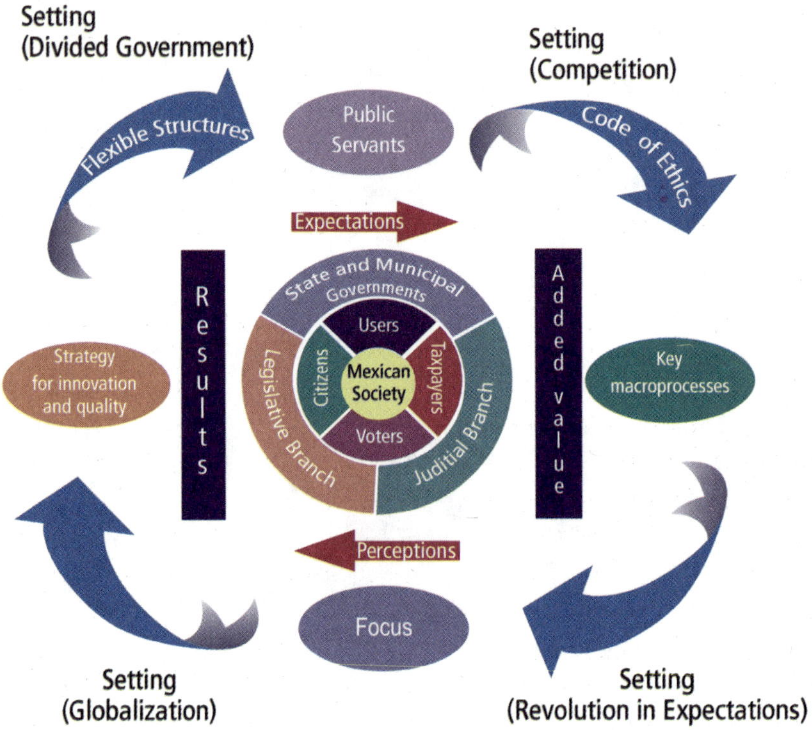

What Do We Call Innovation in the Government?

Innovation in the government is a movement of a cultural and structural nature that seeks to radically reform the Federal Public Administration's direction, capacity and speed of strategic response, reappraising everything from a number of perspectives.

It is a cultural and structural movement because it links all public servants around a purpose. Using strategies for change, they reexamine key macro-processes to improve the capacity to govern and produce results that benefit Mexican society.

Main Features of the Strategic Model

1. External Customers to be Served

a. Mexican society. The Federal Government's raison d'être is society itself. To hit the target as to what society demands and needs, one must have reliable information.

The population's needs are a target in constant movement. Society is not a monolithic block but a series of segments with social, cultural, historical, political and economic features which give them their own identity and differentiate them from one another.

b. The Branches of Government (Legislative and Judicial). For the first time, Mexico is living a real democratic system based on genuine separation of powers in which none is subject to another, rather what prevails is a scheme for jointly responsible collaboration.

c. The Levels of Government (States and Municipalities). Today more than ever attention should be paid to State and Municipal Governments, the result of a growing federalism. Moreover, the Federation allocates a significant percentage of the budget to States and Municipalities, which have the closest contact with citizens.

What most concerns Mexican society about the Federal Government's work is the results it obtains, results that generate significant, evident and close value. Those results are precisely the central objective of the Federal Government's Innovation and Quality Model.

The results, that is, deeds, not words, are ultimately what justifies or disqualifies a government. The government's work culture had centered more on activities and inputs, not on results. This had to be changed.

Perception, being important, cannot be sustained over time unless it is backed by results.

The Innovation and Quality Model seeks to give added value to what the government does; Innovation implies being responsible for visualizing needs not perceived by citizens and acting to satisfy them.

That is why you have to try to go beyond expectations.

In the past, the President of the Republic was Chief Executive and at the same time controlled the Legislative and Judicial Branches, paving the way for an absolute presidential power that totalized and centralized decision-making. However, the 2000 elections not only brought alternation in the Executive Branch but also intensified the process of dispersion of power

2. The Milieu and its Main Characteristics

It is especially important, in the design and application of any type of model of organizational change, to take the milieu into account, as it is not static in time, nor is it hewn in stone. When a paradigm changes, everyone goes back to zero. To understand the importance of a change in the milieu, suffice it to recall here the deplorable terrorist attacks of September 11, 2001, in New York and March 11, 2004, in Madrid, events that globalized insecurity.

Certainly the changes that could be called paradigmatic, such as the appearance of the Internet, cellular telephony, everything relative to the human genome, are events that do not happen every day, and therefore it is also important to consider changes which, although having lesser importance and impact, make it necessary to make a series of adjustments and tactical redefinitions of the model.

a. Competition

One of the main characteristics of the milieu has to do with competition. This applies to all spheres and fields: economic, military, religious, biological, professional, academic, political, cultural, electoral, social, sports, etc.

A model cannot be designed if you do not know who the competitors for investments, financial resources, human talents, accesses to strategic areas and geopolitical spaces are. It is essential to understand the motivations, interests, history, credentials and offers of those who are also participating in the game. The relationship with the competition would necessarily have to be based on open, transparent, legal and ethical rules directed toward a win-win scheme. It is possible and desirable to create collaborative associations even with our competition. Some authors call this relationship co-opetition (Nalebuff, Barry/Brandenburger, Adam M. *Co-Opetition*, Norma).

In the electoral field, the most common occurrence in democratic societies is for the results to lead to divided governments. Such has been the case in Mexico since the 1997 mid-term elections. And even more radically since the July 2, 2000 elections. In the past, the President of the Republic was Chief Executive and at the same time controlled the Legislative and Judicial Branches, paving the way for an absolute presidential power that totalized and centralized decision-making. However, the 2000 elections not only brought alternation in the Executive Branch but also intensified the process of dispersion of power.

Globalization produces major pressures and demands on governments. Above all, globalization has altered the variety and intensity of topics on the diplomatic, economic and political agendas

Added to the separation of powers and the autonomy with which both the Legislature and the Judiciary take their decisions, for the first time the majority of state governments do not belong to the same political party as that of the President. On the other hand there is the plural composition of Congress, for no party obtained an absolute majority in the 2000 federal elections. No one can deny that in any country, for any government it is easier to undertake substantive, in-depth reforms when the ruling party has a majority, which was not the case.

In a situation with a divided government, in terms of its composition, the leeway for political maneuver is reduced, and it is therefore necessary to establish mechanisms based on negotiation, dialogue and consensus-seeking.

Furthermore, we have the competitiveness factor. We cannot successfully face competition unless we are competitive. One arises from the other. Competitiveness encompasses both the individual and collective planes. In this context, having a competitive government becomes a strategic factor in furthering the country's competitiveness.

In regard to this climate of competitiveness in which democracy and government efficiency play a key role, it should be recalled that the 2004 Index of Economic Freedom, published by a number of foundations and institutions at world level, in 2003 Mexico stood in 63rd place among 155 countries classified, far below its main trading partners. The points scored include a series of categories such as trade policy, government tax burden, intervention in the economy, monetary policy, capital flows and foreign investment, banking and financial activity, wages and prices, property rights, regulations and informal market.

In short, competition is a reality in our milieu and competitiveness, in a win-win scheme, is the strategic response.

The change in expectations that this knowledge engenders has serious political, economic, social and educational consequences for the emerging countries and may be considered a Copernican change in peaceful coexistence among societies

b. Globalization

The phenomenon of globalization has existed for a long time, regardless of differing points of view with regard to its origins. There are those who place its beginnings in the great Venetian trade, for others the Austro-Hungarian empire was a form of globalization; still others believe it originated in the interdependence that began in western countries in the seventies and eighties. Everyone recognizes its existence, irrespective of the position they adopt toward it. It is therefore essential to understand this phenomenon and its main characteristics, precisely because of the implications and repercussions it will likely have on our countries, governments, institutions, localities, families and personal lives.

Globalization produces major pressures and demands on governments. Above all, globalization has altered the variety and intensity of topics on the diplomatic, economic and political agendas.

Many new topics have arisen in recent years: the transition of communist bloc countries to free market economies, a much more varied trade agenda, growing concern over the environment, a new international financial architecture, humanitarian aid programs for the poorest countries, etc.

These are topics that have resulted in a generalized concern, such as food security, international organized crime, terrorism and the globalization of international security.

The phenomena we have witnessed in recent years compel us to reexamine our country's relations with the exterior. The advances that have taken place in relatively short time-spans in the fields of telecommunications, information technology, electronic commerce, among others, have radically transformed cultural patterns that until recently were well-defined and well-established within each country.

c. Revolution in Expectations

"The Revolution in Expectations" is a term coined by David Konzevik and refers to one of the consequences of the major technological changes, especially as of the nineties.

In the past, the news most of the world population received from abroad was scarce or nonexistent.

People in villages had no contact with the outside and knew a few hundred people, all equals among themselves, in their whole life. In the Middle Ages, an individual heard about ten pieces of news about the outside world in his or her entire life. Now they are what a human being hears while he shaves.

Instant world news, the current trend in various media, has allowed peoples to know other ways and levels of life, in real time. And as Ovid said: "One does not want what one does not know."

> The change in expectations that this knowledge engenders has serious political, economic, social and educational consequences for the emerging countries and may be considered a Copernican change in peaceful coexistence among societies.

Millions of individuals who used to live and die without being known by the rest of society are today demanding basic goods and services at once, trying to redress centuries of deficiencies in a few years.

This is its extreme manifestation, for the desire to "live like the neighbor" is by no means limited to indigenous or marginalized groups.

This revolution in expectations is being put forth today in all the Latin American countries, regardless of the economic program or ideology of their leaders. From Cuba to Argentina the phenomenon is the same, and the way of managing it largely depends on the country's degree of democratic openness.

Some manifestations are migration, roadblocks, demonstrations, demands and pressures.

The outcome of this information society is that the highest growth is that of the inhabitants' expectations.

The difficulties in governance that this situation entails could lead us to thinking that governing today is the art of managing expectations.

Innovation in the government will be successful to the extent that its actions are linked and are based on identifying society's demands and needs

d. Democracy

To explain the importance of democracy as a worldwide trend, it is worth recalling here a particularly significant fact. When Mexico was negotiating a trade agreement with the European Union, Italy asserted its vote to apply what was called the Democratic Clause. By means of this clause, the signing of the agreement would remain in suspense until the 2000 elections were held, the results were known and there was full certainty as to the cleanness of the electoral process. Once Vicente Fox's victory was known in the world, the agreement was unblocked. That clause was, to be sure, of a political nature, but it also involved an issue of competitiveness: if Mexico was not fully recognized as a democratic country, the agreement would not go through. Somehow the members of the European Union wanted to deal with a country in equality of democratic conditions, with all that this implies, and implicit was the notion that a country with democratic rules would have to have clearer, more honest and more transparent rules of the game for everything concerning international trade and financial relations, without excluding respect for human rights.

Indeed, since then, European direct investment in Mexico has increased substantially, as have trade exchanges, although we know that there is enormous potential there which we must continue developing.

3. The Importance of Having a Well-Defined Aim

To be successful in the design and implementation of any model of innovation and change, there must be a Strategic Approach that enables all the stakeholders in the transformation process to be clearly aware of the most important issues, topics or expected results.

Why is a Strategic Approach advisable? Because without a doubt all the factors involved in a process of change are limited. In the case of the public administration, the time an authority has for governing is limited. The financial and budget resources available for addressing social demands and the commitments made during its campaign are limited. The political capital a leader has for furthering the legislative reforms and political accords he or she pursues is limited and fluctuating. The legal and regulatory framework within which he or she must take his or her decisions is also limited.

Some ideas or elements that could help us as references in the process of determining the central purpose or Strategic Approach we need could be the following, among others:

Nothing succeeds in focusing work teams and organizations as much as the definition of customers to be served and specific needs to be met. This exercise is fundamental to any Strategic Planning process

a. Shared Vision and Mission
b. Social Demands and Priorities
c. Policies of Relations
d. Positioning
e. Definition of Customers
f. Negotiation of Goals

> The purpose of innovation in the government should be to improve the capacity to govern in order to address Mexican society's desires and expectations, thereby recovering trust in its authorities.

a. Shared Vision and Mission

Its strength stems from a common interest: sharing a future we want to build together. The shared vision raises people's aspirations, modifies public servants' relations, encourages experimentation and the desire to run risks and makes it easier to get to where we want to get.

b. Social Demands and Priorities

First of all, it must be understood that Mexican society is not a mass entity but a series of diversified segments. Furthermore, as we have already commented, each person assumes different roles (citizen, customer, taxpayer, voter, etc.). Depending on the role they assume, needs and expectations in relation to the Federal Government vary. Understanding this is essential for us to take the right approach and serve society well.

Innovation in the government will be successful to the extent that its actions are linked and are based on identifying society's demands and needs.

The public administration's most valuable asset should be its people. For things to work outside, they must also work inside. The challenge of shaping an innovative government requires investing strongly in public servants

Many of these demands and priorities are expressed and heard during the electoral process itself. Once you take office, they become government commitments and should be translated into measurable and quantifiable goals.

c. Policies of Relations

Defining policies of relations with the different social, political, economic, religious and military stakeholders, from an institutional point of view, is a highly valuable process when you want to have a Strategic Approach.

In order for such policies not to be a sterile exercise, it is advisable for them to be negotiated with the parties involved, for only thus will it be possible to ensure a sound point of departure and a clear destination.

Since the series of bodies that make up the public administration have legal status, policies of relations cannot be established without an institutional character. It is not a question of an exercise in defining relations from a personal point of view.

d. Positioning

A powerful tool for defining the central purpose is undoubtedly defining the positioning. The following is a simple way of explaining it: you cannot score a ten in all subjects.

A simple formula for explaining positioning would be the following: we have to chose the few subjects in which we should and want to score a ten and avoid failing them at all costs.

All the knowledge that has been developed around what is known today as political marketing, combined with a generous dose of talent, honesty and common sense, can doubtless be a fundamental help in defining positioning.

e. Definition of Customers

Nothing succeeds in focusing work teams and organizations as much as the definition of customers to be served and specific **needs** to be met. This exercise is fundamental to any Strategic Planning process.

Without the foregoing, all services and all processes make no sense and all activities, tasks and efforts are a waste of time and money.

f. Negotiation of Goals

Negotiation of goals from the highest levels of a government, administration or institution is undoubtedly a powerful tool for focusing everyone's attention on the most important results to be pursued.

For this process to really be useful, it is worth bearing a few recommendations in mind.

- It should be initiated and backed by the highest-level authority.
- Consider a few high-impact, highly motivating and challenging goals.
- Define goals in terms of results, not of processes, activities or indicators, much less resources.
- Fulfillment or non-fulfillment of goals should have consequences previously negotiated by the parties.

The leaders' worth is measured by their contribution to the paradigms of others, by their ability to have a significant influence on the lives of those who surround them. Leadership is for serving others, not for using them. A leader's first and most crucial decision is to serve others

4. Internal Customers to be Served: Public Servants and their Needs

The public administration's most valuable asset should be its people. For things to work outside, they must also work inside. The challenge of shaping an innovative government requires investing strongly in public servants.

It is public servants at all levels in the public administration who make it possible for things to happen and for the results to take place. In the final analysis it is the results, not the actions, that justify the work of any government. This is why investing in public servants becomes a priority task.

One essential step is knowing and diagnosing their main needs and building the processes that lead to meeting those needs.

Some of the most important elements that can help in satisfying personnel are:

a. Quality Leadership
b. New Paradigms
c. Mobilization and Participation

The challenges the government is facing require leaders who can create the "YES" after so many decades of "it can't be done"

The challenge is to create the atmosphere and build the means to bring together all public servants in the process of change

d. Empowerment
e. Motivating and Creative Climate
f. Personal Development
g. Security and Hygiene
h. Family Balance

a. Quality Leadership
In this field what counts is the everyday example and evidence. Not spiels or speeches.

The leaders' worth is measured by their contribution to the paradigms of others, by their ability to have a significant influence on the lives of those who surround them. Leadership is for serving others, not for using them. A leader's first and most crucial decision is to serve others. The rest is learning the how, the means and the techniques. First comes the attitude and then the instruments.

Leadership is not for suppressing complaints, it is for raising their category and level. Leaders should be agents of change; innovation is a popular mandate.

The challenges the government is facing require leaders who can create the "yes" after so many decades of "it can't be done."

Quality leadership is based on characteristics such as honesty, vision, innovation, competence and generation of enthusiasm, on genuine principles perceived as such by colleagues, for this gives rise to credibility. Leadership will be the main modeler of the new organizational culture.

> A leader needs to have knowledge and an open mentality; if he or she adheres blindly to tradition, he or she will no longer be a leader and will have nothing to contribute to Change and Innovation. Leaders must be capable of improving what works and creating new options of service and quality and making their collaborators follow them, follow them with enthusiasm, creativity, commitment and shared goals.

b. New Paradigms
When one hears "That's how it used to be done," one could ask:

"What happens if we do it this other way? What happens if we don't do it any more?"

At the same time, one should be able to stimulate the creativity and commitment of one's collaborators, who should also open up to the new paradigms.

c. Mobilization and Participation

Public servants' mobilization will not take place unless their deepest needs are discovered and responded to. Only this will prevent the struggle for change from becoming polarized and politicized.

Mobilization is the process whereby public servants are taken at least to the point where they accept the changes, and in the best of cases to the point where they are ready to act to carry them out.

If leaders do not mobilize personnel and allow them to participate, the results and the commitments acquired will not occur satisfactorily. The challenge is to create the atmosphere and build the means to bring together all public servants in the process of change.

d. Empowerment

It is not enough to mobilize public servants, transmit energy to them and gain their willingness for the daily struggle; one must provide them with the tools, set monitoring systems in motion, then stand aside and let them act.

Empowerment is considered a control strategy that seeks to make an impact on the lever of power structures. It implies displacement of authority and responsibility, as a result of which the upper structures, far from weakening, become stronger.

Empowerment is ultimately a matter of trust and freedom.

e. Motivating and Creative Climate

If a motivating and creative organizational climate is achieved, the results will come in addition. In an atmosphere of credibility, empowerment, enthusiasm and trust, everyone wins.

The key role played by leaders in shaping a highly productive and fully human organizational climate has been psychologically proven.

Measurement of the organizational climate should be viewed as a

There is no prize, however appetizing it may seem, worth paying with the price of giving up the family

compass, an aid for ratifying the course, not as a police or punitive instrument.

Innovation demands permission to be able to make a mistake, to experiment: this only happens within a framework of freedom.

It is necessary to transform the public sector into a good workplace for people, a place where public servants face challenges and take advantage of opportunities, and these should be dependent on service to citizens.

f. Personal Development

To be sure, the traditional hierarchical organization in the government is not designed to meet public servants' higher needs, such as self-esteem, pride and self-realization.

This is why leaders must understand the "almost sacred" nature of their responsibility for the lives of so many people.

An important challenge for public servants in their development is learning to manage their emotional life intelligently.

Personal development is the discipline of growth and personal learning.

For public servants with a high level of personal development, a vision is a vocation and not just a good idea.

If leaders take care of their collaborators' growth, these will take charge of providing good services to citizens.

Personal development requires a platform of credibility and trust, and the latter can only be built from a code of Ethics lived from personal example and from daily life.

The purpose of any strategy is to succeed in differentiating ourselves and providing ourselves with a competitive advantage sustainable for as long as possible. Strategies point to the major routes of action to reach our goals

Leaders have the responsibility to create the conditions so that public servants are themselves responsible for their growth and development. No one can do for others what they themselves are not motivated and determined to do for themselves.

Motivation is a door that opens from the inside.

g. Security and Hygiene

Hygiene factors are only perceived when they do not come up to expectations. They are usually associated with order, cleanliness, logistical aspects, discipline, timetables, salaries and wages.

The challenge in this field is to achieve a balance between Tradition and Innovation in the age of globalization

Their importance is almost always perceived when they are lacking or when they fail.

No one would want to Innovate and lose his/her job at the same time; if one has security, one's attitude changes favorably. No one likes to contribute ideas that only serve to dig his/her own grave.

Some examples of these factors? Physical workplaces, order in the filing system, handling of correspondence, agenda management, payment of the payroll, prevention of occupational accidents, and maintenance of equipment and installations.

These factors should be managed as processes that translate into decent services for public servants.

h. Family Balance

It is very common for many politicians, officials and public servants to pay a very high price in this field because they do not know how to balance their family life with their political vocation. This does not necessarily have to be so... There is no valid reason for betting on a win-lose situation.

Public office is often only temporary. The family is forever. The family should be present in everyone's agenda, priorities, plans and hearts. The family should be an important customer to be served.

Those who believe that to "serve the country" they must push the family into the background are fooling themselves.

There is no prize, however appetizing it may seem, worth paying with the price of giving up the family.

5. Strategies for Innovation and Quality

Strategy design is a basic feature of any model of organizational change. Making the changes that the government, the public administration or any institution needs requires overall, innovative, futurist strategies of rupture with the past.

For any strategy to be considered as such, it must have concepts (theory), techniques (tools) and vehicles (organization schemes and structures).

It would be an illusion to think that significant results can be obtained by operating with the same old rules of the game. We would end up stuck in real "necks of bottlenecks"

The purpose of any strategy is to succeed in differentiating ourselves and providing ourselves with a competitive advantage sustainable for as long as possible.

Strategies point to the major routes of action to reach our goals.

Some of the strategies that the Federal Government, headed by President Vicente Fox Quesada, has suggested for furthering innovation and quality in the agencies of the Federal Public Administration as a whole are:

a. Quality Management

Without a doubt, the evolution of quality systems in the world is an enormous advance in terms of improvement of administration and management models and practices.

From quality control systems that worked as customs houses in laboratories that analyzed raw materials, to quality assurance systems, to the establishment of the current ISO 9000 standards, we have fortunately been able to confirm that as the approach expanded to the entirety of the world of management and administration, better results are obtained as regards internal and external customers' satisfaction and trust in institutions and organizations.

b. Federalism and Local Government

The aim is to strengthen state and municipal governments' strategic response capacity so that they are able to serve citizens more and better.

This strategy should essentially be an exercise in decentralization of power, authority and resources.

c. Tradition and Innovation

The challenge in this field is to achieve a balance between **Tradition** and **Innovation** in the age of globalization. Experience teaches us that it is not possible to scorn history, undo everything and build anew as on a blank page. What works should be handled "with kid gloves." What does not work should be abandoned. The closure of agencies, cancellation of programs and reduction of structures tends to be a particularly painful and difficult exercise which meets with enormous resistance and which institutions and governments often end up postponing or leaving half finished.

Nowadays specialists in processes of change consider *Learning* and *Unlearning* equally important.

A government that wants to be innovative must be capable of attracting extra-governmental resources. Budgets are not sufficient for financing strategic projects or commitments undertaken during political campaigns

d. Open and Transparent Government

> Making a custom out of accountability to society on the use and allocation of public resources and informing it of the progress made in the challenges and commitments undertaken is one of the best ways of guaranteeing transparency.

Endowing the public administration as a whole with a system of "total electricity" would undoubtedly favor the fight against and inhibition of practices based on corruption. It is in an atmosphere of opacity that authoritarian decisions, lies, impunity and dishonesty take root and develop.

Here it is a question of making what is public truly public, and of putting everything to do with the government and its administration in full view of the citizens, as if in a "glass house."

e. Legal and Regulatory Reforms

Any process of change should bear in mind, as of the design stage, the legal and juridical framework. Although it is true and accepted that leaders are only permitted to do what the law expressly authorizes, it is also true that such frameworks should be modified in light of the new challenges and the changes imposed by globalization and demanded by society.

It would be an illusion to think that significant results can be obtained by operating with the same old rules of the game. We would end up stuck in real "necks of bottlenecks." Legal restrictions can stifle any attempt at innovation, and therefore innovation should impregnate the world of regulations, rules and laws.

f. Joining up the Rearguard and the Vanguard

This is a question of building the game rules, collaboration mechanisms and spaces that make it possible to share learning experiences among work teams in different areas, tiers and levels of government.

Public institutions should further not only the necessary tax reforms, which are essential, especially as income-distribution mechanisms, but also other creative schemes to enable them to attract funds from civil society, private initiative or international agencies

Development in any organization is obviously not uniform. Agencies have evolved in different ways and are not at one same level of development. This due to many reasons, among the most important being their history, leadership styles and culture, among others.

g. Benchmarking

This term refers to a sort of comparison of our processes, services and results with the best practices of other organizations and governments in order to have points of reference and learn from all the ideas that might be useful, by adoption or adaptation, for improving our work. Here the key consists of two elements: information and an attitude of improvement. It begins with full understanding or knowledge of our own processes and services. Attention is concentrated more on the process than on the result. It is a "vaccine" against self-complacency.

Undoubtedly, benchmarking is valuable not only in the field of organizational change, but also in that of political strategy.

h. Entrepreneurial Financing

A government that wants to be innovative must be capable of attracting extra-governmental resources. Budgets are not sufficient for financing strategic projects or commitments undertaken during political campaigns.

Factors such as population growth, increased life expectancy, appearance of chronic diseases, the "revolution in expectations", educational level, access to information, and the accumulation of generational problems such as retirement pensions, turn into real pressures for leaders and public administrators who have an influence in practice on leeway for maneuver.

Therefore, "public institutions should further not only the necessary tax reforms, which are essential, especially as income-distribution mechanisms, but also other creative schemes to enable them to attract funds from civil society, private initiative or international agencies."

One scheme that has gained growing acceptance in the world is the one called Service Delivery Projects (SDP), which involves joint participation by the public and private sectors. This scheme, which began in 1992 in the United Kingdom, contributes to more efficient use of public spending, increases resources for investment in social infrastructure and helps the government to provide better quality public services.

i. Informatics and Telecommunications

The use of information technology is essential to any innovation effort. It is important to understand that it is not a question of assigning more computers to a problem without redesigning, for we would merely be digitalizing errors. We are in the age of access, in a world moving on from information based on atoms to information packaged in bytes, and we must therefore take advantage of the new technologies to respond swiftly to the challenges we face as a government, as an institution and as a country.

The results of process redesign backed by leading-edge information technology are simply astounding.

The secret of innovation in this field is to introduce administration systems at the speed of the Internet.

j. Outsourcing

The government should devote itself to coxing, not to rowing. The government should focus on strategic and substantive processes. In this regard, secondary or adjective processes or services can and should be subcontracted or outsourced using any other legally permissible and politically viable arrangement.

k. Total Connectivity

This strategy can produce a truly revolutionary synergy in which one plus one equals three. Who would have imagined what we would be capable of doing with a computer and telephone connection, today called Internet? What would happen if we could connect all of a government's or an institution's financial resources, know-how, public relations and political capital? It is almost impossible to imagine the quantum leaps we could take.

The object of this game would be to connect and integrate everyone with everyone and everything with everything. We are talking about a marvelous idea which if explored offers unlimited possibilities and it would be a mistake to reduce this concept to digital or electronic connections.

I. Appreciative Inquiry

David Cooperrider of Case Western Reserve University and his colleagues and fellow "explorers" designed this strategy for organizational change.

One fundamental principle of appreciative inquiry is that it is a question of a generative process, which means that it is a moving target and people who use it create it and recreate it.

This strategy introduces the concept: **What works here?** It contradicts the traditional method for change that consists of identifying the problem, making a diagnosis and finding the solution.

The idea from the appreciative point of view starts from the principle that in any society, organization or group there is something that works. Its approach is based on visualizing the **Future**, on the positive results we want to achieve on the basis of past experiences that have been successful.

Innovation consists in work teams developing "suggestive proposals" that describe the ideal state we aim for and that favor an atmosphere conducive to doing more of what actually works.

There are those who look for things that went wrong and try to fix them; here it is a question of finding things that turned out well and building on them.

6. Key Macro-Processes to be Redesigned

The key macro-processes are those that have the greatest impact on the government's operation and performance, as well as on its users' and customers' satisfaction. To be considered key, all macro-processes should be strong, structured and systematized.

The following is a powerful dynamic:

- re-visualizing them – rethinking them
- redesigning them – renewing them (innovation)

- controlling them
- continuously improving them
- re-visualizing them again

It is essential to increase the government's capacity to acquire, generate, distribute and apply information strategically and operationally

Macro-processes are the basis of organizational redesign. By way of illustration we present some examples of key macro-processes focused on public servants:

- Information and measurement
- Continuous education and training
- Communication
- Personnel selection
- Organization of work teams
- Assessment and compensation
- Management of strategic projects

It is important to point out that it is imperative for the success of this task to identify the customers, know their needs, negotiate the services to be provided and the quality characteristics of same, define the processes that will meet their needs, determine the performance indicators or measurers of each process and assign a leader to each one of them.

a. Information and Measurement

When the measuring process starts, public servants immediately begin to think about the government's goals. In the world of quality there is a well-known axiom: "if I can measure it I can control it, and if I can control it, I can improve it." Certainly, if the results are not measured, it is not possible to distinguish success from failure. It is essential to increase the government's capacity to acquire, generate, distribute and apply information strategically and operationally.

b. Continuous Education and Training

In modern times university degrees are not sufficient. A résumé is only a letter of introduction, but what is really important is talent, abilities, attitudes and the results you have obtained. If we think that education

The emphasis should center on incorporating the best talents into public administration and not on complying with standards and policies of control that stifle innovation and creativity

is over once we leave the classrooms, obviously we are wrong. Education is forever because nothing is definitive: the environment and circumstances change, customers' needs and expectations also change, and possibilities multiply.

It is a question of continuing to set aside an appreciable amount of time in our agenda both for learning and for unlearning. The options available today are varied and interesting. They go beyond just courses and workshops. They have to do with strategic conversations, illustrative travels, surfing the Internet, interactive games, e-learning, open and modular education systems, distance learning, etc.

c. Communication

It is advisable to further communication on change, on the benefits, on the new culture wanted in the public administration, on why there is innovation. That is why it should be the task of all leaders.

Communication is important because it is linked to the process of accountability—to which all democratic governments are bound—and because it constitutes a powerful motor for bringing together all the players in the process of change.

What is not known or not understood is rejected. Only what is known and understood can eventually be accepted, desired, favored, defended.

d. Budget and Finances

In the government the most important lever, the system that most strongly manages conduct, is the budget. Budgets are viewed as an instrument of power.

To improve the government's operation and effectiveness we must develop a budgetary system based on services—investments—or results, not on activities or inputs.

The budget and public finances go hand-in-hand. This is why responsible management is necessary in this field. And a sound point of departure is to improve the accounts in terms of the public balance and achieve fiscal equilibrium.

Budget implementation should be assessed by the results, not just by the spending allocated.

The redesign of this macro-process should reflect an enormous respect for taxpayers. This makes the task of reducing current expenditure and favoring spending on social investment inevitable.

If what is wanted is to improve performance, it is necessary to begin by creating both positive and negative consequences. Therefore the lever to be changed is Incentives

e. Career Civil Service

Its main goal should be to create the systems and conditions that make it possible to "attract, motivate, train and retain the best men and women in Public Service."

This enables officials at all levels to make a career within the public administration. It seeks to professionalize the task of public servants to guarantee changes of government with the maximum efficiency and the least disruption.

It also seeks to offer public servants opportunities for development and progress for their service to society.

The emphasis should center on incorporating the best talents into public administration and not on complying with standards and policies of control that stifle innovation and creativity.

f. Organization of Work Teams

How do we organize ourselves? The answers can be manifold and varied. They range from systems of cross-administration, taskforces, networks, matrix schemes, temporary project teams, and many more. The important thing here is to leave behind atrophied organization charts dating back to the age of the Industrial Revolution and bet on other options that cut across bureaucratic systems.

Organizational design should not be carved in stone since we will have to adjust it in terms of results, circumstances and changes in the environment.

Organization based on work teams is precisely the opposite of organization based on power domains. Inter-departmental work teams are an excellent answer in solving problems which in most cases have multi-causal origins.

g. Assessment and Compensation

The processes of measurement and reward have to reinforce the new work culture in the public administration. It is necessary to acknowl-

Many processes are at the service of a project, as well as thousands of material inputs and use of intellectual capital, as happens in projects that are familiar to all: a Formula I race, a heart operation, the launching of a rocket into space

edge a superior contribution and sanction mediocre performance. In the government sphere this exercise is highly complicated and difficult, but it is possible to turn it into an innovative practice.

In this process the results are also important, not only the processes or activities.

Management by performance based on results establishes both financial and psychological incentives so as to promote Innovations. If what is wanted is to improve performance, it is necessary to begin by creating both positive and negative Consequences. Therefore the lever to be changed is Incentives.

h. Strategic Projects

Projects are the perfect answer for contending with change. This involves understanding the difference between the world of projects and the world of processes. The former are for seizing the opportunity, the latter for exploiting it. Projects are led, processes are managed. Projects are subject to limited resources and deadlines.

This is why working on the basis of projects represents an excellent alternative for breaking bureaucratic barriers, focusing on results, rendering accounts and delivering promised services on time.

The tool known as Cross-Administration makes possible a splendid combination of processes and projects in which the former are subordinate to the latter.

Cross-Administration is a powerful tool for achieving results in highly complex, crisis settings, with limited resources, with deadlines, highly changeable or high-risk.

As in all complex processes, all the supply mechanisms have to be optimized and made to coincide, that is, all the elements that make up the solution. The most important features of Cross-Administration are:

- It connects projects to processes
- It gathers resources from everywhere (what is called entrepreneurial financing)
- It is based on an overall, holistic vision
- It requires strong, reliable processes (ISO 9000, just in time, online service)

- It builds up teamwork, connectivity and synergies inside and outside the organization (partners' networks, strategic alliances)
- Every project has a leader and every process an "owner"
- Overcomes departmental barriers and runs through the bureaucracy
- Is based on a win-win scheme
- Focuses on results in clearly-defined timeframes

Many processes are at the service of a project, as well as thousands of material inputs and use of intellectual capital, as happens in projects that are familiar to all: a Formula I race, a heart operation, the launching of a rocket into space.

In order to be successful they require high levels of creativity and trust among team members and excellent coordination.

In Cross-Administration the most important thing is not the project but the participants' conviction to make their best effort to achieve success. If this is achieved, there will be an integrated team that will operate with basic criteria (corporate values) that allow coordination (direction) to obtain the best results.

The training of this human capital will be invaluable, for on becoming individually incorporated into other projects they will intrinsically contribute the values acquired.

The reorganization of government structures should be a continuous exercise. Vertical, centralized structures should be replaced by horizontal, virtual, nuclear, online, matrix ones by project, according to the changing expectations of Mexican society

7. The Organizational Structures to be Redesigned

Current organization charts are schemes of the past, of the Industrial Revolution. They no longer work. They were designed for an environment and an age that no longer exist. The reorganization of government structures should be a continuous exercise. Vertical, centralized structures should be replaced by horizontal, virtual, nuclear, online, matrix ones by project, according to the changing expectations of Mexican society.

8. The Culture of the Public Administration

> For any change to be radical and lasting, it should be made from the roots. This has to do with the values and principles that govern conduct, orient decisions and determine public policies.

The most common way is for organizations and institutions to express them in terms of a code of ethics and display them in a code of conduct.

In terms of communication, it is essential for all members of the institution to understand simply and clearly the attributes and qualities that are truly important. We are talking about the values that determine the modus operandi and the style of institutional life.

Central values are necessary to help people take their day-to-day decisions. They are, in fact, our instrument for ethical navigation, that is, we use them as a compass.

Politics is essentially philosophy in action.

Paradigms

If we want innovation in government to be successful, we need a new way of conceiving it and visualizing it, that is, to have new paradigms for reflection, action and transformation. If we do not have new ideas and initiatives that respond to the new needs, both internal and external, Federal Government public servants will have no alternative but to cling to the old schemes.

Paradigms are powerful because they affect everything we see and determine the way in which we behave and think.

Possible synonyms of paradigms are mental models, beliefs, hypotheses, ideas, myths, value judgments, dogmas, patterns of behavior, theories that are somehow like lenses that enable us to see reality. Hence the importance of adopting new ones and abandoning the old ones.

A paradigm is a set of rules (written or unwritten) that establish or define limits, and that indicate how to behave within the established limits in order to succeed.

The discipline of managing paradigms is in itself a decisive innovation in building strategic or intelligent governments.

9. The Results To Be Achieved

Undoubtedly what justifies any model in terms of its effectiveness is the results and their continuance in time. This is true of private enterprises, social institutions or governments. The results should be measured and evaluated by customers and citizens.

Chapter 5

Model of Quality in the Federal Government

Since the beginning of his administration, President Fox, aware of society's demands, pledged to introduce, develop, maintain and improve in all federal agencies and entities a model of quality that would make it possible to transform the Federal Public Administration into a world-class government with a reliable, transparent, innovative image and a solid culture of quality. This involved replacing traditional public-management schemes with the most advanced administrative and technological systems, assessing their performance with standards of competitiveness, promoting the advancement and effectiveness of public service, redesigning its processes and services, and directing its work toward the fulfillment of expectations and needs as a whole.

To respond to these commitments, the Federal Government established its quality policy, aimed at addressing three priority aspects:

- Service quality
- Integrity of public servants
- Society's perception of the reliability and effectiveness of the Federal Public Administration

Toward Service Quality

- An efficient and effective government with a quality management model.

- A reliable government in its policies, processes and services, through certification of its quality management systems.
- A government with tangible, improved results that continuously applies measurements in the definition of strategies and implementation of its actions to enable it to assess both resource management and the impact of its projects.

Toward the Integrity of Public Services

Public servants with a strong sense of commitment and service to citizens, an attitude of continuous improvement, a culture of teamwork, the adoption of schemes that empower their participation, transparency in the management of resources and decision-making based on facts and data.

Toward Society's Perception

- Implementation of actions to allow healthy coexistence and better quality of life in society.
- Services aimed at providing added value by means of clear awareness of expectations and in keeping with international standards.
- Knowledge of the degree of satisfaction perceived by customers and citizens for continuous improvement of public services.

To comply with the Executive's guidelines, we have the talent, responsibility and commitment of all public servants, who constitute the Public Administration's strength and who through the Federal Government's Quality Network accept the challenge of achieving the quality goals in 2006.

Based on particularly valid international experiences, as has been pointed out, but bearing in mind substantive social, cultural, political and economic aspects of the public administration's own reality and tradition, President Fox's administration, in accordance with its own view of what an effective and honest public administration should be, set about designing its own quality model. Thus the INTRAGOB Quality Model emerged, which is aimed at fully satisfying the expectations and needs of customers and citizens with regard to the products and services provided by the Federal Public Administration.

The INTRAGOB Quality Model also seeks to consolidate a culture of quality, improve productivity, competitiveness and technological innovation, as well as strengthen the responsible role of the personnel of all the agencies and entities before society.

The main objective of the Quality Process is a radical transformation of the Federal Public Administration so as to show a level of maturity in the INTRAGOB Quality Model that is reflected by the quality of processes, products and services, and by an enhanced image of public servants and of the agencies and entities. The Process and its results should be assessed from the citizens' point of view, which will contribute to an increase in productivity, competitiveness and savings. To that end, this document describes the guidelines for implementing this model.

Emphasis of the Elements of the INTRAGOB Model

- Improve the quality of public-sector products and services having a high impact on the citizenry in the short term.
- Consolidate a Culture of Quality in the Public Service.
- Achieve an honest and transparent Public Administration.
- Render accounts and results systematically.
- Promote savings and utilization of resources.
- Unify a vision of continuous improvement, innovation and competitiveness in the administration of government agencies and entities.

The INTRAGOB Quality Model focuses on satisfying the needs and expectations of customers and citizens, as the linchpin of efforts for quality, continuous improvement, innovation, competitiveness, integrity and transparency by the Federal Public Administration's agencies and entities, with the aim that the results obtained should have a direct impact on the citizenry's perception of service quality.

The principles of Customer Satisfaction and Service Quality are directed toward optimizing processes and services that enable their needs and expectations to be satisfied at the lowest cost, so that customers and citizens obtain and perceive the tangible and intangible aspects of quality

Within the framework of the 2001-2006 National Development Plan, the INTRAGOB Quality Model contributes to the six lines of action of the Presidential Agenda for Good Government:

- Honest and Transparent Government
- Professional Government
- Quality Government
- Digital Government
- Government with Regulatory Improvement
- Government that Costs Less

In short, a world-class government...
An innovative and total Quality Government.

INTRAGOB Model

Principles of Quality

The **INTRAGOB Quality Model** is a new philosophy of management of the Federal Public Administration aimed at satisfying customers' and citizens' expectations in a comprehensive manner, maintaining and improving results, and developing a preventive vision that promotes the furtherance of strategies and action plans through processes and systems.

The following principles constitute a platform for deploying the **INTRAGOB Quality Model:**

Customer and Citizen Satisfaction

The focal point of agencies' and entities' systems is identifying and becoming fully aware of the needs and expectations of customers, citizens and society as a whole and incorporating them into the improvement cycles of internal processes, as well as into related processes, products and services, in order to fully satisfy said needs and expectations by means of assessment and quality management systems, and thus respond in a timely, reliable manner with added value.

Service Quality

The Federal Public Administration is committed to responding consistently to customers' and citizens' expectations and requirements, with a clear understanding of product and service quality objectives and goals. In this action all public servants carry out their duties with responsibility, integrity, transparency and professionalism, as well as with a clear attitude of service whose added value is evident through professional, respectful, honest, timely and cordial attention.

The principles of Customer Satisfaction and Service Quality are directed toward optimizing processes and services that enable their needs and expectations to be satisfied at the lowest cost, so that customers and citizens obtain and perceive the tangible and intangible aspects of quality.

Quality of Life at Work

Recognizing that public servants are its most valuable element, the Federal Government upholds the responsibility entrusted to it of efficiently administering the wealth of the Nation and providing products and public services with quality.

Thus, public servants further and support the processes of quality, innovation, competitiveness and transparency in the agencies and entities; they participate, undergo training, and assume leadership and commitment to achieve goals and personal satisfaction as individuals and as an essential part of the Public Administration, in a work climate of respect, order, discipline and belt-tightening, translating into better quality of life at work.

Together, each agency or entity and its union direct their efforts toward the attainment of institutional objectives.

Organizational Communication

The Public Administration is committed to the advancement of public management and its public servants as a fundamental feature of democracy, by adhering to the principles of integrity and transparency

Through clear, effective and open communication, the synergy between dissemination of guidelines and achievements is being developed in the Federal Public Administration, which allows effective empowerment of the personnel, greater identification by employees with the agency or entity and a shared outlook in the establishment and fulfillment of goals.

The participation of all the organization's personnel is encouraged in order to generate synergies by using internal and external means of communication to continuously disseminate institutional strategies, plans and programs and their results clearly, directly and openly.

Efficient use of Resources

The human capital and financial and material resources used in the organization should be managed rationally with responsibility, effectiveness, efficiency, integrity and transparency.

Respect for the Environment

All of the Public Administration's activities should be carried out with environmental conservation and improvement in mind, respecting the cultural setting of the communities in which government facilities are located and in harmony with society in order to strengthen sustainable development.

Integrity, Transparency and Honesty

The Public Administration is committed to the advancement of public management and its public servants as a fundamental feature of democracy, by adhering to the principles of integrity and transparency.

It is the duty of public servants to adjust their conduct to principles of integrity, which entail acting with honesty and favoring the truth.

Likewise, public servants must guarantee access to government information of a public nature and make open, honest, rational and efficient use of resources, clearly showing the reasons and results of their decisions and actions.

The strategy for effective implementation of the INTRAGOB Quality Model requires the alignment of plans, projects and actions to national goals and priorities, to the legal framework, and to institutional purposes aimed at obtaining results over the short, medium and long terms

Measurements

It is necessary to determine the degree of satisfaction of customers and citizens, as well as of public servants, with the firm purpose of continuously improving processes and their results, identifying points of control and critical success factors in order to fully comply with their expectations and requirements.

To assess the progress of the INTRAGOB **Quality Model** and its effectiveness in improving the quality of public services, we must define and implement systems to measure performance, effectiveness, efficiency and savings in the execution of processes and in the delivery of services provided to customers and citizens, in accordance with their requirements.

- **Performance indicators** that show process performance.
- **Effectiveness indicators,** to measure systems operation in accordance with their design and the expected results.
- **Efficiency indicators,** to measure utilization of the resources used to attain the objectives of the systems, as well as the savings achieved.

Continuous Improvement

It is important for all public servants to contribute their know-how, abilities and experience to processes, through innovation proposals to improve the effectiveness of the value chain, the products and services, and for them to know and identify the role they play in their agency's or entity's productive process; the processes of greatest impact must therefore be identified, defined and prioritized according to the powers granted by their current legal framework, and according to customers' and citizens' needs, expectations and complaints. To do this, it is necessary to clearly define in each area the owners of the processes and their respective sections of control, and facilitate the establishment of work teams that have a positive influence in the chains of value for each product or service. Each link in the chain pertains to a process.

The above principles are the elements that sustain and guide the efforts for continuous improvement, innovation, competitiveness, integrity, transparency and professionalism in the products and services that the agencies and entities of the Federal Government provide to their customers and citizens; however, the strategy for effective implementation of the INTRAGOB **Quality Model** requires the alignment of plans, projects and actions to national goals and priorities, to the legal framework, and to institutional purposes aimed at obtaining results over the short, medium and long terms.

Quality Values

These are the conducts that distinguish the Federal Public Administration's public servants and enable them to act with integrity and transparency to **dignify public administration** and add value to each process carried out in order to satisfy the expectations, needs and requirements of the customers and citizens who demand quality products and services.

Participatory Leadership

This is the ongoing commitment by the heads and union representatives of the Federal Public Administration's agencies and entities to furthering and facilitating the development of a Culture of Quality, competitiveness, integrity and transparency, and thus promote by example the values of Quality of the Federal Government.

Vocation for Service

This is the enthusiastic attitude of public servants to carry out their duties with timeliness, courtesy and care, committed to their agency's or entity's mission, and thus show their work motivation in providing timely, full, reliable and transparent service.

Teamwork

This is the organizational structure that makes it possible for all the personnel to work together in daily operations and to improve processes and systems in a synergic manner in order to achieve the goals of continuous improvement, innovation and competitiveness.

Order and Discipline

This is the series of actions of the personnel aimed at achieving respect and harmony at the workplace by complying with policies, regulations and institutional procedures in the context of quality.

Recognition

These are the incentives that the personnel receive, at all levels of the organizational structure, and that motivate them to develop all their potential to achieve results with competitive standards.

In order for the INTRAGOB **Quality Model** to fully and consistently satisfy agencies' and entities' objectives and continuously improve results, innovation and competitiveness, it is essential to adopt a preventive, innovative vision. This vision should guide and trigger activities in a participatory manner, based on improvement systems and processes that consolidate a Culture of Total Quality, competitiveness, integrity and transparency in the Federal Government.

To that end it is necessary to establish, develop and improve permanent work programs that underpin implementation of systems defined in the criteria of the INTRAGOB **Quality Model** in all the agencies and entities of the Public Administration.

Criteria of the INTRAGOB **Quality Model:**

1) Customer and Citizen Satisfaction
2) Leadership
3) Development of Personnel and Intellectual Capital
4) Management of Information and Technology
5) Planning
6) Process Management and Improvement
7) Impact on Society
8) Outcomes

Below is a description of the requirements to be considered in each of the criteria of the INTRAGOB **Quality Model.**

1. Customer and Citizen Satisfaction

1.1 Knowledge of Customer and Citizen Needs and Expectations

Implies the development of formal systems to identify and determine customer and citizen needs, requirements and expectations, within the sphere of authority conferred on it by its legal framework.

1.2 Communication with Customers and Citizens, Capacity for Timely Response to their Complaints and Claims

In order to build positive, transparent relations with customers and citizens, each agency and entity of the Federal Public Administration is interested in listening, responding and relating to customers and citizens effectively. These relations should occur in terms of quality of the services provided, integrity, attention, courtesy, communication,

INTRAGOB Quality Model

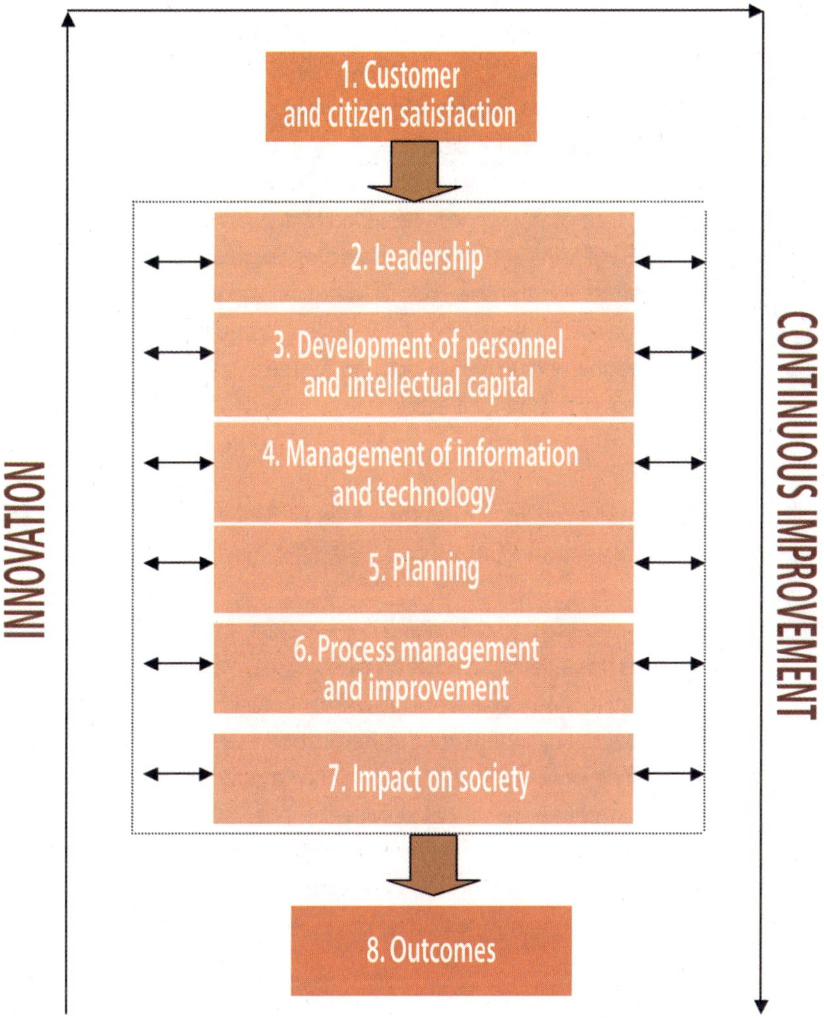

The concept of professionalization and the methodologies used are basically directed toward the development of the individual and the group, as well as the career plan, since it is precisely people who sustain and project the organization as a whole

timeliness, and with reliable, transparent information that is obtained to know their needs and requirements by means of well-defined collection methods and mechanisms to ensure the objectivity and validity of said information.

The INTRAGOB **Quality Model** involves customers and citizens in the process, by responding in a timely and effective manner to their opinions, proposals, complaints, disagreements and reports regarding performance of the services provided by the organization.

The agencies and entities should establish systems to assure the effectiveness and transparency of the organization to provide an effective response to customers' and citizens' requirements, needs and expectations, including service guarantees, specific commitments, pacts, programs and joint actions.

1.3 Systems to Determine the Level of Satisfaction of Customers and Citizens

It is also necessary to design and implement systems to determine and measure the level of satisfaction of customers and citizens, including comparative studies carried out within the agencies and entities, and those effected by independent external bodies or by customers themselves. The organization should maintain a training program aimed at ensuring that the personnel serving the public continuously improve their service skills. These personnel are systematically assessed as regards their knowledge of execution of procedures, information, service delivery and their honest conduct.

2. Leadership

In their daily actions, the heads and the managerial team of Federal Government agencies and entities, as well as their union representatives, advance their leadership on the basis of example and practice and promote the approach of higher value to customers and citizens by means of their personal performance in line with the INTRAGOB

Quality Model. This is carried out in all the processes of the organization, in all its areas and levels, within the framework of an ongoing commitment. The model's principles and values of quality, integrity and transparency are linked and correlated to internal policies, systems and processes, consistent with achievement of its goals and objectives, turning it into a competitive and transparent organization.

Agencies and entities should implement and further systems, methods and practices to improve participatory leadership, and promote the principles and values of quality, integrity and transparency, translated into codes of conduct shared by all members of the organization.

Operative, administrative, managerial and unionized personnel should participate jointly and permanently in the task of promoting a creative, integral and transparent work model in which the development of knowledge and the application of all the personnel's abilities are of particular importance

3. Development of Personnel and of Intellectual Capital

3.1 Teamwork

The public officials responsible should design and implement systems that advance teamwork, in order to increase the participation of all personnel in the attainment of the goals of quality, productivity, competitiveness, savings and transparency. They should also favor an increase in the personnel's level of responsibility, authority, capacity for innovation and contribution of ideas so as to promote actions of continuous improvement, self-control and empowerment.

3.2 Professionalization and Personnel Development

The concept of professionalization and the methodologies used are basically directed toward the development of the individual and the group, as well as the career plan, since it is precisely people who sustain and project the organization as a whole. Thus, the professionalization system should bear in mind essential aspects regarding principles, values, codes of conduct, strategies, approaches and tools for improving quality, productivity, competitiveness, and professional and individual self-improvement.

Professionalization is associated with career civil service schemes

Agencies and entities adhere to and comply with the criteria of applicable laws and regulations, and continuously promote access to public government information

available for the Federal Public Administration to the extent that the maturity of agencies and entities permit this.

3.3 Intellectual Capital

Intellectual capital is the value generated by the information and knowledge required to provide Federal Government services.

It is made up of people's knowledge and abilities, technology, processes and the characteristics of each organization.

Data placed in their context become information. Analysis of information produces knowledge. When knowledge is institutionalized to be used in an organized manner and it increases the Institution's pool of experience and culture, it becomes the organization's intellectual capital. The organization's system for Intellectual Capital Management involves the training, development, application, efficiency and improvement of the organization's resources required to maintain and increase the information and technical and technological knowledge applied to providing services in accordance with the established characteristics of quality and competitiveness.

3.4 Recognition

Recognition (individual and/or group) is given by means of systems of compensation, promotion and incentives to personnel for their advances and fulfillment of results and goals in quality, productivity, competitiveness and savings, and for the application of values and codes of conduct. There is a consistent methodology that makes it possible to determine the degree of satisfaction of personnel in their work and on account of their work.

3.5 Improvement of Quality of Life at Work

The system for improvement of quality of life includes, among other aspects: well-being, health, finances, security, attention and decent, respectful treatment. Operative, administrative, managerial and unionized personnel should participate jointly and permanently in the task of promoting a creative, integral and transparent work model in which the development of knowledge and the application of all the personnel's abilities are of particular importance.

Public servants become involved in the development of the quality process through the systematic assessment of effective communication, work climate and leadership.

3.6 Permanent Atmosphere for Quality

Agencies and entities should establish systems for the proper atmosphere, familiarization and appropriation of the INTRAGOB **Quality Model** on the part of all those involved. Therefore, an important role is played by the different internal communications media of the agencies and entities—audiovisual and graphic media, registers, information activities and others—in creating a favorable atmosphere for quality, innovation, competitiveness and reinforcement of the culture of integrity and transparency.

4. Management of Information and Technology

4.1 Management of Information

The Federal Government has information systems in its agencies and entities at the different stages of productive, administrative, commercial and communication processes with customers and citizens. By means of these systems an analysis is made of information for strategic planning, improvement and innovation of processes and administration, and indicators to measure the organization's performance.

Information systems should include data and systematic practices to analyze the information and the reliability of sources. Information systems should influence the organization's decision-making and create higher value for customers and citizens in processes, products and services, with quality and timeliness.

The* INTRAGOB *Quality Model is the result of rational utilization of all the resources, cost reduction, savings, valuing the importance of customers and citizens, teamwork, pertinence of individual initiatives and comprehensive, transparent management

Agencies and entities adhere to and comply with the criteria of applicable laws and regulations, and continuously promote access to public government information by customers and citizens.

4.2 Management of Technology

Agencies and entities should establish systems to:

- Identify know-how, technology and experts in processes.
- Share the innovations and knowledge learned.
- Encourage, administer and protect know-how, technology and the experience gained.
- Further, through Management of Technology, the empowerment of personnel, teamwork, strategic planning, profitability and updating of technological projects, customer and citizen satisfaction, integrity and transparency.
- Encourage the generation of knowledge.

5. Planning

5.1 Strategic Planning

This system should be used to implement and assess the vision, mission, priorities, objectives, strategies, performance indicators, effectiveness indicators, efficiency indicators, cost/benefit studies, action lines, and innovation and technology programs and projects of each agency and entity. The foregoing should include the contributions of all the personnel, customers, citizens and suppliers, focusing on maintaining the institution's leadership in quality and strategies, as well as the manner in which strategic, operative, financial, quality and integrity and transparency objectives come together in harmony.

5.2 Operative Planning

Suppliers should be involved in the adoption of programs focusing on reinforcing the integrity, development and application of codes of conduct in their companies, since they represent a key link in the value chain of Federal Government organizations

Implies the implementation of plans and systems development, technological architecture and formal processes, through which productive actions for quality, productivity, innovation, competitiveness, integrity, transparency and honest conduct, by means of work programs that determine goals and resources.

6. Process Management and Improvement

6.1 Development of Services and Processes

This is the preventive and support part of the INTRAGOB **Quality Model**.

It includes everything to do with design and redesign of services and processes with the greatest impact; it includes systems and procedures, as well as their orientation toward continuous improvement. It places special emphasis on agencies' and entities' technical, technological and administrative processes to ensure that customers consistently receive higher value in products and services.

It should include systems and methodologies for process analysis, cost-benefit studies, efficiency, the value chain, improvement and redesign of key processes and support processes. It should be oriented toward the simplification and deregulation of processes, competitiveness through innovation and updating of the technological architecture, and programs of integrity and transparency. To that end, information on the expectations, complaints, reports and disagreements of customers and citizens should be considered in order to respond to their needs in a timely and effective manner.

6.2 Implementation of the Management System

Process management and improvement takes into account the implementation of systems for quality management, environmental management and security and health at work.

The INTRAGOB **Quality Model** is the result of rational utilization of all the resources, cost reduction, savings, valuing the importance of customers and citizens, teamwork, pertinence of individual initiatives and comprehensive, transparent management. The Federal Government incorporates the above into its processes in accordance with the provisions of current Mexican and international standards in this field: ISO-9001:2000/NMX-CC-9001-IMNC-2000; ISO-14001:1996/NMX-SSA-14001-IMNC-2002; and NMX-SAST-001-IMNC-2000.

The aspects of quality management, environmental management and security and health at work are a commitment and responsibility of all Federal Government personnel; they involve a series of measures, actions, programs and procedures aimed at improving each institution's productive and administrative processes in order to increase agencies' and entities' productivity.

6.3 Suppliers

With the aim of satisfying the needs and expectations of customers and citizens, as well as of the agencies and entities themselves, it is necessary to implement, maintain and improve the system for the management of quality of supplies and the system for assessment and development of suppliers, ensuring that procurement processes are transparent. Suppliers should be involved in the adoption of programs focusing on reinforcing the integrity, development and application of codes of conduct in their companies, since they represent a key link in the value chain of Federal Government organizations.

7. Impact on Society

7.1 Improvement of the Milieu

Within the framework of the INTRAGOB **Quality Model**, through the agencies and entities, and with the resources generated by their internal savings, efforts aimed at improvement of their sphere of influence in the legal, physical, social and economic milieu should be increased by means of the establishment of systems and specific actions to promote the culture of quality, minimizing environmental impacts. All of this should encourage and make it easier for other organizations in the community to develop their own Total Quality programs and foster citizen participation in the definition of policies and programs through pacts, accords and agreements on collaboration with social organizations and society in general.

A government that does not base itself on higher, universal values shared by the majority of public servants is doomed not to transcend

8. Outcomes

8.1 Created value for Personnel and the Agency or Entity

The results of systems related to leadership modules, personnel development and management of intellectual capital, management of information and technology, strategic planning, process management and improvement, should be analyzed in order to identify their quantitative and qualitative impact on personnel satisfaction, growth, profitability, savings, productivity, integrity and transparency, achievement of objectives and performance and on each agency or entity.

8.2 Created Value for Customers, Citizens and Society

The results of systems related to customer and citizen satisfaction modules, management of information and technology, strategic planning, process management and improvement and impact on society should be analyzed in order to identify their quantitative and qualitative impact on customers and citizens, on ecosystems, on the community and on each agency or entity.

8.3 Value Created by the Culture of Quality

It is necessary to analyze the results of systems for customer and citizen satisfaction, personnel development and management of intellectual capital, with the aim of assessing improvements in the competitive position, increase in response capacity, transparency and integrity, capacity for change, learning and growth of work centers.

The indicators to measure the value created for the agency or entity, customers, citizens and society and by the culture of quality, integrity and transparency, are correlated with the maturity of the INTRAGOB Quality Model.

The results of these indicators should also be compared to those of leading regional, national and international organizations.

The INTRAGOB Model has a Code of Ethics for public officials based on the following criteria:

1. Procurement of the Common Good
2. Integrity of public officials
3. Honesty
4. Impartiality
5. Justice
6. Transparency
7. Accountability
8. Cultural and ecological setting
9. Generosity
10. Leadership

A government that does not base itself on higher, universal values shared by the majority of public servants is doomed not to transcend.

Systems Improvement for the INTRAGOB Quality Model

The systems used in criteria 1 to 7 should include indicators for the assessment of their efficiency and effectiveness, as well as of the cost/benefit analysis of the resources employed.

Work programs should be established for dissemination, training and implementation of the systems used.

The information derived from the indicators used is analyzed to control and improve processes through data and charts to make it possible to determine the levels and trends of the results obtained.

The methods, processes, technological architecture and systems are subject to cycles of continuous improvement.

The cycle of design and implementation of systems for innovation and continuous improvement of the criteria that make up the INTRAGOB Quality Model is carried out according to the stages shown in the following diagram.

Cycle of Design, Innovation and Improvement of Systems Applied to The INTRAGOB Quality Model

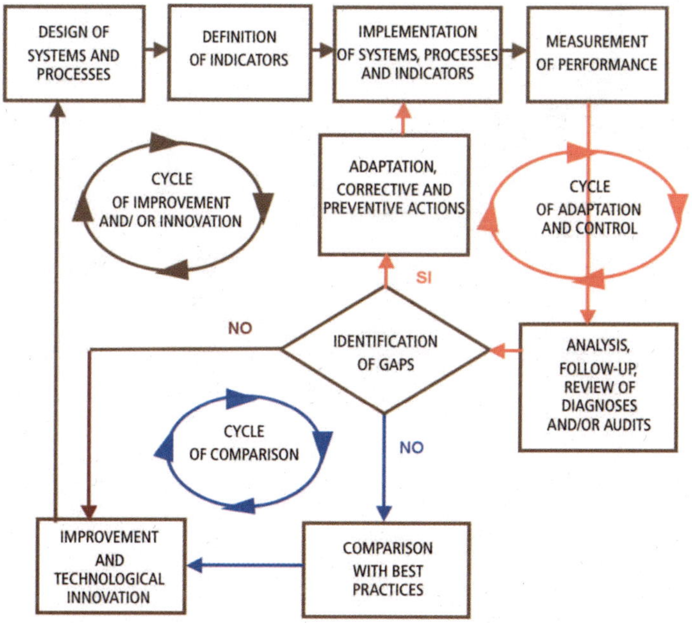

Chapter 6

Innovative Practices

INNOVA and INTRAGOB Awards

As we have seen in earlier chapters, today Innovation and Quality are an imperative for governments seeking to provide efficient, effective and honest service to citizens and customers.

President Fox's administration is making a singular effort to ensure that federal institutions incorporate those concepts into their responsibilities in order to offer better world-class quality service.

To that end, the Office of the Presidency for Government Innovation was created and the Ministry of the Comptroller and Administrative Development (SECODAM) was transformed into the new Ministry of Public Administration, in order to assure successful results in *Good Government* by means of the facilitation and implementation of strategic projects.

Among these projects are the awards and recognitions which, as shown by the experiences of the United States with the Malcolm Baldrige Award, Japan with the Deming Prize, and the European Union with the European Quality Award of the European Foundation for Quality Management (EFQM) are an incentive and a motivation of singular merit for making substantial changes in organizations, as regards both internal administration and added value in their relations with the customer-citizen.

Added to this is the fact that the creation and application of international quality standards such as ISO-9000 has become widespread.

The INNOVA Recognition Award is presented to the entities and agencies of the Federal Public Administration that distinguish themselves by the development of innovative services with high added value for citizens and that contribute significantly to the six lines of action of the Presidential Agenda for Good Government

The implementation of the INTRAGOB Quality Model supports institutions in fully satisfying citizens' expectations and needs and, in general, those of customers of the products or services provided by the Federal Public Administration; similarly, it contributes to the consolidation of a culture of quality, to improved productivity and competitiveness, to technological innovation and to responsible performance by public servants before society

In 2002 President Fox's administration established the prizes and awards for innovation and quality for the best practices of federal government agencies and entities.

The INNOVA Recognition Award is presented to the entities and agencies of the Federal Public Administration that distinguish themselves by the development of innovative services with high added value for citizens and that contribute significantly to the six lines of action of the Presidential Agenda for Good Government.

This award fosters creativity and innovation, increasing the Federal Government's competitiveness and having an impact on the modernization of the public administration, as well as on the advancement of public servants as the main agents of change. Its main objectives are:

- Identifying and recognizing the best practices in innovation in the public administration.
- Fostering public servants' creative participation by incorporating their contributions into the innovation of public services.
- Strengthening the management of knowledge in order to increase the country's intellectual capital with regard to public administration, by generating, seeking, recognizing, disseminating, sharing and transferring successful cases of innovation.
- Creating synergic effects of exchange of successful experiences.
- Developing the necessary abilities in public servants to analyse cases of innovation.
- Strengthening the progress of the Presidential Agenda for Good Government in the Public Administration.

President Fox presents the Recognition Awards during the National Week on Innovation and Quality in the Public Administration, which is organized every year in November.

As of the 2004 edition of the INNOVA Recognition Awards, the Awards Committee may grant special recognition to innovation practices which, in addition to showing important results in the Good Government Agenda, can be exemplary by being outstanding in the six lines of action of said Agenda.

The winning agencies and entities of the INNOVA Recognition

Award go on to another phase of assessment in which the additional criteria of impact on citizens, regional scope and degree of innovation are considered. The practices that obtained the highest points receive the National Award for Innovation in the Public Administration (INNOVA prize) in the categories of agency and entity.

The INTRAGOB Prize is presented to units of the Federal Public Administration that distinguish themselves by their maturity in introducing the culture of quality and that are therefore an example to be followed. By means of a transparent, objective and reliable assessment process, the agencies and entities that have the best practices of total quality developed by public servants who live the day-to-day culture of continuous improvement are selected.

The implementation of the Intragob Quality Model supports institutions in fully satisfying citizens' expectations and needs and, in general, those of customers of the products or services provided by the Federal Public Administration; similarly, it contributes to the consolidation of a culture of quality, to improved productivity and competitiveness, to technological innovation and to responsible performance by public servants before society. Furthermore, the prize is a tool that makes it possible to analyze the progress of systems and processes aimed at total quality. The benefit begins with the self-evaluation the participants carry out during the drafting of their participation reports; subsequently, on participating in the INTRAGOB Prize, the evaluating group analyzes the information submitted, in order to offer the participants an external point of view.

On March 3, 2003, at the Official Residence of Los Pinos, during the presentation ceremony for the 2002 INTRAGOB Prize, collaboration was formalized between the Office of the Presidency for Government Innovation and the Trust Fund of the National Quality Prize, for technical and administrative support, as well as for coordination of the evaluation and selection processes of the Federal Government Recognition System, which includes the Intragob Prize, the Innova Recognition Award and the INNOVA Prize.

The INTRAGOB Prize, the INNOVA Recognition Award and the INNOVA Prize have a Technical Committee, a body whose function is to further and support the general process, assuring the consistency of actions related to promotion, recognition and dissemination, to its mission, vision and strategies, as well as providing the guidelines and resources necessary for their accomplishment.

There is also a Technical Committee made up of a group of specialists in the lines of action of Good Government, which defines the guidelines of the Prizes for the design, improvement and innovation of the instruments used in the evaluation process, such as the participation guide, evaluation tools, training courses, etc.

The Awards Committee, always basing itself on the report of the Innova Assessment Group and through a transparent, objective and reliable process, selects the winning agencies and entities and its decision is final and unappealable.

Below we present a list of the winners of the Intragob Prize and the Innova Prize, as well as some of the agencies and institutions that have certified their work centers 100% under standard ISO 9000.

1. INNOVA Prizes

Ministry of Foreign Affairs (SRE)

MIDIS System for the Passport Issuance Process

1. Situation of the Ministry in 2000

Faced with the growth of forgery of identity and travel documents, which increased during the eighties, as well as the possibilities of fraud and lack of security that the Mexican passport had shown during those years, the Ministry of Foreign Affairs diagnosed that the traditional equipment used for issuing passports was obsolete in 2000 and it was necessary in the short term to change all of the pertinent infrastructure (hardware, software).

Another type of problems the Ministry was facing in the passport issuance procedure was:

With regard to the document:

- Need to adapt to the passport security measures issued by the International Civil Aviation Organization (ICAO).
- Quality.
- Erasing of the holder's photograph.
- Lack of security.

With regard to errors in operation:

- Deficient operative work due to waste; there were no controls.
- Detachment of forgery-proof segments.
- Inconvenience of signing all passports by hand.
- Discretionary authority.

The above were some of the reasons that led the Ministry of Foreign Affairs to make an investment to modernize the passport issuance process and put it in the technological vanguard, while at the same time providing it with the necessary features to ensure the security that said document needs.

2. Brief Explanation on the Implementation of the Practice of Innovation

The implementation project for the MIDIS system (for passport issuance) was carried out by means of outsourcing, with which the General Directorate of Delegations avoided investment in:

- Analysis, design and development of the application.
- Purchase of hardware and support equipment.
- Staff training.
- Preventive and corrective maintenance.
- Acquisition and distribution of inputs and consumables.

The digitized passport showed modifications in its preparation and presentation; among these changes it is important to mention:

- The booklet was designed totally in Mexico by SRE personnel.
- Filling out of the data sheet is carried out by means of inverted printing on a new laminate [Multi-layer Infilling System (MLIS)].
- It is designed as a production line that begins with entering data and images (photo, fingerprints and signature) and ends with the digitization of documents.
- The database is shared with other agencies [National Population Register (RENAPO)].
- Inclusion of biometric measures for positive identification of holders.
- Simplifies passport renewal.
- Rapid access to digitized documents.
- Operations registered automatically.
- Compulsory digitization of support documents was incorporated.
- Delegates' handwritten signatures and observations stamps eliminated and incorporated into the programming.
- The final check, always carried out by the holder upon receiving his passport, was included at the beginning of the process, eliminating up to five intermediate checks.
- Registration and manual control of booklets was eliminated through the use of bar codes in booklets and laminates.
- Use of digital fingerprints of holders and officials was incorporated.
- Authorization is the exclusive responsibility of the delegate or subdelegate.
- Greater transparency was imparted to passport issuance by controlling each stage of the process.
- Cases in which an application can be located by identifying verification documents were ordered and classified for the first time by incorporating them into 39 business rules.
- The discretionary authority that existed in the previous system was eliminated.
- Immediate detection of duplicates and namesakes.

3. Why Was it Decided to Implement this Innovation Practice over other Alternatives?

The Ministry of Foreign Affairs opted for the implementation of the Multiple Identity Document Issuing System (MIDIS) for production of the Mexican passport because it makes the following possible, among other things:

Introduction of data: Data can be introduced manually, importing them from a magnetic tape or disc, or downloading them from an existing database of national registers by means of a telecommunications link. The system can be made up of external or existing databases, to export data to the historical archive or to be shared with other entities or state functions.
Capture of images: The issuing authorities can choose between capturing images of face, signature and fingerprints "live" or using scanners to do so from printed applications sent by mail.
Printing: MIDIS has a flexible configuration that makes it possible to print a diversity of identity documents on a wide range of materials, including paper, Teslin, PVC and Fortas. The printing server makes possible automatic prints by lots or by priority printing lines.
Quality control: A quality control station enables the operator to carry out a visual inspection of the quality of the images; documents that do not comply with the specifications are sent back to the system to be reissued. Likewise, all the applications should be checked against the list of unresolved offenses before being printed out.

All these components can be divided into four discrete operator stations for more vanguard systems, or can be combined into one single station for cases of reduced production.

Another important factor in improving the security of the document was the application of the MLIS, which complies with the measures established by ICAO. The following are some of the features of this System:

- Protection against fraud and forgery. From the lowest level to the highest that exist.
- Secure passport issuance process. Allows absolute control of the entire passport issuance process.
- Flexibility of use. Can be processed from the central base or from the Delegations.
- High-security, long-lasting passports. The Mexican passport is guaranteed to last a long time, having undergone photo-resistance, rapid aging, folding, rubbing and flexibility tests.
- High production rate and a trace of transparent auditing.
- Visible and mechanical reading security features.

    - Special inks. Some security measures require ultraviolet light, others can only be revealed by means of a hand visual display unit that cannot be obtained in a commercial market. There are new security features that demand the use of even more specialized detectors to check concealed features.

    - Personalization operations. These range from the inclusion of an OCR-B code and a 2D bar code to the incorporation of a "ghost image" of the holder's photograph.

4. General Results and Results with Impact on Citizens

In response to strong demands from the user population, the system led to changes and improvements in the Passport Regulations which needed the presentation of certain requirements for securing a passport, such as:

- National Military Service Card.
- Second identification.
- Complementary documents in the case of time-barred birth certificates.
- National Vaccination Card (for children under six).

Moreover, the previous passport had a total of ten security measures: five visible and five invisible; now it has 38 security measures, of which 21 are visible and 17 invisible.

With regard to the security of the document, biometric technologies have been successfully integrated. The holder's fingerprint is encoded in a 2D bar code. Comparison of the fingerprint contained in the bar code with that of the holder confirms his identity.

The preventive and corrective maintenance services for the computer equipment used in the Ministry's Production Centers are paid for by the company that supplies the above-mentioned systems.

Together with the Ministry, the supplying company carries out a continuous training program for all the personnel who handle the passport issuance equipment, and gives an introductory course on the MIDIS system to delegates and sub-delegates responsible for issuance of the documents in each of the Production Centers.

As one of the many advantages for citizens, the high-security mechanical reading passports that use MLIS enable passengers to move more swiftly through airports and border control points.

As an important part of the modernization of the equipment and the training provided to the personnel who handle the MIDIS System in Delegations, this will be replaced in 2004 in all the Production Centers and the Central Site in order to avoid its obsolescence while in service. This replacement of equipment will include updating of software to streamline processes, since features will gradually be incorporated so as to remain in the vanguard, and also to reduce the percentage of waste and shorten passport delivery times to the holders.

Ministry of Agriculture, Livestock Rural Development, Fisheries and Food (SAGARPA)

Transparency in Payment of Supports for the Rural Sector through Information Technology

Profile of the Practice of Innovation

1. Background

In SAGARPA there is an area called General Coordination of Supports (CGA), whose function is to provide supports (subsidies) to farmers who are the beneficiaries of the PROCAMPO and Marketing Programs, and interact, as of 2001, with the Mexican Coffee Council (CMC) to generate the payment for the delivery of supports from the Coffee Harvest Emergency Support Program and the Coffee Price Stabilization Fund.

The amount managed by the CGA with the four above-mentioned programs totals almost 20 billion pesos, and therefore to make its distribution transparent and more efficient, three projects were implemented by the three General Directorates belonging to the CGA.

The decision was taken to bring them together into one single project called "Transparency in the Payment of Supports for the Rural Sector through Information Technology," since the three General Directorates partly participate in at least one process of the three projects.

1.1 Objectives

a) Draw up a geo-referenced National Register of Perennial Crop Farmers and Lands in order to know reliably who are true farmers and the characteristics of their lands, processing and operating the respective data in a Geographical Information System (SIG). This will facilitate updating and the elimination, as far as possible, of periodic censuses; it will also facilitate decision-making and the definition of sectoral policies, as well as to give impetus for product marketing and the farmers' development.

b. Obtain simple alternatives that are easy to introduce and operate and that make it more efficient and transparent to channel the supports, as well as to fully identify farmers, without this implying any cost for them.

c. Have a system on the Internet whereby the supports granted and the progress of planting and harvesting can be known, providing names and surnames, and making the use of public resources transparent by making the information available to the public in general, using as a basis the most up-to-date technology available.

Now only true farmers of perennial crops will receive support, eliminating doubtful payments, thus ensuring that public resources will be correctly allocated and redistributed among those who really require them. A reduction of approximately 120,000 hectares was made with respect to what had been declared

1. National Register of Perennial Crop Farmers and Lands	General Directorate of Information Systems for the Operation of Direct Supports
2. Means of Payment in Supports and Identification of Farmers	General Directorate of Means of Payment, General Directorate of Programming and Assessment
3. System of Information on Supports on the Internet	General Directorate of Information Systems for the Operation of Direct Supports

1.2 Problems

Support for farmers of perennial crops used to be delivered on the basis of simple lists on which farmers were only requested to write their names to be able to process and receive their support or benefit, without checking whether the person on the list was really a farmer, or whether the area or lot(s) he declared he cultivated actually existed.

At the time of delivery and change of instrument for the payment of supports by means of checks there can be corruption, and therefore the aim was to disburse the resources for the payment through electronic means, which guarantees that the payment reaches the farmer in full and without intermediaries.

Previously neither the amount of the support nor the beneficiaries of the program were made public in some medium, and the field check in PROCAMPO was carried out randomly, covering less than one percent of the area supported.

1.3 Mission of the Agency and Impact of the Innovation Practice on the Mission

The innovation practice has a direct impact on the majority of points of SAGARPA's Mission, as the form of payment of the supports has been improved and the information on Perennials Product Systems is obtained and put in order. These Systems are the basis for marketing, conduct better support policies, focus development, redistribute and have greater equity in supports, increase farmers' profitability, use science and technology and make the institution's operations transparent.

2. Impact

2.1 Benefits of the Project for Mexico and its Population

Now only true farmers of perennial crops will receive support, eliminating doubtful payments, thus ensuring that public resources will be correctly allocated and redistributed among those who really require them. A reduction of approximately 120,000 hectares was made with respect to what had been declared.

A work team was formed, made up of representatives from the three levels of government, *ejido* farmers and farmers' organizations, and State and Regional Product Systems Councils were created, thus strengthening the rural sector's integration.

Electronic payment and identification have been a key factor in achieving transparency and reducing the possibility of corruption in the delivery of PROCAMPO Supports, which include almost 2.7 million farmers annually, distributed throughout the country. We have thus contributed to a cultural change in the sector due to the use of electronic means of payment and the incentive to save, which helps to improve the general economy of rural areas.

2.2 Impact of the Innovation Practice in Strengthening the Presidential Agenda for Good Government

- **Honest and Transparent Government**

The operation of support programs becomes transparent and corruption is reduced by having plots geo-referenced, as well as by making direct deposits to farmers' accounts. In PROCAMPO, 85 percent of farmers have a favorable opinion of the service. The payments, account deposits and register advances, among others, are contained as indicators in the Program of Transparency and Fight against Corruption.

- **Professional Government**

More than 2,000 brigade members were trained in GPS technology and in the Product Systems. Over 100 technicians were trained in GPS, Geographical Information Systems, Censuses and Product Systems. The best brigade members were hired on the basis of a selection examination.

- **Quality Government**

Based on declarations and surveys, farmers are satisfied with the support programs, as well as with their more timely delivery. Their audits have been considered of world-class quality and have been recognized by the Inter-American Development Bank as an innovative project in 2001.

- **Digital Government**

All the information collected is stored, consulted and developed in digital media. Payment of supports is made by electronic means, and the program's information is available on the Internet.

• Government with Regulatory Improvement

The documentation and information on farmers and lands is collected only once. With electronic payments procedures are reduced and farmers' capacity to avail themselves of their support improves. No requests for information are required since the information is available on the Internet for the public at large.

• Government that Costs Less

In the first year of operation of the coffee programs, savings of almost 110 million pesos were achieved. In comparison with Colombia, SAGARPA's register was taken 65 percent faster and at a lower cost. A standardized Coffee Information System was created at the national level. For PROCAMPO, the cost per banking operation was reduced.

2.3 Number of Persons Involved in the Process

CGA structure: 125 persons. Register Coordinators and Supervisors: 50. Brigade members: 2,000. CMC structure: 130. Leaders of organizations, Mayors, *Ejido* Commissioners: 350.

2.4 Scope of the Benefits

The scope of the benefits of this project is national, since it includes coffee farmers and PROCAMPO beneficiaries. Taken as a whole, they add up to almost 3.2 million people.

2.5 Type of Impact of the Final Benefit

The impact has been favorable for the institution and society, for direct costs were reduced, public resources were optimized and service to farmers and accountability were made transparent and improved.

3. Customers

3.1 Type and Number of Customers/Citizens Benefited

Farmers were benefited by means of direct or indirect actions. Coffee growers: 470,000 and PROCAMPO farmers: 2.7 million.

3.2 How Is the Service Provided?

For the registers, windows are opened in the localities where farmers of the Product System in question live. For PROCAMPO, farmers go to the Rural Development Support Center (CADER) or to an authorized alternate window.

4. Impact on Employees

4.1 Impact of Innovation on Employees

Training in satellite technology and geographical information systems, field surveys and agronomy and constitution of Product Systems.

4.2 Level of Employee Involvement in the Process

All those involved participated 100 percent in the actions they were responsible for. There has been an improvement in the labor climate as a result of greater integration and interaction with internal and external areas, such as the CMC, the three levels of government, *campesino* organizations and banking institutions.

5. Processes

5.1 Existence of this Type of Practices in the Local and International Contexts

The geo-referenced Registers of Perennial Crop Farmers are an example at the international level, for there is no similar integration by Product System with the amount of variables (170) considered and included in a SIG in any other part of the world. Electronic payment to farmers who are beneficiaries of Support Programs is also an international example, as well as the manner of identifying them.

5.2 Viability of Implementing Similar Processes in the Local and International Contexts

Registers of Farmers of any type can and should be administered in the manner in which this was done, and their methodology can be reproduced perfectly in any part of the world.

It is also possible to reproduce the electronic means of payment with the farmer's debit card identification, as long as the country where it is going to be applied has a minimum of banking and telecommunications infrastructure.

Publication on the Internet of an information system related to the characteristics involved in this project can also be reproduced at any level: municipal, state and/or national.

Ministry of Labor and Social Welfare (STPS)

New Schemes for Information and Labor Linkage

—*CHAMBATEL, CHAMBANET* and *MI CHAMBA*—

Since 2003 CHAMBATEL has had a Contact Center to address demand in Mexico City and the metropolitan area. It is endowed with cutting-edge technology and the capacity to deal with up to 5,000 interactions daily (calls, e-mail, fax and chat)

1. Objectives

The main objective of information and labor linkage programs is to provide citizens with attention and information schemes that are efficient, responsive and pleasant, supported by the new technologies, in order to reduce times and costs for people seeking employment.

2. Background and Problems Encountered

Until the year 2000, the STPS's linkage actions, through the National Employment Service (SNE), were basically aimed at developing personalized attention services based on job vacancy systems and holding direct linkage events, such as Employment Fairs. Thus, the SNE only had two service channels to cater to job seekers and companies.

Job vacancy services require people to go to SNE offices to obtain information on job offers, and to fill out forms to receive the service. This involves transportation costs for the unemployed, who sometimes do not have resources available in view of their labor situation. Likewise, with this service scheme it was not possible to provide attention to the differently abled, since most SNE offices do not have the necessary levels of accessibility. Furthermore, the SNE did not have a periodic, free publication in which to widely disseminate available job offers.

Despite the significant results shown by direct linkage schemes, the General Coordination of Employment (CGE), the STPS unit responsible for coordinating the SNE, considered it necessary to develop more flexible, modern mechanisms to address the unmet needs of job seekers and companies.

Therefore the STPS, through the CGE, applied itself to the task of developing and promoting new forms of information and labor linkage for job seekers with regard to more effective alternatives for access to

Chambanet is an Internet labor linkage system available to companies and individuals since March 6, 2002. Through Chambanet companies can register and publish their job vacancies, as well as seek, select and contact the candidates who have the profile to fill them

job opportunities in less time and at a lower cost. Thus, the CGE implemented a comprehensive strategy of labor linkage services based on the design, development and implementation of new products whose basic support is the use of information technology and telecommunications, as well as other media that are insufficiently used for these purposes, such as print media, with the aim of providing citizens with timely access to information on job supply and demand.

Within the framework of this strategy, the CGE made three new programs available to citizens: *a)* A free telephone information service on job opportunities known as *CHAMBATEL*; *b)* a free newspaper on job offers, *MI CHAMBA*, and *c)* an Internet labor linkage system called *CHAMBANET*.

For the design and implementation of these programs basically three strategic lines of Innovation and Quality were followed: *1)* service quality, *2)* administrative deregulation and simplification and *3)* use of information technology and telecommunications.

3. CHAMBATEL

CHAMBATEL is one of the labor linkage services offered by the STPS, since the telephone is a means of growing access for the majority of the population (15.5 fixed lines in service for every 100 inhabitants as of September 2003, COFETEL). Thus, *CHAMBATEL* facilitates the linkage of people seeking employment with job vacancies that arise in the productive sector. The service is offered free of charge (the user does not pay for the call or the service) on telephone number 01-800-111-6000, from anywhere in the country, and the call is taken by personnel specializing in labor counseling.

> On calling *CHAMBATEL* the job seeker obtains, in no more than 10 minutes, the necessary information to contact up to three job options in keeping with his labor profile. With this information the person can immediately call the companies to arrange for an interview and negotiate hiring terms after

ensuring that the conditions and wages are suitable, with a significant reduction in time and cost of the job search.

This service is mainly designed to have a direct effect on reduction of the time and cost involved in the search for employment in urban labor markets by making use of the advantages of information technology and telecommunications.

CHAMBATEL was placed at the disposal of citizens on February 21, 2001, in Mexico City and the metropolitan area, and it is currently available in the country's thirty-two federative entities. *CHAMBATEL* also includes actions of mass dissemination, business promotion and follow-up on the service provided to employers, in order to maintain the job offer database up to date and ensure the validity and quality of the information.

Since its implementation, the STPS has carried out continuous improvement actions to make this service more efficient. Since 2003 *CHAMBATEL* has had a Contact Center to address demand in Mexico City and the metropolitan area. It is endowed with cutting-edge technology and the capacity to deal with up to 5,000 interactions daily (calls, e-mail, fax and chat). Furthermore, it has a Company Service Center devoted to promoting the program among companies in order to increase the number of job vacancies. This has resulted in the program having greater reach among individuals and companies, as well as in better service quality.

4. MI CHAMBA

MI CHAMBA is a free-distribution periodical publication designed to offer the population a flexible mechanism for information on job opportunities. Since October 2001 *MI CHAMBA* has been published and distributed fortnightly, in a 16-page color format, letter size, and with an edition of 65,000 copies in Mexico City and its metropolitan area. Each issue provides information on more than 2,500 vacancies, which enables job-seekers to establish direct contact with job opportunities they are interested in according to their labor profile, which in turn helps to reduce time and cost in the search for a job. Similarly, the companies that publish their job offers in MI CHAMBA can count on a larger number of candidates to fill their vacancies. MI CHAMBA is distributed through different channels, such as: department and self-service stores, government offices, business chambers, unions, non-governmental organizations and educational institutions, among others. At present MI CHAMBA is published in the 32 federative entities and has succeeded in positioning itself among the citizenry as an effective medium for occupational linkage and guidance.

5. CHAMBANET

CHAMBANET is an Internet labor linkage system available to companies and individuals since March 6, 2002. Through CHAMBANET companies can register and publish their job vacancies, as well as seek, select and contact the candidates who have the profile to fill them. Job seekers, for their part, can register their résumé, as well as seek, consult and apply for the job offers they are interested in, from any part of the country.

CHAMBANET is above all an interactive tool for seeking employment and human resources and its operation does not require the intervention of personnel other than the users themselves, except in support and administration processes. Its operating scheme is defined by the different processes carried out by individuals and companies to enter the system, carry out information searches, identify and establish the pertinent contacts, as well as those that include the administration of their data through their personalized web pages.

The following are the main features of the site that should be underscored: *a)* available on the Internet at *www.chambanet.gob.mx*; *b)* access 24 hours a day 365 days a year; *c)* national coverage; *d)* free service for individuals and companies; *e)* security in information and user access by means of a personalized code; *f)* administration of information by the STPS and exclusive use for purposes of linkage; *g)* information on conditions of use of the system and about the site; *h)* e-mail for doubts or advisory assistance; *i)* questionnaire for comments or opinions on the site; *j)* links to sites of interest related to the labor sphere, and *k)* entry of applicants and companies backed by the SNE.

As of April 2004 citizens have had a new version of *CHAMBANET*, which offers, among other things, new search options, quicker mechanisms for entering information, a personalized module for graduates of the National College for Professional Technical Education (CONALEP), notification by e-mail of new job offers, access to and downloading of the newspaper *MI CHAMBA* in PDF format, and consultation via chat to *CHAMBATEL'S* job offers.

With the implementation of CHAMBATEL, CHAMBANET and Mi CHAMBA, 3,488,551 job seekers were served and 878,664 persons were placed in a job

6. Impact and Benefits

The new information and labor linkage schemes in operation since 2001 have achieved a better positioning of the image and services provided by STPS to citizens, and in particular the SNE as a modern, dynamic instrument in keeping with the challenges of the labor market. These services have transformed the bureaucratic notion of the processing office to arrive at a concept of immediate attention, without useless procedures and documentation and supported by information technology and telecommunications. Likewise, these programs have had an influence on the rise in formal employment indexes, which contributes to reducing the social pressure caused by unemployment and the absence of opportunities for improvement and professional development.

The main benefits that have been achieved with these programs are:

a. Free service.
b. Immediate, timely information on employment options.
c. It is unnecessary for people to go to the offices to obtain information.
d. It is not necessary to fill out forms to have access to the services.
e. Citizens do not have to buy newspapers and publications to find job offers.
f. Expenses associated with the search for employment and the engaging and hiring of personnel are significantly reduced.

g. The time and cost for people coming out of unemployment, as well as for companies to fill their vacancies are significantly reduced.

In addition to these benefits, in the case of *CHAMBANET* individuals and companies have access, through the Internet, to an extensive database of job offers and candidates, to registering their résumé and to job offers online the same day, in addition to obtaining contact information on job vacancies and on candidates they are interested in, as well as accessing a personalized page to manage their information.

Furthermore, the results achieved with the development of these services have been significant. In the year 2000, the SNE had only two substantive programs to offer labor linkage services: the Labor Exchange and the organization of Employment Fairs. During the period 2001-2003, a total of 2,565,557 job seekers were served through these two programs, and 762,209 persons were placed in a job. With the implementation of *CHAMBATEL*, *CHAMBANET* and *MI CHAMBA*, during that same period these figures rose substantially, since 3,488,551 job seekers were served and 878,664 persons were placed in a job. Likewise, with these new schemes it has been possible to extend the benefits of the labor linkage services offered citizens by the Federal Government to other segments of the population. Thus, it has been made possible for persons with some disability to have access to information on job opportunities free of charge and practically without moving from their homes.

At present, almost 50 percent of the population using the labor linkage services offered by STPS do not need to go to the employment office or fill out a form to access information on available job offers.

CHAMBATEL was the innovation linchpin of the STPS's new labor linkage programs and also of the government initiatives whose purpose was to bring society closer to responsive, modern services. Their shaping and development were decisive for the design, development and consolidation of other programs, since *CHAMBATEL* proved that the new government was capable of producing short-term results with modern operating schemes and a real impact on society's pressing needs, such as seeking employment. Similarly, with the *CHAMBANET* service, the STPS became incorporated immediately into the digital government model of the Good Government Agenda. The statistics of access to *CHAMBANET* show the site's growing performance and a good impression among users. With the services offered by *CHAMBATEL* and *MI CHAMBA* people can avoid unnecessary travel to obtain information on job offers, the purchase of publications to find job offers, as well as other related expenses such as transportation and telephone.

The time for coming out of unemployment and the costs associated with this labor situation have also been significantly reduced. For companies, these schemes have been highly favorable for their hiring and personnel selection processes in all job categories, by enabling them to make timely contact with suitable candidates for the profile of their job vacancies. Thus, they reduce the times and costs of the search for the personnel they require and speed up their selection processes.

In the case of *CHAMBANET*, in addition to the benefits already mentioned, individuals have online access to an extensive database of job offers, the possibility of registering their résumé online on the same day, obtaining information for contacting the job vacancies they are interested in, a personalized web page for managing their information, links to labor-sector sites of interest and access to the web pages of State Employment Services (SEE). *CHAMBANET* offers companies free online access to an extensive database of job seekers, publication online of their job vacancies, information on contact with the selected candidates, a personalized web page for managing their information and links to labor-sector sites of interest.

To facilitate access to *CHAMBANET* to a larger number of persons and broaden its benefits, the STPS has designed an important program consisting of the installation of cybernetic kiosks in the country's main cities so that people can consult the job offers available on *CHAMBANET* free of charge.

Tax Administration Service (SAT)

New Electronic Payment Scheme

The *New Electronic Payment Scheme* was created to simplify compliance with tax obligations and modernize payment of federal contributions.

This scheme includes two forms of payment:

- Tax Card. At bank windows.
- Internet. By means of electronic transfer of funds through bank portals.

1. Introduction

The SAT has been developing the eSAT strategy as part of the automation project of the services offered by the Federal Government recognized in SAT's Strategic Planning, with which it seeks to provide and broaden services to taxpayers through electronic media.

The *New Electronic Payment Scheme* is one of the components of the eSAT strategy which represents a radical, innovative change in tax culture by introducing and furthering the use of informatics technology as a means to comply in a transparent, modern, easy and secure manner.

2. Background

Prior to August 2002, payment of federal taxes was carried out quarterly in most cases and through printed tax forms. The Tax Miscellany Resolution that year established the modification for making payments by electronic means, in line with the provisions of the laws in force, which provide for the obligation of making monthly payments.

The modification of the Tax Miscellany Resolution to make payment of the taxes corresponding to the month of July onward entered into effect as of August 2002, and to that end the *New Electronic Payment Scheme* was established.

3. Description of the New Electronic Payment Scheme

- **Tax Card**

The purpose of this card is to streamline tax payments made at bank branches; this avoids errors and saves time in entering data, and also guarantees that the payment is credited directly to the taxpayer's tax account.

The Tax Card contains the taxpayers' necessary tax identification data for compliance with their tax obligations. This instrument is used by taxpayers with low administrative capacity:

a) Individuals with business activities who earn less than one million seven hundred and fifty thousand pesos a year.
b) Individuals with activities other than business whose annual income is less than three hundred thousand pesos.

- **Internet**

Payment through the Internet makes possible the electronic transfer of funds for tax payments made by taxpayers in their bank portal.

This form of payment is compulsory for:
a) All legal persons.
b) Individuals with an annual income of more than one million seven hundred and fifty thousand pesos.

This form of payment is optional for individuals who have a Tax Card.

4. Advantages and Benefits

In comparison with the previous form of compliance, the *New Electronic Payment Scheme* has various advantages:

For Taxpayers	For the SAT	For Banks
Security, because errors in entering data are avoided and a receipt is issued, with a digital seal, which due to its characteristics make it forgery-proof and constitutes the pay slip.	Data flow and payment through the same channel with minimal errors.	Data flow and payment through the same channel with minimal errors.
Facility for payment from any computer connected to the Internet anywhere in the world and with longer hours.	Reduction in the service load due to lower influx of taxpayers.	Reduction in service load at branches due to lower influx of taxpayers (customers).
Guarantee that the payment is credited directly to the taxpayer's tax account.	Timeliness in the control of taxpayers' obligations (from 25 days to 48 hours).	Possibilities for increase of bank customers through the Internet.
Extension of the deadline for payment from one to five days, according to the sixth number of the Federal Taxpayers Register (RFC).	Reduction in possibilities for fraud and corruption.	Reduction in possibilities for fraud and corruption.
Elimination of tax forms.	Reduction in handling of volumes of paper.	Reduction in handling of volumes of paper.
Reduction in administrative costs and the risk of carrying cash.	Savings in storage and transfer of papers and archives (consumables, messengers, vehicles, gasoline, fares, etc.)	Reduction in spending on processes and back-office personnel.
Option for those who have a Tax Card to also pay via Internet.	Saving of processing costs due to centralization of information and processes.	
Replacement of proprietary *software* with an Internet setting.	Medium-term amortization of investment and spending on computer equipment, workstations, printers and maintenance.	

5. Actions for the Development and Implementation of the New Electronic Payment Scheme

The *New Electronic Payment Scheme* has required a series of tasks that have involved the following actions, among others:

- Design and production of 6,370,500 Tax Cards delivered to more than 82 percent of taxpayers.
- Meetings with the Bankers' Association of Mexico to establish points of agreement for the receipt of electronic payments.
- Training and certification of 16 banking institutions to operate the new scheme.
- Design and preparation of five electronic forms with self-fill-out guide for bank and SAT Internet web pages; 14 informatics applications and updating of five of SAT's main institutional systems for receiving bank and SAT operations.
- Design and publication of a special SAT Internet site to make tax declarations, correct data, consult information on the new payment scheme, practice in the payment guide, check addresses and telephone numbers of the institution's offices, print out help sheets, request electronic identification codes and consult authorized banks, among others.
- Training for tax counselors to operate applications for tax payments.
- Establishment of an alternate Telephone Service Center for receiving taxpayers' doubts.
- Talks, conferences, courses and workshops, nationwide, with different sectors linked to tax matters.
- Wide dissemination through:
    - Mass media.
    - Chats on Internet pages.
    - Printed matter for national distribution.
    - Production and broadcasting of radio and television spots.
    - Strategic alliances with various institutions to disseminate information through their Internet pages and distribute published material.

There is no possibility of diverting funds, since the payment is credited directly to the taxpayer's tax account

6. Strategic Lines of Innovation and Quality

The *New Electronic Payment Scheme* complies with all the strategic lines issued by the Office of the Presidency for Government Innovation.

7. Transparency and the Fight against Corruption

- Direct dealings with taxpayers have been reduced, which prevents possible acts of corruption and fraud on the part of public servants, bank employees and intermediaries.
- There is no possibility of diverting funds, since the payment is credited directly to the taxpayer's tax account.
- There is greater transparency in payments and possible acts of corruption are avoided, because the payment receipt for federal contributions issued by SAT and bank applications is forgery-proof and can be authenticated.
- Taxpayer-tax authority relations are transparent since transactions can be consulted online on the next working day after payment is made.

8. Professionalization of Public Service/Cultural Change

External Changes

- Encouragement and raising of awareness for the population regarding the use of the Internet as a modern, swift and secure means to carry out their tax operations.
- Reengineering of the payment process aimed at facilitating taxpayers' compliance.

9. Culture of Quality in Public Service

- Automatic data processing; attention is centered on the taxpayer.
- Fostering of the culture of service through Integral Taxpayer Assistance Modules.

- System of dynamic attention to cover demand peaks in the service.
- Electronic access channels to SAT to draw closer to taxpayers and provide them with self-service, favoring remote service and avoiding unnecessary travel.
- Greater interaction and integration between taxpayers and SAT.

Taxpayer-tax authority relations are transparent since transactions can be consulted online on the next working day after payment is made

10. Use of Information Technology and Telecommunications

- Payment of taxes is mostly made online through bank Internet pages, whereas declarations in zeros and data correction, as well as consultations and assignation of codes, are carried out through the SAT Internet page. This makes it possible, on the one hand, to have timely information and, on the other, to have online statistical information to allow greater control of compliance with tax obligations.
- The use of electronic forms with self-fill-out guide used by banks and SAT are standardized simultaneously, which reduces development and updating times.
- Tax payment receipts in banks contain a digital seal which, due to its technological characteristics, make it forgery-proof and subject to authentication.
- Taxpayers' tax identification data are taken from the Tax Card, which contains a bar code and a magnetic band with said information.
- 97 "Internet Rooms" located in SAT offices throughout the country, equipped with a total of 693 computers, to offer taxpayers who do not have this medium the opportunity to carry out their operations.

11. Deregulation and Administrative Simplification

- Payment is made without turning over the calculation of the declaration.
- The entering of information is automatic, which eliminates the work and cost of document administration.

- Accounting and tax compliance information can be consulted online in a timely manner.

12. Government Savings and Cost Reduction

- Use of paper approximately 23 percent lower in 2002 and 70 percent less in 2003.
- Less time in receipt and entering of information.
- Lower processing costs.
- The administrative personnel in charge of data processing can be reassigned to other activities of collection and attention to the public.
- Amortization of investment in computer equipment, workstations, printers and maintenance over the medium term.

Internal Changes:

- Training of advisers and counselors to help taxpayers in the use of payment applications and to clarify their doubts.
- Establishment of a culture of service to taxpayers through the concentration of services in the Integral Taxpayer Assistance Modules.

13. Profitability (Cost-Benefit)

The launching of the *New Electronic Payment Scheme* required the efforts of three general administrations of the Tax Administration Service which carried out the activities described above.

The new form of payment of taxes is in line with the worldwide trend of offering services through new technologies with proven effectiveness, such as the Internet.

Work and modifications have been carried out to reorient systems and processes in such a way that the activities that were previously effected manually and with human intervention are carried out today by making use of the existing tools and technologies.

In this regard, the financial investment for production of Tax

Cards, the establishment of Internet Rooms, the purchase of machines that read bar codes and magnetic bands, etc., is significantly low compared to the benefit obtained to meet taxpayers' needs as regards responsible, timely compliance with their tax obligations, which responds to the mission, vision and strategic objectives of the Tax Administration Service.

Notices of Zeros /1

	Total	2002	2003	2004
Module	5,595,405	691,907	3,552,893	1,350,605
Internet	24,197,130	3,335,280	14,499,053	6,362,797
Total	29,792,535	4,027,187	18,051,946	7,713,402

1/ From August 2002 to May 2004

Correctives /2

Month	Total	2002	2003	2004
Module	179,414	17,698	116,371	45,345
Internet	768,985	23,389	491,397	254,199
Total	948,399	41,087	607,768	299,544

/2 From September 2002 to May 2004

CIEC /3

Year	Total	2002	2003	2004
Internet	1,854,674	157,727	1,313,370	383,577
Module	485,102	33,480	389,517	62,105
Total	2,339,776	191,207	1,702,887	445,682

/3 From August 2002 to April 2004

Payment in Banks

Year	Total	2002	2003	2004
Banks	41,297,373	6,570,704	25,650,207	9,076,462

Information on 2004 to April

Results Obtained

Item	Before	Today	Benefit
Number of operations through the Internet	Average of 25,000	25,650,207	Expansion of the taxpayer base using Internet
Number of forms	Printed: 4; Electronic: 5	Printed: 0; Internet: 2	Elimination of paper Proprietary software replaced by Internet setting
Payment options	Only at bank windows	Through the Internet or Bank window. Internet SAT or SAT windows	Easy to comply from any computer connected to the Internet. More means and channels for payment: 66 SAT offices and 16 participating banks with 7,500 branches and 24-hour service on the Internet
Payment due dates	One day only (17 each month)	Six days (17 each month + 5 additional working days)	More days to comply and better distribution of the inflow of taxpayers
Availability of information for control of obligations	25 days	48 hours	Timeliness of information
Internet Rooms at the disposal of taxpayers	0 rooms	97 rooms with a total of 693 computers	Internet access service offered nationwide
Payment slip	Declaration with ink stamp and cashier's handwritten signature	Electronic receipt with digital bank or SAT seal	Innovation, security and transparency

Ministry of National Defense (SEDENA)

Introduction of the Integral Administration System

1. Background

Within the framework of the 2001-2006 National Development Plan and the Operation and Development Program of the Ministry of National Defense relative to the same period, the Integral Administration System was introduced in order to make its Budget Management processes more efficient by means of an informatics tool that uses leading-edge technology through a unique application that incorporates all of the activities carried out in the General Directorate of Administration (DGA).

Initially these activities included the two final stages of the Budget Management process provided for by the Ministry of Finance and Public Credit, which consist of the Allocation and Control of Spending as well as its Registering, considered within the functions that rest with the (DGA) in accordance with the Organic Law of the Army and Air Force.

This was based on an analysis of the problems affecting the DGA, and it was detected that the information related to the budget was handled using non-integrated software tools, which hindered their use by virtue of the fact that disperse information was used in independent files, which favored duplication and inconsistencies. This evidenced the need to integrate financial, budget and procurement operations in order to consolidate the information generated in a single database to avoid unnecessary duplication.

One decisive factor in developing this system was having an information bank capable of providing information in due time and form for timely decision-making, which enables units, agencies and installations to have sufficient economic and material resources for the performance of the missions entrusted to them.

To comply with this commitment a multidisciplinary team was formed with qualified personnel from the Ministry with the aim of assessing and analyzing traditional management, and thus the seven

The systematization of administrative processes, strictly in keeping with institutional regulations and doctrine, diminishes the points considered critical in budget management, which makes it possible to forestall irregular conduct within the framework of procurement and budget management

basic processes of the (DGA) were upgraded in a precise, efficient and innovative manner, with an approach centering on the expectations and needs of internal and external users in order to offer citizens quality service.

As a result of this analysis it was determined that the installation of an Enterprise Resource Planning (ERP), when applied to the government sector known as Government Resource Planning (GRP), would diminish the problems faced, obtaining added value derived from the incorporation of new areas. On the basis of the above the Integral Administration System (SIA) was implemented institutionally, which made it possible to merge the budget, financial and material resources management processes of the entire Mexican Army and Air Force.

At present an extension process is under way which already incorporates various functions in the planning, programming and budgeting processes at national level, as well as control of warehouses and the payment scheme for all Mexican Army and Air Force personnel.

2. Setting and Objective

The Integral Administration System has been introduced in the Ministry of National Defense to manage budget and material resources appropriately, with functional and institutional scope and nationwide coverage through its own communication schemes. Its objective is to modernize and innovate budget management processes in order to improve the transparency, productivity and effectiveness of budget allocation and monitoring, using the best practices at world level with the support of new technologies and with a quality approach.

3. Description of the Practice

In its first phase, the SIA included the two final stages of the Budget Management process provided for by the Ministry of Finance and

Public Credit, forming the modules of Budget, Accounting, Inventory Control and Procurement, which facilitated operations related to Allocation and Control of Spending, as well as its Registering, incorporating the budget, financial and material resources management processes carried out by the Mexican Army and Air Force in an expeditious and efficient manner.

In a second phase, the SIA incorporated into its operating scheme the Materials Planning and Warehouse Control modules, initially combining the General Directorates of Informatics, War Materials, Transmissions, Quartermaster Corps and Health, as well as their respective general warehouses, which makes available an effective tool for appropriate control and management of stock.

In addition a third phase has been contemplated for 2005 and 2006, in which the centrally installed application will be extended to the Military Regions as regards Budget Allocation, Control and Registering, and Procurement, as well as introducing the maintenance module for the goods administered by this Ministry.

The development of this system will facilitate incorporation of the scheme for electronic payments made between the Ministry and the Treasury of the Federation, through its Integral Federal Financial Administration System (SIAFF).

The implementation of the Integral Administration System has a direct impact on the six strategic lines of the Presidential Agenda for Good Government, the following benefits being identified:

To bring training to fruition a radial scheme is used which consists of training a leading training group which in turn becomes an instructor of other groups, giving rise to a multiplier effect that covers the training needs of the different levels of users

4. Honest and Transparent Government

The systematization of administrative processes, strictly in keeping with institutional regulations and doctrine, diminishes the points considered critical in budget management, which makes it possible to forestall irregular conduct within the framework of procurement and budget management.

Being a system that integrates budget management processes, the SIA makes it possible to obtain reports and surveys that serve to respond to requests for information on the part of the general public in compliance with the Law on Transparency and Access to Government Public Information.

5. Professional Government

The human factor is considered the pivotal part of the system, so that to develop the SIA's training process a Training Center is used, located in its Central Area, where experts in processes transmit their knowledge to end users.

To bring training to fruition a radial scheme is used which consists of training a leading training group which in turn becomes an instructor of other groups, giving rise to a multiplier effect that covers the training needs of the different levels of users.

The design of training plans is carried out through an analysis of processes, designing the profiles required by users. Once this analysis has concluded, the courses required for their coverage is established, as well as the training program with dates, courses, participants and instructors, creating a simulated setting of the real setting.

6. Quality Government

One key objective considered in developing SIA's infrastructure was achieving a direct impact on the diverse sectors of society by making the management of budget resources allocated to the Ministry more transparent, reliable and efficient, under an operational scheme based on the Demming Cycle, in order to comply fully with the general missions assigned to it, which have an eminently social approach by providing the Ministry with more and better human and material resources aimed at strengthening national security and development, which consolidate the stability of the Mexican State.

In order to offer quality products and services, the Central Area of SIA implemented a Quality Management System (SGC) certified under standard ISO 9001:2000, in which the basic processes that materialize in the SIA were identified and documented in a Quality Manual and

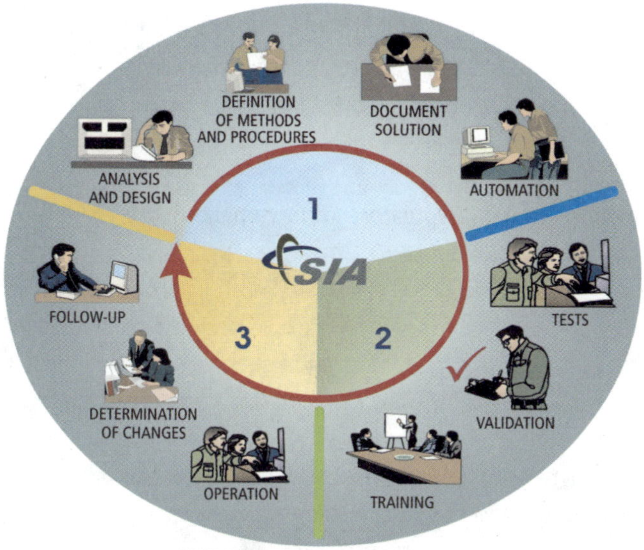

CONTINUOUS IMPROVEMENT PROCESS

incorporating control mechanisms that enable the system's performance to be evaluated and improved. Furthermore, various means were implemented to determine users' expectations, as well as their degree of satisfaction, and these have become the main tools through which the continuous improvement process operates.

7. Digital Government

The Integral Administration System (SIA) is an informatics tool that encompasses the Ministry's budget and material resources management processes, automating their use and distribution, which facilitates its exchange and utilization for decision-making by including operative and support applications in decisions.

To achieve process integration a GRP of a leading company at world level was installed, which incorporates the best practices and allows their extension to other sectors of this agency in a modular and integral manner.

Furthermore, a web page is available by means of which technical support is provided, in addition to having a regulations library containing all of the applicable legislation, which makes it possible to have highly useful complementary information for the personnel.

8. Government with Regulatory Improvement

One of the objectives of the system is simplifying processes and making application procedures more flexible and secure, avoiding the growth of procedures, provisions and instructions that turn out to be unnecessary and tend toward the bureaucratization of systematized processes.

For this reason, the system includes mechanisms to obtain administrative deregulation by interrelating activities in workflows, which results in a reduction in the preparation of additional procedures for the exchange and utilization of information.

Its implementation required the redesign of processes that improved response time and eliminated obsolete practices that slowed the fulfillment of activities.

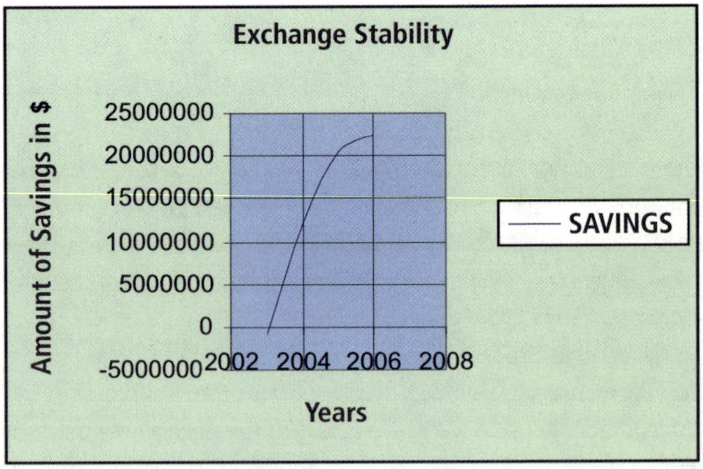

9. Government that Costs Less

The SIA makes it possible to know at all times the status of application of the Ministry's budget, the result of which is timely decision-making, in addition to making acquisitions transparently and in accordance with the policies, bases and guidelines governing Procurement, Leasing and Services, by providing reliable, timely information for the awarding process for purchase contracts following objective and precise criteria for better application of resources, which generates substantial savings allocated, with prior approval from the Ministry of Finance and Public Credit (SHCP), to reinforcing the activities carried out by Army and Air Force personnel in benefit of the civil population.

10. Conclusions

The implementation of the Integral Administration System constitutes an innovative practice that can be reproduced at all levels of the Public Administration, since it combines budget management processes with strict adherence to current regulations, with an operational model focusing on the requirements of users and the population, assuring compliance with the highest quality standards by providing continuous improvement mechanisms.

National Institute of the Workers' Housing Fund (INFONAVIT)

Digital Alternatives for INFONAVIT Service

With the commitment to complying with its constitutional mandate, INFONAVIT adopted a strategy of furnishing communication channels with its clients and collaborators, supported by information technology. Through the use of digital technologies such as Internet, telephones and kiosks, in an average month INFONAVIT deals with over two million applications, focusing on customer service within a framework of absolute transparency. The objective is to integrate a network of processes equipped with information technologies to the main actors in the housing market to be able to offer simple, economical and efficient services to its 12 million beneficiaries.

Since its founding in 1972, INFONAVIT has extended three million credits for low-cost housing, of which one million were extended between 2000 and 2003, a figure that will double before 2006, that is, in six years INFONAVIT will extend two million housing credits for families in benefit of almost 10 million Mexicans, thus contributing to the development of a sector with enormous impact—construction— with around 23 million jobs generated in six years.

INFONAVIT took up an aggressive stance on innovation which has enabled it to reduce its past due portfolio from 21 percent to 9 percent in only three years. Likewise, an orderly monitoring has represented income of more than four billion pesos in 2003, roughly 400 percent more than in previous years. This has been reflected in the market's confidence in the Institution and has contributed to an AAA rating on the part of the world's most important Financial Rating Agencies, such as Standard and Poor's. For the first time in its history INFONAVIT has placed debt certificates on the Stock Market—Low-Cost Hosing Stock Market Certificates (CEDEVI).

1. Objective of the Service

Offer easy and transparent service alternatives to 12 million workers and to almost one million employers, as well as incorporating into its processes other entities (notaries, BANSEFI, Government, etc.) that participate with INFONAVIT in the ultimate task of providing people with their own home.

Generically, the project includes:

- The portal *www.infonavit.gob.mx.*
- The portal *www.micasa.gob.mx.*
- The Transparency and Access to Information portal.

- The INFONATEL Contact Center.
- The INFONAVIT kiosks.
- The management control system.
- Automation of appraisals.

During the current administration, the strategy has been to simplify and standardize processes, focusing on the use of information technology to provide service and consultations in a remote manner through the Internet or by telephone. This did not entail making the Institute's offices in the country disappear, but rather complementing them. As an example of this, in these three years the concept of INFONAVIT Service Centers (CESI), which are Customer Service offices, certified with ISO 9000, with modern, suitable facilities for providing service of excellence and with employees transformed into *advisers*.

2. The CESI Were Worthy of the INNOVA Recognition Award 2002

The CESI deal with the specialized services that require physical presence, whereas alternate channels, such as the Internet portal *(www.infonavit.gob.mx)*, the INFONATEL telephone service center (INNOVA Recognition Award 2000), the housing portal *www.micasa.gob.mx*, and the kiosks, cater to the large volume of customer requirements. Since they started at the beginning of the current administration, the alternate channels have contributed to combating bureaucratic practices and corruption, since they have carried out more than 60 million operations that would have required a visit to one of the Institute's offices somewhere in the country.

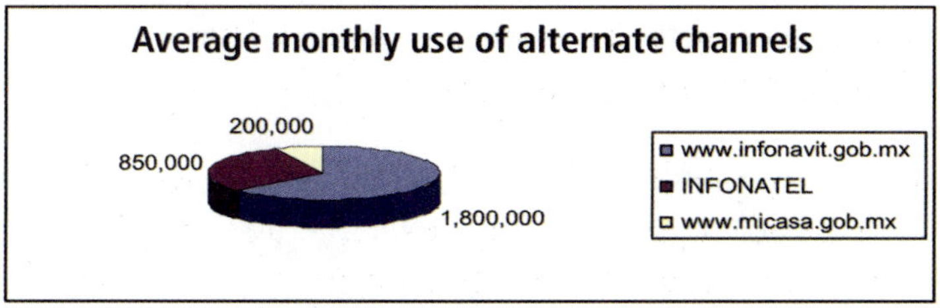

3. Problems before the Implementation of the Practice of Innovation

All the procedures and consultations were carried out at the traditional windows, the consequence of which was repeated visits with long lines, service personnel overwhelmed and unable to show citizens a friendly, efficient attitude, which gave rise to a favorable setting for corruption and an unreliable image of INFONAVIT.

4. Impact of Innovation

The alternate channels strategy contributes to Good Government, for it enables it to cost less, to have quality, to be of a highly professional nature, it offers digital services, improves regulation—both internal and toward the customer or citizen—and improves the user's perception with regard to honesty and transparency.

5. Benefit for Mexico

The procedures established give certainty to borrowers and suppliers in the process of marketing the supply, since the result of their appraisal can be consulted freely and transparently.

Moreover, the mortgage reflects the market value without ceasing to ensure the quality of housing by means of verification by qualified and certified third parties.

The alternate channels have had an impact such that the figures have been outstanding in less than two years.

In one year, the portal has been visited by almost 15 million people; it is a site where the Institution's three major categories of customers are segmented: workers, employers and developers, as well as having a section for the public in general.

- The portal for dissemination of housing supply, *www.micasa.gob.mx,* is an electronic catalogue of low-cost housing where workers can find almost one million houses throughout the country by means of a simple search mechanism. Similarly, almost a thousand promoters can automatically upload their houses to the site. From November 2001 to date, the portal has catered to 3.5 million people.

- The INFONATEL Contact Center has an area of almost one thousand square meters, located in what used to be an INFONAVIT warehouse which was conditioned under the principles of excellence, austerity and efficiency, to house almost 400 telephone advisers and a first-world technological platform which enables us to process 850,000 incoming and outgoing calls a month and work with a philosophy of administration of relations with the customer (all matters become cases). Today, INFONATEL offers around 200 electronic procedures.
- INFONATEL provides more than 200 services related to contributions, statements of account, extensions, regularization, release of credits, change of regime, contributions and payments, transfers, etc.
- INFONATEL makes interaction with customers easier, while making internal operations more transparent and efficient.
- The *Interactive Kiosks*—there are currently six—are devices similar to a computer with the characteristic of being made for rough use and for public places. Their touch-screens and their capacity for multimedia sound makes them easy to use. This project is in its pilot phase and has served more than 50,000 people in a year.

6. Economy in Human and Material Resources

Cost reduction through the elimination of report functions as part of the process of extending credit, evaluation and appraisal of housing in the work of the delegations and central regulatory areas, which do not add value to substantive processes.

7. Appraisal in Less Time and at Lower Cost

In addition to the citizen and customer attention portals, there is the automation of the appraisal request process, which makes it possible to obtain statistical data for the issuing of the housing price index. This enables values to be monitored and possible deviations to be determined, as well as the behavior of commercial values for timely decision-making by housing agencies.

Access to the appraisal system through the Internet is available 16 hours a day. It favors the saving of time, material resources and costs; furthermore, the information is contained in a database at a central server, to minimize impacts in the case of a contingency. Offering the Institute a technological platform allows real-estate appraisal professionals to make appraisals in less time and in a standard manner, making the process easier and reducing the time. The result is diminished costs in preparing appraisals and consequently, in the rates beneficiary workers pay for said services.

8. Continuous Improvement

There are procedures and systems that standardize real-estate appraisal processes, making it possible to establish quantitative quality indicators which, by being periodically monitored, will facilitate continuous quality improvement processes.

9. INTRAGOB

The methodology of the INTRAGOB Quality Model has been used, establishing quality objectives and defining a set of preventive actions, as well as a process of continuous improvement through the High-Yield Strategic Unit implemented by the General Directorate.

In addition, a strategic committee is incorporated into the subdirectorates and coordination offices which reviews goals, effectiveness and efficiency indicators and improvement projects on a quarterly basis.

Office of the Attorney General of the Republic (PGR)

Federal Investigation Agency (AFI)

Negotiation and Crisis Management Procedure

The positive impact that the creation of the procedure for dealing with kidnappings by means of Negotiation and Crisis Management in the AFI has had on society has been reflected by the rate of complaints heeded

1. Problems Encountered: the Situation before Implementing the Practice of Innovation

The increase in recent years in our country in the incidence of the crime of kidnapping, under a pattern of organized crime, had complicated the role of the Mexican State's police forces. One example of this was the mechanism with which the Federal Judicial Police operated, with a reactive methodology, with minimal or no investigating capacity. That attitude gave rise to a high rate of mistrust in society, causing a rift with the authority and inhibiting the reporting of kidnappings, although in fact such a rift also had a bearing on the rift with regard to other crimes. In addition, previously the aim was to evidence the flagrancy of the criminal by means of confrontation for his arrest, which put the life of the victim at risk.

All this conduct produced a considerable lag in specialized, sensitive and professional attention to this crime from the point of view of the victim, but on establishing the AFI, a very important step was taken by creating an effective police investigation model based on the following points:

- Compartmentalization of information;
- Specialization of police functions in analysis, investigation or operation;
- The case of kidnapping favored specialization in negotiating capacity, crisis management within the victim's family and the life of the person kidnapped.

Based on this, the AFI has succeeded in being an effective assistant for the Office of the Public Prosecutor of the Federation.

2. Implementation

To implement the practice of the negotiation procedure, intensive work of awareness-raising has been carried out on the changes demanded by society, and therefore training and dissemination of the objectives of the procedure to the personnel in charge of putting it into practice has been favored.

The initial step consisted of appropriate recruitment of personnel, seeking mainly a solid foundation of personal values which, reinforced by close supervision by superiors, would reduce the possibility of corruption.

The next step consisted of intensive, continuous training on the practice of the Negotiation and Crisis Management procedure.

The final stage consisted of making a cyclical analysis of results evaluated directly by citizens themselves, which has made it possible to categorize the effectiveness of the Innovative Practice.

3. Selection of the Practice

It was decided to carry out this practice in comparison with other options for dealing with kidnappings because, as regards the methodology of the Negotiation and Crisis Management procedure, it is unique in the AFI in the country and in other parts of the world. In dealing with kidnappings, only Colombia carries out activities similar to the ones that have the methodology used by the AFI.

The positive impact that the creation of the procedure for dealing with kidnappings by means of Negotiation and Crisis Management in the AFI has had on society has been reflected by the rate of complaints heeded, by the creation of files and voice bank, and by the identification of gangs of kidnappers, all of which stems from intelligence work that makes it possible to create pertinent lines of investigation that systematically help to arrest criminals without endangering the life of the person kidnapped.

4. General results and results with an impact on citizens

4.1 General Results of the Project for Mexico and its Population

The work of dealing with kidnappings is backed by a quality certificate under International Standard ISO 9001/2000

The fight against kidnapping by the personnel of the Federal Investigation Agency has made it possible to lower organized crime's levels of profitability by reducing kidnappers' demands, since the amounts demanded by them have been reduced by 94.32 percent on average in comparison with those paid previously. This has favored the discouragement of this offense in organized crime.

According to surveys carried out by the AFI at the end of the advisory assistance provided to relatives of kidnapping victims, the following results have been obtained in the degree of customer satisfaction:

Year	Rating Obtained
2003	9.5
1st half of 2004	9.9

Likewise, gangs of kidnappers have been arrested, as shown below.

Year	Number of Gangs of Alleged Kidnappers	Number of Alleged Kidnappers
2002	14	109
2003	19	114
1st half of 2004	12	70

4.2 Results with an Impact on Citizens

The impact produced by the Practice of Innovation as regards financial savings in society is highly important, since only an average of six per-

In the context of the expectations for change demanded by society, personnel with higher education have been recruited, thus seeking a solid base of personal values which, reinforced by the close supervision of superiors, reduces the possibility of corruption

cent of the amount demanded is paid for the release of the person kidnapped; this protects the assets of the affected families and avoids the closure of companies due to the entrepreneur's fear of becoming a victim once again.

The work of dealing with kidnappings is backed by a quality certificate under International Standard ISO 9001/2000.

There is a section on kidnapping in the Office of the Attorney General of the Republic's web page in which citizens are informed of the telephone numbers for direct attention for their complaint.

Advisers' activities are based on the Federal Penal Code, in Article 366 *bis*, as well as on the Federal Law against Organized Crime and the Federal Code of Penal Proceedings.

In the context of the expectations for change demanded by society, personnel with higher education have been recruited, thus seeking a solid base of personal values which, reinforced by the close supervision of superiors, reduces the possibility of corruption.

4.3 Benefits (Local, State, Regional or National)

A toll-free number is available to take calls from anywhere in the country, and there is close coordination with the Attorney General's offices of state governments to provide advisory assistance to the relatives of kidnapping victims as soon as they request it.

The AFI is the only institution that has a Sub-directorate of Negotiation and Crisis Management in which an advisory procedure is applied whose main objective is the recovery of the person kidnapped, in contrast to the traditional reactive scheme of other institutions.

4.4 Impact of the Final Benefit (for the Institution or for Society)

- Increase in the probabilities of the person kidnapped returning alive.
- Increase in the probabilities of reduced duration of the kidnap.

- Diminish recidivism toward one same family.
- Minimize the psychological impact that negotiation of the kidnap has for the families of persons kidnapped.
- In the presidential goals for 2003, the AFI attained the objective of arresting 19 criminal gangs involved in kidnapping and, for 2004, up to June, 12 gangs have been arrested.
- The Institution's image at national and international levels is improving with the good performance and the results evidenced in the media.

Type and Number of Customers/Citizens Benefited

Year	Cases Attended
2001	67
2002	107
2003	169
1st half of 2004	90

Bearing in mind that each family has at least three members, it is estimated that a total of approximately 1,299 citizens have benefited directly. It should be emphasized that anybody, regardless of age or financial position, is vulnerable to forming part of the statistics as a victim of kidnapping.

Once the request for help has been received, the service is provided in a personalized manner in the customers' residence.

Mexican Social Security Institute (IMSS)

e-Government and Technological Development in the IMSS

The IMSS provides health-care services to more than half of the country's population, as well as care and education for children of women workers, savings for retirement due to age or disablement, protection against occupational hazards, subsidy for maternity, compensation for the handicapped and support for social activities to improve living standards. Its success is judged by its capacity to stabilize the population's living standards in relation to three main sets of risks: health spending; income in retirement, disability and death; and loss of employment for women workers who are pregnant or have small children.

With 20 years of constraints in levels of investment and spending on infrastructure, and emerging challenges stemming from increases in the cost of medical attention, in view of changes in the demographic and epidemiological profiles of the country's population, in addition to the growing cost of its own labor obligations and evasion in the payment of social security contributions, the IMSS is facing the greatest challenge in its history: guaranteeing the financial sustainability in the medium and long terms of Mexico's main social security institution.

The Beginnings. During the Eighty-eighth General Assembly of the Mexican Social Security Institute, held in March 2001, President Fox instructed the Director General to follow a strategy based on the application of six lines of action as a fulcrum for the transformation of the Institute:

- Promote a culture that strengthens streamlining, efficiency and transparency in the management of financial resources.
- Incorporate information technology into the Institute's substantive processes as the cornerstone of its transformation.
- Establish a Program of Professional Management of Human Capital.
- Guide IMSS processes toward a culture of quality and customer service.
- Make IMSS management a glass box in which the public and society in general form part of efforts for transparency and eradication of corruption.
- Guarantee the Institute's financial sustainability through the creation of Financial Reserves and the Professionalization of Financial Management.

Therefore a component of Information and Communication Technologies (ICT) was incorporated into the Institute's strategy, giving rise to the Program of e-*Government and Technological Development* as an element of cohesion for the substantive areas: Medical Benefits, Incorporation and Collection of Social Security, and Economic and Social Benefits, with shared support and services areas.

Lighting the flame. It was President Fox himself who, with the aim of supporting the development of e-Government services in the IMSS to provide better services to companies, those insured, beneficiaries, retirees and pensioners, submitted for the approval of the Legislative Branch, in October 2001, a series of amendments and additions to the Social Security Law, which were approved with the unanimous vote of all the political parties in December that same year. These amendments made possible the creation of the legal framework that provides validity and legal certainty to the use of the patient's electronic medical record and electronic signature, without distinction with the handwritten signature, to carry out electronic transactions and the storage of data and information in electronic media, the use of the Sole Population Registry Code (CURP) in substitution of the Social Security number and the issuance of a sole means of identification for all its beneficiaries.

The first efforts, in 2001 and 2002, concentrated on integrating and optimizing investment and current spending on ICT Communication Technology assets. It should be mentioned that at the beginning of the administration, the infrastructure was supported by more than 1,200 dispersed computer applications, without database managers, operating in offline processing, whose main components had been developed in the seventies and eighties, the majority of these being incapable of communicating with each other.

The Directorate of Innovation and Technological Development was created as the area responsible for this transformation process to integrate and optimize policies, and manage projects, investment and spending related to Information and Communication Technologies.

To begin with, this Directorate defined four strategic lines:

a) Promote the development of applications with strategic impact that support the processes of each of the substantive areas and generate added value to their respective customers, especially those of predominantly internal use.

The impact in annual savings, both for the Institute and for taxpayers, is higher than 250 million pesos, which continues to increase as the penetration of the service advances and which, together with the Monthly or Bimonthly Issue on CD, makes it possible to economize more than 700 tons in paper consumption and 2,000 man/years in distribution costs and logistics

b) Unify the development platforms of computer programs and database management, and favor the use of support systems for decision-making with databases shared among the substantive areas.
c) Promote the methodologies of the Project Management Institute (PMI) for the management of technology projects, and Capability Maturity Model (CMM) for Administration of the Life Cycle of applications. The objective of certifying the Institute's development areas with CMM level 2 was established for 2006.
d) The use of Internet navigators with open architecture was established as a user interface for all new applications, in substitution of proprietary interfaces.

Thus began the consolidation of the more than 100 computer mini-centers and three area informatics centers in two National Information Technology Centers, with mirror operation, located in Monterrey and Mexico City, which were inaugurated in August 2001 and support the operation of information systems in a setting of high availability. Likewise, and to reduce operating costs, the conditions of hardware and software maintenance contracts were renegotiated, in accordance with current regulations, with IBM and Microsoft, which resulted in savings of more than 3.7 and 13.6 million dollars, respectively.

To interconnect all the Institute's units, tenders were invited for the contracting of the Virtual Private Network service for voice, data and video for around 3,000 service points, which was awarded in 2002 to the company *Uninet* (a subsidiary of *TELMEX*'s), with a value of some 66 million dollars, for a period of 40 months, obtaining the best cost/benefit ratio of any network in the country, and at least five times more economical that that used or contracted by any other agency or entity of the Public Administration. In terms of coverage and broadband, this network is second in importance after *TELMEX*'s own infrastructure. In a parallel manner, the cost per minute for long distance was reduced from 0.99 to 0.70 pesos in cities open to pre-subscription, whereas the average cost of a local call fell from 1.46 to 1.03 pesos. This resulted in annual savings of more than 60 million pesos.

The Patient's Electronic Medical Record, which incorporates data and information on all medical events during the life of beneficiaries, can be available online in each and every one of the Institute's medical units

Once the technological component had been completed, five high-impact initiatives were put into operation in the e-Government program to strengthen the Good Government Strategy of the Office of Government Innovation of the Presidency of the Republic:

a) e-Taxes: to support the process of incorporation and collection of social security, based mainly in the IMSS from your Company initiative.
b) e-Health: to improve the provision of medical services.
c) e-Transparency, through the initiative "IMSS is going to Buy, IMSS Bought;" as the linchpin for strengthening the transparency and fight against corruption policies.
d) Institutional Resource Planning (PREI), an integral system of financial administration and support for managerial decisions: for the promotion of strict management of financial resources and transparency in the allocation of expenditure.
e) e-Supply: to improve service levels in supply of medication and curing material for the Institute's customers.

e-Taxes. To strengthen the Institute's incorporation and collection process, as the country's second fiscal authority, with annual collection of more than 90 billion pesos, the Program IMSS from your Company was promoted, which enables companies or employers to carry out their affiliation movements through the Internet 24 hours a day, 365 days a year, with the consequent savings in operating costs, both for employers and the Institute, minimizing points of risk of corruption by eliminating transactions in person. Today it has a number of private suppliers, among them Terra, bCentral, Levicom and *Eje Comercial*, as well as *Tramitanet*, operated by the Ministry of Public Administration, where transactions are carried out free of charge. The affiliation movements of slightly over 60 percent of the workers enrolled in the IMSS —more than seven million—are carried out through these Internet portals, and companies and employers can make their payments through bank portals. This process reduces percentages of errors in data processing, from 9 percent to 0.1 percent, by entering data at the origin, that is, in the company.

To put the Electronic Medical Record and the Family Medicine System into operation, the Institute has installed and equipped with computer and communications infrastructure the 105 largest Family Medicine Units (UMF), which cover 39.2 percent of the potential population served, out of a total of 1,200 UMF

The impact in annual savings, both for the Institute and for taxpayers, is higher than 250 million pesos, which continues to increase as the penetration of the service advances and which, together with the Monthly or Bimonthly Issue on CD, makes it possible to economize more than 700 tons in paper consumption and 2,000 man/years in distribution costs and logistics.

To solve the problems associated with the processes of Affiliation, Validity and Certification of Rights, Collection and Oversight at the root, the Affiliation, Collection and Oversight System (SIAREFI) was launched, with results expected in 20 to 30 months, with the taking of requirements and generating the Technical Specifications resulting from the Reengineering Project. The second phase, programmed for 2004 and 2005, includes the development of computer applications and the implementation of the information systems and their quality management systems for ISO 9000:2000 and Six Sigma certification, which will reduce, over a period of five years, the deviation or error index in transactions to a level below 3.64 errors or defects for every million transactions carried out.

e-Health. To support the process of improvement in the provision of medical services, the Institute launched the programs of Family Medicine and the Patient's Electronic Medical Record, which incorporates data and information on all medical events during the life of beneficiaries, can be available online in each and every one of the Institute's medical units. This makes it possible, for instance, for a patient assigned to a medical unit in Chiapas to receive service at another unit located in the state of Sonora, with the same information base, to improve treatment of his or her ailments.

The Family Medicine Information System, which together with a series of comprehensive improvements in the processes of care for beneficiaries at the first level of health care, improves the experience in 85 percent of the more than 120 million medical events per year, incorporates the following applications:

- An Electronic Appointments Agenda for Family Medicine Unit services, as support for the Prior Appointments Agenda, in operation in more than 600 Medical Units in the country, and a coverage of over 75 percent of the population attended, which reduces average waiting times from two hours to less than twenty minutes;

- The Integral Health Care Module implements an Electronic Clinical Registration Sheet with the efficiency to keep details of personalized outpatient medical care, and implementing the forms used by the physician and specialized nurses which feeds the Patient's Electronic Medical Record in first-level units; and
- A Preventive Health Care Module aimed at registering the events of the Integrated Health Programs (PREVENIMSS).

Electronic Medical Record was recognized in April 2003 by Steve Ballmer, President of Microsoft Corp., at the Summit of Government Leaders, held in Redmond, Washington, as the most innovative application and with the greatest potential for reproduction in other countries for the development of electronic government services and the improvement of services for citizens

To put the Electronic Medical Record and the Family Medicine System into operation, the Institute has installed and equipped with computer and communications infrastructure the 105 largest Family Medicine Units (UMF), which cover 39.2 percent of the potential population served, out of a total of 1,200 UMF.

However, to be able to have a system of medical information that makes possible interoperability and exchange of data, the Institute defined as compulsory a series of international standards to make up the patient's electronic medical records and the health systems, and it is the first institution in Mexico to adopt standard HL7 V3 for the exchange of data and interoperability, and DICOM for the incorporation of digital images. Also, since the year 2002, the IMSS has promoted the establishment of Chapter HL7 Mexico, which makes it possible to make the local adaptations required to normalize institutional needs before International HL7 Agencies, which incorporates the main health and educational institutions of the public and private sectors and the developers of health software. In addition, the IMSS has represented Mexico in international forums to define the workings of the Electronic Medical Record.

This program was recognized in April 2003 by Steve Ballmer, President of Microsoft Corp., at the Summit of Government Leaders, held in Redmond, Washington, as the most innovative application and with the greatest potential for reproduction in other countries for the

To strengthen transparency in allocation of expenditure and financial management the most ambitious initiative in Latin America was launched for the implementation of a GRP (Government Resource Planning) system known as Institutional Resource Planning Program (PREI)

development of electronic government services and the improvement of services for citizens.

e-Government and Transparency. The IMSS, one of the largest purchasers of goods and services, with an annual amount of more than 30 billion pesos, launched, as part of its Transparency program, the Internet portal known as "The IMSS is going to Buy, the IMSS Bought," which consists of two sections. The first contains a description of the goods and services that the buying areas plan to acquire, as well as their Technical Specifications, through a novel concept of publication of "Pre-Bases" which enables suppliers or potential participants in bidding process to review specifications even before the calls for tenders are published definitively. Suppliers can also make suggestions or comments and foster the participation of a larger number of providers, reducing at the same time the phenomenon of induction of bases or the levels of corruption. The second section shows the goods or services that have been acquired. It is compulsory for all buying units to disclose the terms and conditions under which goods and services were contracted, placing at the disposal of the general public all the data on what, when, how much, where and how it is going to be acquired, and subsequently from whom and under what conditions.

Institutional Resource Planning. To strengthen transparency in allocation of expenditure and financial management, and as a factor for integration between the Institute's substantive and support areas, which facilitates better planning, control and monitoring of financial operations, the most ambitious initiative in Latin America was launched for the implementation of a Government Resource Planning (GRP) system known as Institutional Resource Planning Program (PREI). By means of this initiative, the functions of Accounting, Budget, Treasury, Fixed Assets, Accounts Payable, Balanced Control Board and Managerial Information System will be integrated under a common platform in the Institute's more than 3,000 buying and paying units. This project, with a duration of three years, from 2002 to 2005, began operations in a partial manner only six months after having started, and more than

5,000 users have been trained as part of the project. The PREI is based on the application of the Six Sigma methodology, helps to minimize errors in transactions, and provides for the normalization of processes and the incorporation of the Quality Management System.

45 computer classrooms were equipped and put into operation in the training centers administered by the SNTSS, through which training was provided to more than 32,000 people in the use of information technology tools

e-Government and Institutional Supply. The Institutional Supply System or SAI supports the management of the supply process and includes consolidation of requirements, bidding processes, contracting, reception, warehousing, supply and control of inventories of consumer goods and investment. It began operations in November 1999 amid a mass of complaints, both internal and from institutional suppliers, and as of 2001 it was redesigned, incorporating around 4,000 modifications in functioning that made it possible to achieve operative stabilization and put an end completely to users' complaints, thereby strengthening operations in more than 1,200 drugstores and 40 warehouses. As a complement, the system of support for decisions, based on Brio, was set in motion, which concentrates information to support decisions at national, regional or delegation level, and which supports monitoring of optimal levels of supply in all drugstores and warehouses, and follows up on more than 300 codes of the most used medicines and the 100 medicines of the most critical level. This system was the tool that helped to increase the percentage of prescriptions filled for beneficiaries from levels of less than 65 percent in January 2003 to record levels of 92 percent at the close of 2003, which reduced the high rate of complaints received with regard to supply.

Institute-Union Work. One highly important aspect in setting these initiatives in motion has been the participation of the National Union of Social Security Workers (SNTSS). In the Family Medicine, "IMSS from your Company," SIAREFI and PREI initiatives, joint working groups were created made up of members of the National Executive Committee of SNTSS and the Institute's executives; the result was that the implementation of said programs took place in a bilateral and jointly responsible atmosphere, which made it easier for more than 40,000 people to form part of the initiatives.

The IMSS commitment to the development of e-Services is even greater. The aim is for 90 percent of transactions related to the processes of affiliation, issue and collection, as well as all payments, should be carried out through the Internet by the end of 2006

Development of Human Capital. No technological development program can be successful without a Human Capital Management program. The Institute began a managerial development program for the leaders of change of these initiatives. Between 2002 and 2003 more than 100 executives have taken courses in senior management business development programs of the Pan-American Institute of Senior Business Management (IPADE), and more than 150 officials have taken managerial development diploma courses at the Autonomous Technological Institute of Mexico (ITAM) and the Monterrey Technological Institute of Higher Studies (ITESM). One hundred employees have been trained in administration and quality certification systems and Six Sigma. Similarly, 45 computer classrooms were equipped and put into operation in the training centers administered by the SNTSS, through which training was provided to more than 32,000 people in the use of information technology tools.

A distance education initiative was also launched, which provides specialization courses for family physicians and a degree course in nursing, developed jointly with the National Autonomus University of Mexico (UNAM), through 24 new videoconference halls in the country.

e-Government Vision in the IMSS. The Institute's commitment to the development of e-Services is even greater. The aim is for 90 percent of transactions related to the processes of affiliation, issue and collection, as well as all payments, should be carried out through the Internet by the end of 2006. The Institute's e-Health program will allow intercommunication between all clinics and hospitals, as well as accessibility of the medical records of all beneficiaries online. Along the same lines, "IMSS is going to Buy, IMSS Bought" must publish all the information related to procurement and contracting processes, making sure that the outlays registered in the Institute's accounting are equal in amount to the information published in said portal. To that end, as a result of the implementation of the PREI, the Institute's financial and operative information will be available to the public in general through the Internet. These initiatives are expected to be strengthened over the next few years in benefit of millions of users and beneficiaries of social security in Mexico.

Comparison of e-Government Practices *vs.* Best Practices Worldwide

e-Health is a world-class, leading application, and exchanges of experience and the negotiation of standards with international agencies and organizations are conducted on equal terms. There is recognition at world level for the application of this initiative in Mexico

Applications concerning collection, such as "IMSS from your Company," which facilitate compliance with fiscal obligations through the Internet, are at an average level of maturity in comparison with similar best practices in countries such as France and Canada, or the Ministry of Finance in Mexico.

e-Health applications, for their part, such as the Electronic Medical Record and the Family Medicine Model, can perhaps be compared to similar projects in the degree of depth and penetration in countries such as the United Kingdom, Australia, New Zealand and the United States. Nonetheless, those efforts are still in the early stages, and although they will also have national coverage, they have not achieved the penetration and normalization reached by the Institute.

This is a world-class, leading application, and exchanges of experience and the negotiation of standards with international agencies and organizations are conducted on equal terms. There is recognition at world level for the application of this initiative in Mexico.

The financial management applications that make up the PREI project, when compared to the initiatives of *Government Resource Planning*-GRP of OECD countries, positions the Institute at mid-level in three years; however, to date there is still a lag of over five years. The applications launched in this first stage are standard, with tools available on the market, and therefore there is no advantage over existing GRPs in similar institutions.

The Institute's e-Supply practices, such as SAI and Brio, even though they constitute the procurement system that generates the greatest volume of purchase orders through the Internet in Mexico, compare unfavorably with the levels of service offered by these applications in any world-class government institution, by virtue of the fact that it does not form an integral part of a GRP. However, an important aspect is how, through the system of support for decisions, Brio succeeded in increasing agreements on service levels in supply of medicines, reaching record levels in the Institute's entire history in less than a year.

On the transparency portal, such as "IMSS is going to Buy, IMSS

Bought," there is no reference at world level as to its penetration or scope with which it can be compared.

Ministry of Communications and Transportation (SCT)

First e-Mexico Satellite Digital Connectivity Network

1. Problems Existing in 2000

In the year 2000 there were almost 60 million inhabitants in Mexico without access to basic telecommunications services, either because of lack of infrastructure or because they did not have the resources to pay for such services. This required a comprehensive solution, in technical and economic terms, to confront this situation.

In his inaugural address on December 1, 2000, the President of the Republic, Vicente Fox Quesada, announced the project of the e-Mexico National System in order to integrate the efforts of various agencies and entities of the Public Administration, as well as the operators of telecommunications networks, among other actors, in a national connectivity project that would incorporate cutting-edge technologies and online contents, particularly those with a social impact for Mexico. This program came under the coordination of the Ministry of Communications and Transportation.

Three main headings were defined for the development of the e-Mexico National System: Connectivity, Contents and Systems. Given their characteristics, they are managed independently for purposes of execution; however, they must be kept coordinated as a whole.

> The backbone of this system is the First e-Mexico Network of Satellite Digital Connectivity, through which comprehensive communication services are offered that provide Internet access to the country's localities, initially through the creation of Digital Community Centers (CCDs), as principal vehicles that enable the different localities that comprise it to be linked and become an engine of the development of the community.

With this First e-Mexico Network of Satellite Digital Connectivity all Mexicans are being connected through an interactive digital network which, by means of voice, image and data transmission, provides access to information and knowledge.

The Connectivity framework of the National e-Mexico System was designed in the Ministry of Communications and Transportation with the aim of providing high-speed Internet access to the population that does not have this service, whether because of lack of infrastructure for providing these services, or because the population does not have sufficient resources to contract the services offered by license holders

2. Brief Explanation of the Implementation of the System

As a starting point, a satellite network was conceived which would provide access to the Internet in the short term, with an initial coverage of 3,200 connectivity points, with a lower cost than those established on the commercial market. Likewise, the quality required to achieve communication from any point where electric power is assured. All of this supports compliance with the Good Government Agenda.

Between June and July 2002 the Inter-ministerial Collaboration Agreements were signed between the Ministry of Communications and Transportation and each of the participating agencies and entities: Ministry of Public Education (SEP), Ministry of Health (SSA), Ministry of Social Development (SEDESOL), National Institute for Federalism and Municipal Development (INAFED) of the Ministry of the Interior (SEGOB) and the National Institute for Adult Education (INEA), in order to establish commitments to attain the objectives established in the Satellite Digital Connectivity Strategy.

The main commitments assumed by said agencies are the establishment, implementation, operation, protection and maintenance of the CCDs. The SCT is in charge of providing the connectivity for the CCDs selected by the agencies and entities. The term of these agreements is five years, extendable for a further two, which guarantees the continuity of the service.

> Thus, the aim is to guarantee the service for a longer period than the current administration, which will be in benefit of the population, supported by economies of scale by incorporating a larger number of users at lower cost, particularly important for marginalized areas that require social coverage in our country.

One of the greatest virtues of satellite connectivity is that it makes it possible to offer Internet service in any part of the country in a very short time, regardless of the distance or the difficulty in accessing the specific locality, sufficing it to have the locale, the equipment and the electric power to operate it

The population that makes use of CCDs in most cases only pays the recovery quotas required to cover marginal costs for the operation and maintenance of the CCDs.

To begin the first stage, the bidding conditions for contracting satellite connectivity services were published in the Official Gazette of the Federation on October 1, 2002. The winning bidder was the company Internet Directo, S.A. de C.V. (Interdirec), a license holder of the public telecommunications network, with which the respective contract was signed on December 18, 2002. Work on installing the Satellite Network began immediately. To lower costs, the Federal Government, through the SCT, contributes the satellite capacity free of charge for connectivity. This connectivity is provided at an initial preferential rate of 499.00 pesos a month, VAT included, per connectivity point, for 2003. This rate could be updated yearly in keeping with the National Consumer Price Index (INPC) which Banco de Mexico issues.

The current rate of 518.84 pesos monthly, including VAT, which the CCDs pay to Interdirec, represents less than 18.00 pesos per day, which, considering that each CCD has a minimum of two workstations and a maximum of 20 (on average 11 workstations per CCD), allows the operator in charge of the CCD, if applicable, to charge users very reasonable rates, compared to the 10 or 20 pesos per hour charged by commercial Internet cafés in localities that have such services. It should be clarified that the majority of the CCDs offer this service to the public free of charge, recovering costs only for consumables, such as floppy discs, printouts or burnable compact discs, among others.

It should be mentioned that in the inter-ministerial agreements signed with the participating agencies and entities the rate schedule for charging users of the service in the CCDs was left open, which allows each one to determine the charge, and therefore it can obtain resources to cover the direct costs of the CCDs, such as payment for connectivity, payment of the operator responsible for the CCD, some consumable costs as well as for preventive and/or corrective maintenance of computer equipment, among others.

3. Why it Was Decided to Implement this System over other Alternatives?

The Connectivity framework of the National e-Mexico System was designed in the Ministry of Communications and Transportation with the aim of providing high-speed Internet access to the population that does not have this service, whether because of lack of infrastructure for providing these services, or because the population does not have sufficient resources to contract the services offered by license holders.

In this regard, analyses were carried out to determine the type of technology that should be used, and that would comply basically with the following premises: national coverage, short implementation time, low cost for users, the best quality for an efficient service, that would consider the country's social, economic and geographical conditions and that would be in accordance with the Good Government strategy.

Given that the Federal Government, through the SCT, has available capacity as part of the satellite reserve and of coverage and social connectivity programs of domestic and foreign satellite operators, there is the possibility of supporting satellite digital connectivity at sufficiently low prices compared to the same services offered commercially, since the cost of the satellite segment is reduced, which represents a very important part of the total cost of a connectivity service of this nature.

One of the greatest virtues of satellite connectivity is that it makes it possible to offer Internet service in any part of the country in a very short time, regardless of the distance or the difficulty in accessing the specific locality, sufficing it to have the locale, the equipment and the electric power to operate it.

4. General Results and Results with an Impact on Citizens

The benefits produced with the installation of the First e-Mexico Satellite Digital Connectivity Network include all levels of government, since the CCDs provide geopolitical coverage to serve the municipalities of the 31 states and the 16 Political Boroughs of the Federal District. Frequently, service coverage is provided to various localities in one same municipality, and furthermore, supported by SEDESOL's Micro-regions strategy, various neighboring municipalities can be incorporated, which makes it possible for this network to have a local, municipal, state, regional and national nature at the same time.

The benefit for society is becoming more evident every day, since through the CCDs the population is gaining access to numerous individual and collective development opportunities; the integration of individuals and groups in society has been favored, together with the strengthening of democracy and citizen participation, increase in knowledge, training and competitiveness and an improvement in development opportunities and quality of life by raising the level of education and knowledge of the communities where the CCDs have an impact.

The installation and implementation of the first Satellite Digital Connectivity Network aligned the efforts and resources of the participating agencies and entities, whose substantive activities constitute the key factors for the country's integral development.

Each participating agency and entity assigned or used its available infrastructure in the places selected for the installation of the CCDs, thus complying with the provisions of the inter-ministerial agreements. In the case of the education sector, which covers basic education in localities and in some up to higher education, including adult education, by using this network, both students and the public can have access from schools, through the Internet, to national and international portals that provide them with information and knowledge.

In the health sector the CCDs were installed in Health Ministry clinics and hospitals and those of other de-concentrated bodies, such as IMSS and ISSSTE, as a result of which know-how can be exchanged or broadened from the clinics, as well as carrying out practices and consultations relative to their disciplines, without users having to travel to urban centers or other states, by providing better, more timely services at a lower cost for the population.

In regard to social development, the CCDs were located mainly in Community Learning Centers, where different levels of education are provided to the population that did not obtain a place in schools in their locality, or else students who have to travel considerable distances to reach the locality where basic, high school and senior high school education centers are located. With this network, these students can receive training in the CCD itself, in addition to the fact that it generates added value, since adults and economically active people can inform themselves of different work sources or places where they can promote and market the goods and services they produce.

The CCDs located in places where government administrative services are provided were installed in city halls to which the public in general has access, and they are also used by public servants both for their daily work and to access portals of information on government procedures and cultural or legislative resources. Thus, public servants make their duties efficient and have the opportunity to know and keep up to date with actions related to modernization, deconcentration, decentralization and deregulation implemented in the Federal Public Administration.

As has been mentioned, service in the CCDs is provided at minimum cost for the user, and the agencies' commitment is to offer it for at least 20 hours a week. With regard to the network's functioning, the license holder operating the Connectivity Network has an assistance center available which operates 24 hours a day throughout the year to solve connectivity problems.

2. INTRAGOB Awards

Office of the Attorney General of the Republic (PGR)

1. Problems Faced or Situation in which the PGR Found itself in 2000

The organization scheme of the PGR was characterized by having rigid structures for responding to new, changing forms of crime.

Likewise, within the Attorney General's Office there was a complicated bureaucracy, with insufficient professional development, which caused discouragement and lack of commitment among public servants when faced with acts of corruption.

Furthermore, the imbalance in workload distribution and the limited technical-legal training provided to substantive personnel contributed to the centralization of decision-making and zero empowerment of personnel, which gave rise to significant backlogs in Detailed Reports, Preliminary Investigations and in the execution of Ministerial and Judicial Warrants. Police, expert and legal personnel, for their part, were dispersed in the Attorney General's Office administrative units, which favored a lack of coordination and application of the technical regulations issued by substantive units, such as the General Directorate of Coordination of Expert Services and the then Federal Judicial Police.

The lag in the technological area was patent; by way of example, there were only 2,132 personal computers at national level in the agency's offices. The above, combined with budget constraints and the lag in updating the norms governing the function of the Federal Public Prosecutor's Office, pointed up legal inconsistencies before national judicial authorities and international courts and brought out the inefficiency in law enforcement. Particularly evident were impunity, corruption, labor instability of personnel and irregular conduct, in some cases contrary to respect for human rights.

The agency was also facing the growth of the crime rate, the constant and complex role of organized crime, especially that related to health crimes and operations with resources from illicit sources; and in addition, violence associated with irregular conduct and acts of corruption in the Attorney General's Office were on the rise.

As a result of the above, seven challenges were identified for ensuring prompt, expeditious justice according to law and with respect for human rights.

In this context, it became essential to establish a new model of law enforcement aimed at raising quality in providing the service, in order to:

- Recover society's trust.
- Transform law enforcement mechanisms.
- Combat crime.
- Strengthen transparency and accountability schemes.
- Make the fugitive localization system more efficient.
- Foster legality and citizen participation.
- Respect human rights and care for the victims of crime.

To meet the challenges set forth above, **six central elements** were defined supported by the **"Fight against corruption"** National Law Enforcement Program, through information, control and accountability of institutional management.

1. **Reduce impunity rates** by means of crime investigation and prosecution and assistance in the function of public security.
2. **Care of crime victims,** with actions oriented toward providing comprehensive support for victims, which has had an effect on recovering citizens' trust in law enforcement.
3. **Promotion and protection of human rights,** which has involved vigilance, protection and furtherance of human rights and interaction with social organizations.
4. **All-out fight against drug trafficking and organized crime,** which has required concerted action through state, national and international cooperation and participation in law enforcement.
5. **Making the Institution efficient and effective** by means of the implementation of a Model of Total Quality which, through participatory leadership and example, furthers strategic planning and

implementation of public policies, as well as performance management and assessment, and organizational effectiveness and development.

6. **Comprehensive restructuring of the PGR,** and amendment of its Organic Law and its Regulations.

2. Brief explanation of the Implementation of the Quality System

Within the framework of the restructuring and as the principal strategy for making the Institution's functioning efficient, the INTRAGOB Total Quality Model was adopted, supported by the following aspects:

a. Furtherance of **Leadership** from the highest levels; a cascade effect was created down to all levels of the organization. Thus, the Attorney General's Office strategic approach was defined, based on the establishment of its Mission and Vision.

   Mission
   Represent society in the investigation and prosecution of crimes of federal jurisdiction, in accordance with the principles of legality and legal certainty and with respect for human rights.

   Vision
   Ensure, in three years, a functional law enforcement structure and in six, a streamlined system, so that in 2025 the institutions that participate in law enforcement are of excellence, have personnel with a vocation for service and solid training that contributes to citizens living in conditions that promote integral development within the Rule of Law.

   The **principles and values** contained in the Decalogue of Conduct and the Code of Motivation and Conduct of Public Servants were established, whose assimilation is assessed through the application of surveys of Organizational Culture and Quality, which make it possible to measure the degree of adoption of said principles and values.

An **organization for change** was also introduced, made up of the Committee for Institutional Development, Innovation and Quality, composed of four bodies:

1. The first line of command, as regulatory body;
2. The PGR's Quality Network, made up of liaisons of each of the Deputy Attorney General's Offices or equivalent, in charge of implementing the operative application of the guidelines issued by the Committee within their spheres of competence (it is each liaison's responsibility to generate a multiplying effect for the personnel in its control segment);
3. Internal networks per Deputy Attorney General's Office or equivalent with the participation of the general directors and presided by the head of the Deputy Attorney General's Office or equivalent, whose responsibility is to operatively apply the Agreements of the Institutional Quality Network;
4. Quality Committees. Presided by the general directors, they include the participants in Quality Management Systems and their purpose is to ensure that the culture of quality permeates down to the last level of the organization, as well as to implement, maintain and develop the above-mentioned Management Systems through the certification of processes in International Standard ISO 9001:2000. This organization for change was built in 2002 and formalized in 2003.

b. **The strategic planning system**—supported by the National Law Enforcement Program and its strategic hubs—was set in motion and was deployed in Operative Planning through the Digital Alignment System, SPE/DAS-G, which has made it possible to ensure the consistency of strategic objectives with operative ones and their generalized application, by defining programs, processes and projects in all administrative units at central and state levels.

c. **Technological development** was promoted by means of an Integral Informatics Development Plan linked to the strategic approach. Consequently, informatics and telecommunications systems were made available which made it possible to interconnect systems at national and international levels with information on citizens, alignment of goals, crime statistics, cartographies, and security, intelligence and resource administration systems.

   With regard to technology, a process consisting of six subprocesses was defined, namely: detection of technological needs; monitoring and appraisal; acquisition; implementation; impact measurement and technological support.

   It should be underscored that due to the nature of the Attorney General's Office, appropriate systems were established for security and protection of information, consisting of detection of intruders, information back-ups and timely control of informatics viruses.

d. Implementation of the model required the furtherance of **teamwork** as a means to involve the personnel, in order to reinforce the results and achieve better performance, productivity, satisfaction at work and stemming from work, as well as to favor creativity, innovation and continuous improvement; thus, natural work teams, the Organization for Change and the Professionalization Council, among others, were developed.

e. Personnel **training** was favored by strengthening the training (ICAP) and National Criminal Sciences (INACIPE) Institutes, both aimed at the education, training and professionalization of the Federal Public Prosecutor's Office and its auxiliaries. The INACIPE also carries out scientific research and dissemination of penal sciences. In addition, the National Workers' Training Program is being developed, which includes: Service attitude, Teamwork, Personal development, Sensitivity training, Management of nonprofessional disabilities and Occupational accidents, among others. All of this to favor the formation of intellectual capital and develop processes that fully satisfy the requirements, needs and expectations of customers and citizens.

f. Impetus to the creation of **innovative practices** through the system of skills development, since the training focuses on the creation of a quality organizational culture, which has enabled the personnel to know, become involved and transfer their knowledge to the Attorney General's Office's processes, products and services.

g. Identification and certification with international standards of **key processes** as a basis for ensuring increased quality in the law enforcement products and services provided to citizens; proof of this are the 193 certifications obtained in 2002 under Standard ISO 9001:2000.

h. Likewise, the workshops and the Diploma in Planning have allowed knowledge of the strategic approach and the deployment of operative planning in the Institution.

Supported by pioneer infrastructure in investigation systems, 100 percent of the cases of kidnapping reported to the PGR were positively resolved.
Arrests related to health crimes have increased, with more than 15,000 persons related to drug trafficking captured

3. Decision to Implement the Quality System over other Alternatives

This decision was taken to support the presidential commitment to implementing, developing, maintaining and improving a model of quality so as to transform the Federal Public Administration into a world-class government; furthermore, it was necessary to respond to social demands and offer quality products and services, capable of measurement with international standards, to move toward a world-class government.

The above means giving transparency to law enforcement, instilling a solid Culture of Quality in public servants, and adopting innovative systems and processes that ensure full satisfaction of the needs and expectations of citizens/customers.

4. General Results and Results with an Impact on Citizens

The backlog in **detailed reports** has been reduced by 93.5 percent with respect to the amount originally received and an efficiency rate of 96.3 percent has been achieved; with regard to **preliminary investigations**, the backlog has been reduced by 76.8 percent over the year 2000, and the time for dealing with said investigations has diminished by 86.1 percent, whereas in regard to the processing of **preliminary investigations initiated**, a compliance of 84.4 percent has been attained.

In the first two years of administration, 97 percent compliance with **ministerial warrants** was achieved.

The **Integral Real-Estate Planning Program** has given the PGR a new face by means of the acquisition and refurbishing of functional premises, dignifying public servants and raising efficiency and productivity levels.

Supported by pioneer infrastructure in investigation systems, 100 percent of the cases of **kidnapping** reported to the PGR were positively resolved.

Arrests related to health crimes have increased, with more than 15,000 persons related to drug trafficking captured.

In the first two years of administration, 463 **federal trials** were concluded and 424 were ruled in favor of the Federation, which represents an effectiveness rate of 91.6 percent.

From December 2001 to November 2002, of 94 **resolutions** in controversies and **unconstitutional** actions, the opinion issued by the Attorney General was fully and/or partially coinciding in 75 matters, there was no coincidence in 9 and in 10 it was not possible to determine coincidence, since the High Court did not carry out an in-depth study. This represents 89.2 percent **objectivity and juridical quality in** the intervention of the head of this body of federal jurisdiction in the cases resolved by the Supreme Court of Justice of the Nation (SCJN).

More than two thousand public servants were trained and in the Units certified under standard ISO 9001:2000 the taking of satisfaction surveys was established to measure the degree of improvement in attention to external and internal customers.

The work that the Institution is performing to implement the Quality Management System necessarily involves the public servants who work in it, and therefore the number of **trained personnel** has increased, giving the PGR the certainty of having human resources prepared for the transition toward a culture of quality.

National Commission on Medical Arbitration (CONAMED)

1. Institutional Profile

CONAMED is a deconcentrated agency of the Ministry of Health, created by means of a Federal Executive decree published in the Official Gazette of the Federation in June 1996.

The purpose of CONAMED, in terms of the instrument of its establishment, is to "contribute to solving conflicts arising between the users of medical services and the providers of said services," which is basically carried out with the application of methods other than judicial dispute, such as conciliation and arbitration. In line with the above, CONAMED's functions related to cases of dissatisfaction derived from medical acts can be specified in the following terms:

a) Advise users and providers of medical services on all kinds of issues linked to medical attention.
b) Arrange for medical attention in cases in which, due to the nature of the petition and the patient's state of health, the intervention —immediate in some cases—of medical service providers, whether public or private, is required in order to safeguard the patient's health.
c) Deal with, investigate and resolve the cases of dissatisfaction presented by patients or their relatives for possible acts of negligence or inexperience that have caused damage to health in the attention provided in the private or public sphere.
d) Intervene officially in matters of general interest by preparing technical opinions.

e) Issue recommendations based on proven knowledge and aimed at the medical profession, with the ultimate purpose of preventing acts of malpractice and contribute to raising the quality of medical services.
f) Prepare, at the request of the authority, medical reports of an institutional nature, the aim of which is to illustrate the law enforcement and administration of justice authorities, as well as to the internal control organs of institutions providing medical services, on the particularities of medical acts in cases in which malpractice on the part of the health care team is presumed.

In order to specify the nature of the functions in the charge of the CONAMED, it is important to highlight that through the arbitration process the Commission administers justice; however, it is an alternative for dispute settlement that does not seek to substitute the jurisdictional authorities in charge of said function. The filing of complaints in this body contributes to reducing workloads in the Judicial Branch, which also fosters a culture of non-litigious dispute settlement between physician and patient, for due to the characteristics of medical acts —based on the principles of autonomy, beneficence, non-maleficence and justice—it is necessary for differences to be settled in specialized bodies, based on medical science, ethics and applicable norms.

2. Market and Customer Requirements

CONAMED provides its services to the population as a whole, in such a way that it receives complaints of dissatisfaction from patients or their relatives, against both private and public service providers; in the latter case, mainly complaints about medical services provided by the Mexican Social Security Institute (IMSS) and the Social Security and Services Institute for Government Workers (ISSSTE).

Customers' main requirements refer to: a) impartiality, b) that interest be shown in solving their problem, c) be attended by personnel experienced in the subject and quickness in resolution times. The requirements for all the services mentioned will be explained at length in the customer satisfaction criterion.

With regard to the issuance of expert reports, CONAMED's customers, in generic terms, are the law enforcement and administration of justice authorities in the state and federal spheres, and the Ministry of Public Administration through its internal control organs in public institutions providing medical services.

CONAMED receives and deals with an average of 23,000 cases a year, which are attended in the following ways: guidance, specialized advisory assistance, immediate steps, conciliation agreements, decisions or through the issuance of expert medical reports.

3. Situation of the Commission at the Beginning of the Current Administration

In December 2000, the new administration of CONAMED, aware of the commitment to guaranteeing service quality in terms of the needs of patients and their relatives and of the impact that the Commission's actions could have on the health care system, placed special care on identifying the challenges it had to assume. To that end, a careful diagnosis was carried out which included ratification of customers and services, analysis of strengths, weaknesses, threats and opportunities, and assessment of compliance with customers' requirements for each of the services provided.

As part of the diagnosis, the Commission placed special emphasis on improving and giving continuity to the institutional policies established since its creation, strategically reformulating various schemes for settling cases of dissatisfaction. It was concluded that in accordance with the conditions in which the Institution found itself from the administrative and functional viewpoint, and given the nature of its work, it was necessary for it to address the following actions and challenges in order to fulfill its assignment:

- Obtain administrative autonomy, given its deconcentrated nature from the Ministry of Health, ensuring its technical, organic and financial autonomy; furthermore, another image before society was required.

- Rethink the organization structurally and functionally. The Commission had traditional administrative and functional structures that caused attention to matters to be vertical, segmented, with participation influenced and limited to sections of authority and little participation by operative personnel, obviously without coordinated teamwork.
- Shape a sole model of medical arbitration. Assure an operation that complies fully with procedures in a standardized manner, with unified medical-legal criteria and that provides specialized and personalized attention.
- Broaden the coverage of attention; since there were many federative entities without a commission it was necessary to promote before state governments the creation of bodies similar to CONAMED, providing the necessary advisory assistance to guarantee their social usefulness.
- Offer high quality in its services to give it moral support before society; it was therefore proposed that the Institution be certified comprehensively under Standard ISO 9001:2000.
- Strengthen promotion and dissemination of the services provided by the Commission with emphasis on the principles governing its functioning, since there was no clear acceptance of the Institution by the medical profession.
- Disseminate among medical groups, health care institutions and society in general, the common characteristics of the main motives for dissatisfaction and their causes, and propose alternatives for solution, in order to influence the improvement in the practice of medicine.
- Sign collaboration bases with specialty academies and councils to comply with the functions of CONAMED, for example advisory assistance to select among their associates highly specialized physicians recognized as experts in their field, who guarantee objectiveness in analysis and impartiality in the processing of reports and technical opinions.
- Strengthen institutional coordination and sign collaboration agreements with law enforcement agencies, specifically with those that constantly request medical reports, as is the case with the Office

of the Attorney General of the Republic and the Office of the Attorney General of the Federal District.

4. Actions Carried Out

Among the most important strategies implemented the following may be mentioned:

Organizational Restructuring

A first organic and functional restructuring of the Institution was carried out without increasing the number of regular staff. In the substantive area attention modules were set up, made up of a medical officer, a legal support and a technical support, responsible for attention to each case, from its reception to its conclusion. This operative restructuring achieved the following benefits: establishing equitable workloads; collegiate, jointly responsible decision-making among the members of the module, and better utilization of resources through efficient use of the Commission's installed capacity. Furthermore, the function of three general directorates was refocused to support the substantive areas, and the general directorates of Promotion and Dissemination, Research and Teaching, and Innovation and Quality were created.

Subsequently the regular staff was reduced by 25 percent, with the consequent budget savings, due to the increase in institutional productivity.

The Institution's Strategic Planning

One key aspect for the Institution's performance is the strategic planning carried out at the beginning of the current administration, in which the Mission was reviewed, the Vision was defined, a strategic diagnosis was carried out, identifying strengths, weaknesses, threats and opportunities, and strategic objectives were defined, as were the projects required for attainment of the objectives. As a fundamental part of follow-up of this strategic program, the key indicators for measuring attainment of objectives were identified, as well as the goals for each one of them.

The most important indicators are the following: attraction of service demand, effectiveness of the arbitration process, conciliatory capacity, overall effectiveness in resolving matters, issue of recommendations, arbitration efficiency, expert efficiency, customer satisfaction level, fulfillment of commitments, standardization of the arbitration process with state commissions and creation of new commissions to cover the national territory.

Certification in Standard ISO 9001:2000

Included the application of strategies to ensure process standardization and guarantee a high level of quality in services, strategies such as redesign of the operation through modules responsible for attending to cases comprehensively, establishment of a matrix support structure for substantive areas for medical and legal issues, deployment up to operation of a group of standards and indicators to measure daily operations and attention to users, which seeks to foster self-control in the Commission's different operative units. Some of these are described below.

Investigation of Users' Needs

In order to validate the administration's perception of users' needs, a research study on expectations was carried out with different groups of users, which served as a basis for process redesign and for the design of instruments to monitor user satisfaction with the services provided. Also, a mechanism for review of and response to users' complaints was designed.

Redesign and Documentation of Service Processes

Service processes were redesigned with the participation of work teams made up of the personnel who operate them. The redesign involved an analysis of the main problems encountered in the operation and identification of procedures to avoid triangulation and rely on an expeditious process, as well as clarification of criteria for analyzing the issues dealt with by CONAMED.

Leadership and Personnel Development

One fundamental aspect in this process of change has been the participatory leadership practiced and furthered by the head of the Institution. The policy established by the National Commissioner in relation to dealings and interaction between the Institution's different levels of command is characterized by great respect for people, having efficient mechanisms of communication with all the staff—such as periodic meetings with the staff of each general directorate—by a great disposition for dialogue with all the organizational levels, a positive approach toward analysis of the Institution's problems and results, always focusing on continuous improvement, and a clear approach to user satisfaction and compliance with the institutional Mission to society.

Personnel Development

Personnel management has been optimized to guarantee that the personnel are competent to perform the responsibilities entrusted to them and that they develop in an appropriate working atmosphere. In this regard, personnel hiring and selection systems were upgraded, induction processes were implemented for new personnel, and an ongoing training program is maintained in line with training needs which includes technical aspects of the post, quality tools and administrative aspects. Moreover, a study of the labor atmosphere is made annually to analyze the areas that should be improved in the Institution from its employees' point of view.

Online Information System

Information is an important factor for decision-making in the Institution. CONAMED has a System for Attention to Medical Complaints (SAQMED) in which matters are registered and they can be followed up on from reception to their conclusion. SAQMED was redesigned so as to be operated online by the personnel responsible for dealing with cases. Use of this system makes it possible to obtain quick, reliable and timely information for decision-making and is also a functional tool for the personnel, as it enables them to attend to the user in a swifter and more effective manner since it provides the opportunity to create all the types of documents that have to be signed to settle the cases, as well as the most important aspects arising in the different phases of the attention process.

Inter-institutional Coordination for the Integration of Value Chains

New collaboration agreements were signed with IMSS and ISSSTE in which CONAMED's role as an arbitrator and entry into the entirety of the arbitration process were accepted, as well as recognition of state commissions and the possibility of receiving and dealing with issues in a deconcentrated manner through them, when application of the standardized model of arbitration is assured in conjunction with CONAMED.

Follow-up mechanisms have been established for compliance with the delivery of information required by CONAMED by said institutions, for swift resolution of issues in benefit of users.

Relations with the Medical Profession

CONAMED established relations with academies, medical specialty councils, schools and academic associations to analyze, assess and follow up on actions and proposals that lead to improving the quality of medical care and reducing errors. This has made it possible to obtain the recognition of the medical profession, an essential condition for success in fulfilling its Mission.

CONAMED obtained Certification in Standard ISO 9001:2000 granted by BSI (British Standards Institute) and re-certification was maintained during 2002 and 2003

4. Results

a. The Institution's productivity and capacity for resolution have improved by reducing its regular staff by 25 percent and increasing the number of persons served by 53 percent.
b. The number of cases requiring specialized medico-legal attention increased by 23 percent.
c. Whereas in the year 2000 some 54 percent of matters were resolved almost immediately (specialized advisory assistance or immediate steps), in 2003 a total of 75 percent of matters are resolved in this manner.
d. The results obtained by the Commission reflect an increase in conciliation capacity and arbitration efficiency—that is, the number of cases resolved through a conciliation agreement or decision rose from 53.3 percent to 69.7 percent.
e. A high level of user satisfaction is maintained: 96 percent rate CONAMED's service as good or excellent.
f. The number of complaints or dissatisfied users remains at a level close to zero, as shown in the reports of the Internal Control Organ.
g. In this connection, **the sole model of attention to cases of dissatisfaction was also consolidated as a result of the redesign of processes and their documentation,** with the jointly responsible of all the substantive areas, and its application in each of the operative modules has made it possible to **obtain high user satisfaction levels, meet their needs and cover their expectations.**
h. To assure citizens comprehensive, standardized attention throughout the country, CONAMED promoted the creation of the Mexican Medical Arbitration Council, which has permitted the incorporation of ten state commissions into the National Model and nine more are in the standardization process.
i. With CONAMED's support, coverage has been broadened with the

creation of 10 new state commissions, rising from 14 existing commissions to 22.

j. A major achievement for CONAMED has been the issuance of recommendations aimed at the medical community in each specialty; thus progress has been made in another of the strategic institutional objectives: affecting the improvement of the practice of medicine. It is hoped that in follow-up and assessment of the proposed actions, in the short term there will be visible evidence of better medical practice as a result of the impact of these products on the medical profession.

k. Another of the important aspects that have resulted from the coordinated application of institutional dissemination and promotion actions was obtaining a change in the projection of the Commission's work, from being an agency for attention to medical complaints to becoming a promoter of healthy relations between physicians and their patients, but even more so in the role of meta-evaluator of health care services and arbitrator with a clear legal and regulatory framework, which raises the level of discussion and the value of its products; all of these aimed at the citizenry, for better use of this agency and an opportunity to increase credibility and confidence in the country's health care services, in both the public and private spheres. It is still too early to measure institutional projection and its impact, but the results are there for all to see.

l. CONAMED obtained **Certification in Standard ISO 9001:2000** granted by BSI (British Standards Institute) and re-certification was maintained during 2002 and 2003.

m. It is important to mention that in 2003 CONAMED received the INTRAGOB Award granted by the Federal Government to institutions that distinguish themselves by having a comprehensive model of attention that makes it possible to offer high quality services to their users. The award was received by the National Commissioner from President Vicente Fox Quesada.

n. Finally, emphasis should be placed on the educational and communication work that the Institution has established with health care institutions, schools and faculties of medicine and the profession in general in order to establish a policy to prevent medical conflict.

5. Considerations of the CASE

These efforts for change are a **comprehensive process** that seeks to favor the development of a culture of quality reflected in the service and attention received by anyone who establishes contact with the Institution. These efforts are comprehensive, since the strategies implemented cover aspects considered essential for a performance of excellence according to the best known quality models, namely: customer satisfaction, leadership, development of personnel and intellectual capital, management of information and technology, planning, process management, impact on society and results.

The critical success factors identified are: close follow-up on the Institution's advances and results and implementation of the Quality Management System, always looking to satisfaction of the Commission's users; also, the collaboration, commitment and participation of the Institution's senior management; a key factor was also having highly trained personnel in the subject of quality who gave order and direction to the efforts made. Last but not least, having had an awareness building program with 100 percent of the staff, and of course their excellent response for process redesign and documentation, and in general throughout the process of change.

The challenge now faced by the Commission as regards its quality system is maintaining that work motivation, improving systems for measuring user satisfaction and bettering it, establishing more effective mechanisms for alliance with its main suppliers—public institutions providing medical services—and progressing in the promotion of a culture of quality among its staff that leads increasingly to self-monitoring of their own performance, keyed to internal and external users' satisfaction.

The effectiveness of the arbitration process determines the percentage of matters concluded by conciliation or decision during the conciliation and arbitration phase in relation to the total of matters liable to having been concluded under said forms, and therefore does not take into account matters concluded due to lack of procedural interest and irresolvable.

Matters Attended 2000/2003

Issue		2000	2001	2002	2003
Guidance		10,342	7,537	9,071	17,864
Advisory Assistance		1,672	2,464	2,849	3,145
Cases of Dissatisfaction	Immediate responses	692	738	862	941
	Complaints	1,997	1,546	1,114	1,309
Experts' Reports		742	473	664	443
Total		15,445	12,758	14,560	23,702

Source: System of Attention to Medical Complaints. Institutional Statistics System.

Advisory Assistance, Cases of Dissatisfaction and Reports Attended 2000/2003

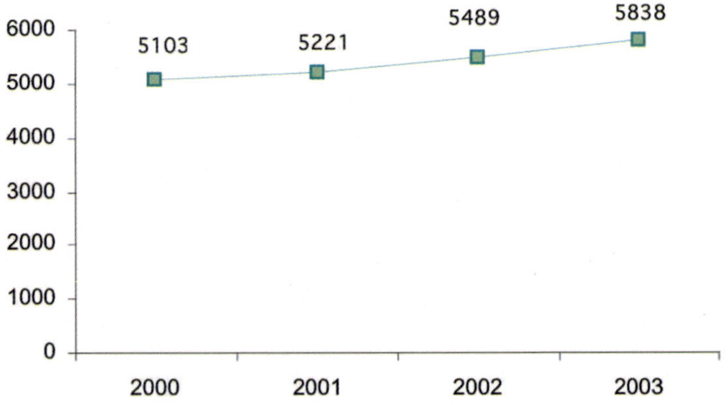

An ongoing satisfaction rate of 95 percent is maintained.

The main factors measured are: expeditious attention (times), impartiality and treatment.

Effectiveness Rate of the Arbitration Process 2000/2003

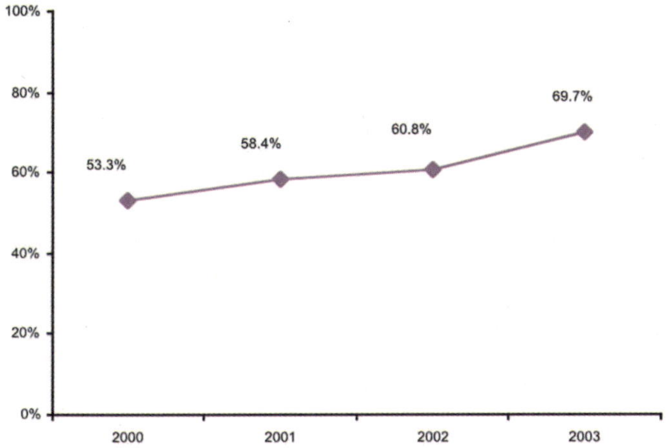

User Satisfaction Registered in CONAMED 2000/2003

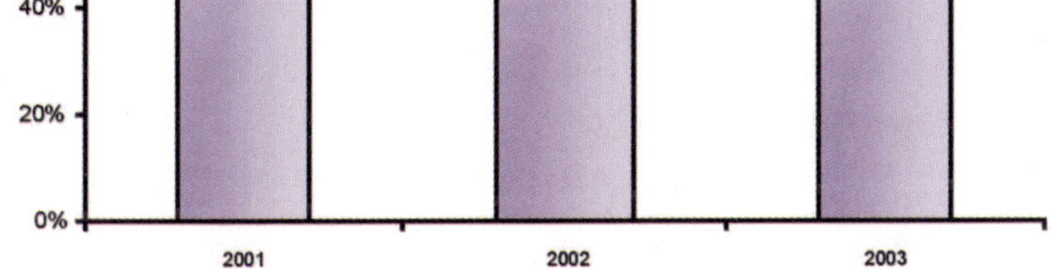

One of the main objectives to be attained by whoever decides to implement a quality model or system is to ensure that the latter is assimilated as a culture by each of the organization's members. This is why the Military Health Service required, on one hand, highly competent personnel in the military culture and in the health culture, and on the other, an open attitude stemming from integration into the culture of quality

Ministry of National Defense (SEDENA)

Women's Specialties Clinic (CEM)

Situation in 2002

CEM forms part of the Military Health Care System and was created to meet the health needs of women and newborns. It began its activities in December 1999 with a team made up of personnel with high professional competence and with the necessary technology for proper diagnosis and treatment.

The design and construction of the CEM's infrastructure complied with the provisions of Official Mexican Standard 197-SSAI in relation to equipment, areas, services and systems that guarantee appropriate medical care.

> In addition to having available what is necessary for carrying out procedures and activities related to the value chain for the health of women who are not pregnant, as well as for mothers and their newborns, the CEM has the Prenatal Education area, in which pregnant women are informed about the process of pregnancy, childbirth and puerperium and the development of breastfeeding. It also has a Section of Combined Rooms which replaces the traditional labor, delivery and postpartum recovery rooms with a comfortable individual room, including a specific room for underwater birth, and a section for Joint Accommodation immediately adjacent, which enables the mother to strengthen the emotional relationship with her child.

Problems Encountered

The development and implementation of a methodology of quality within the public administration's health care organizations should consider systems and processes aligned with the requirements of the

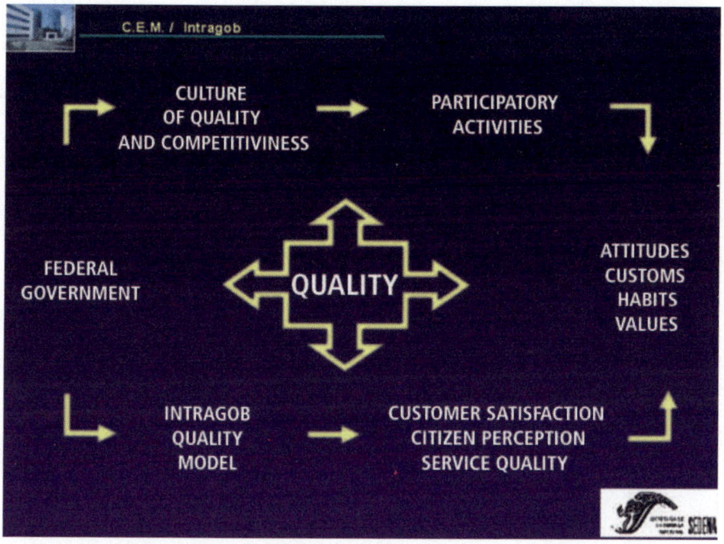

Certification of Health Care Establishments, of the INTRAGOB Quality Model and of Quality Assurance.

Through the implementation of these quality systems, the Federal Government seeks to orient health care services toward citizens' needs. The purpose of quality assurance is to incorporate the culture of quality into the members of all organizations providing services in such a way that activities are carried out in a shared manner with attitudes, customs, habits and values that foster quality.

The material and human resources in the CEM were oriented to medical care for military personnel and their beneficiaries, based on the values of military culture and medical care. The main problem was forming a team with a vision of culture of quality.

Participation in quality models represented a change of paradigm, accompanied by evident resistance to change. This resistance was transitional thanks to the commitment of senior officers, which guaranteed that, without departing from current commitments to medical care, the development of processes and systems consistent with quality models should begin and the quality assurance model should be designed and implemented.

An additional problem was identifying equivalences between the culture of quality and the above-mentioned quality models and the culture of Military Health and the established systematic operative procedures.

Once one has a certain degree of implementation of the quality system, the personnel trained become facilitators and undertake to identify the high-impact measures that will give rise to greater interaction, a better organizational climate and proper incorporation of the culture of quality

One of the main objectives to be attained by whoever decides to implement a quality model or system is to ensure that the latter is assimilated as a culture by each of the organization's members. This is why the Military Health Service required, on one hand, highly competent personnel in the military culture and in the health culture, and on the other, an open attitude stemming from integration into the culture of quality.

Harmonious interaction between these two elements brings about a unity that makes it possible to align individual military and technical competence with the aims of the organization, among them ensuring that Military Health is perceived by the military and beneficiaries as a quality service with warmth that achieves its mission of recovering, maintaining and raising the health of personnel and beneficiaries, and that therefore contributes to raising troop morale; the above, translated into terms of quality, means establishing a positive, loyal and deeply-rooted relationship with the customer and end user.

Implementation of the Quality System in the Women's Specialties Clinic (Certification of Health Care Establishments and INTRAGOB Model)

Implementation of the quality system began with the creation of a work team under the coordination of a head previously trained in quality through diploma courses and courses related to the INTRAGOB Model.

The work team's first commitment was participation in the Pilot Test for the Health Council's Hospital Certification Program.

The certification verified implementation of the quality processes as regards structure, human resources, physical installations, equipment, inputs, medical record, attention and complaints, committees, organization and methods, and government. The CEM was one of the 20 Health Care Institutions that formed part of the Program's pilot test, obtaining 83.5 points, which was the highest grade.

Faced with the need to develop, maintain and improve processes, the INTRAGOB Quality Model was adopted in order to implement it in the CEM. The working group was trained on the Model by means of external advisory assistance, lectures, videos and attendance at different workshops prepared by the INTRAGOB Quality Network.

The maternal mortality rate in 1999, 2000 and 2001 was 111, 154 and 60 per 100,000 live births and subsequently went down to 40, remaining stable as of 2002

Quality Assurance

The Quality Assurance model includes a series of phases that are inserted according to needs and expectations.

Training Phase

Implementation of the quality system was accompanied by actions related to quality assurance thanks to the training of personnel with certain characteristics of military, technical and quality leadership. Participation in courses and workshops made it possible to become familiar with Mexican Quality Standards, Certification Criteria for Health Care Establishments, the Innovation and Government Quality Model and the National Total Quality Model. Certification as assessors in each of these models enabled them to know the mechanics of the assessment process in extra-institutional organizations.

Phase: Active Participation

The development of competences in quality interacts with implementation of the quality system from the outset, by taking an active part in the design, introduction and assessment of processes and systems, transmitting knowledge acquired during training and identifying equivalences with military and technical organizational culture.

Phase: Facilitation

Once one has a certain degree of implementation of the quality system, the personnel trained become facilitators and undertake to identify the high-impact measures that will give rise to greater interaction, a better organizational climate and proper incorporation of the culture of quality. The key in this phase of assurance is becoming integrated as a team. Team proposals stem from analysis of the behavior of processes and systems and are always analyzed by senior management so that in accordance with the quality policy they become instructions.

Phase: Analysis and Comparison

Knowledge of the organization's overall performance and of the characteristics of the organizational climate makes possible intra-institutional forums for referential comparison with regard to progress in the maturity of the quality system and of quality assurance.

Results

The value chain in the organization is structured by the set of procedures and processes related to health, which include detection, study, diagnosis, treatment and follow-up. The key processes are those related to medical care by means of consultation, appraisal and medico-surgical treatment.

As part of the programs governing the organization's technical operational capacity are those related to pregnancy care, delivery, puerperium and the newborn; in this process, the key indicator is maternal and perinatal mortality. Favorable behavior was observed in the cause-effect ratio with the implementation of the INTRAGOB quality model.

The maternal mortality rate in 1999, 2000 and 2001 was 111, 154 and 60 per 100,000 live births and subsequently went down to 40, remaining stable as of 2002.

Beginning the implementation of the model, the processes related to the key indicator were identified, which in the case of obstetric care are prenatal care from 80.5 to 82.6, care during the puerperium and the increase in family planning. In all these cases the trend has been upward.

Maternal Mortality Rate per 100,000 Live Births

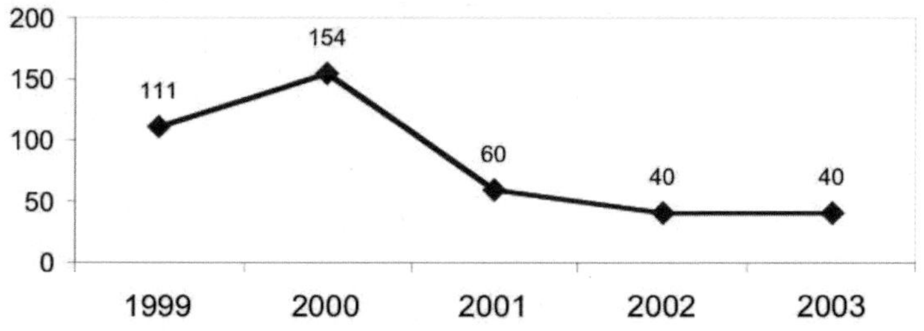

Source: Statistical Annual of the CEM.

Prenatal Care, Customer Satisfaction, Prenatal Care, CEM

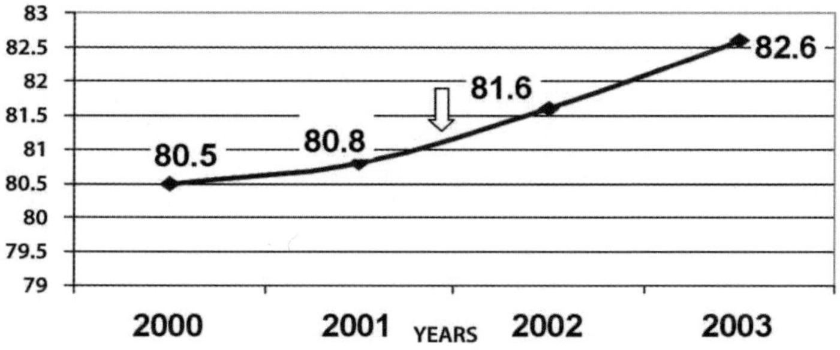

Likewise, it may be seen that the behavior of the other key indicator, which is fetus mortality (MFT) and newborn mortality (MNT), a term known as perinatal mortality, has tended to diminish and stabilize, coming closer to the rate identified in the best world practice, found in the Japanese model of care.

A factor was added in the development of the management system which is not always considered, that is, the system's process of maturity. It was considered that in the first steps any system must break the inertia of certain activities carried out by force of habit, but what is important is to believe in the strength to change paradigms and forge a culture of change

The rate registered in 1999 was 9.5 per 1,000 live births, and 6.8 in 2003. Since the beginning of quality management in the Clinic, areas of opportunity were identified which helped maintain the downward trend in a sustained manner.

It can be appreciated that the implementation of this quality model since 2001 to date has given rise to a positive and stable trend in the results.

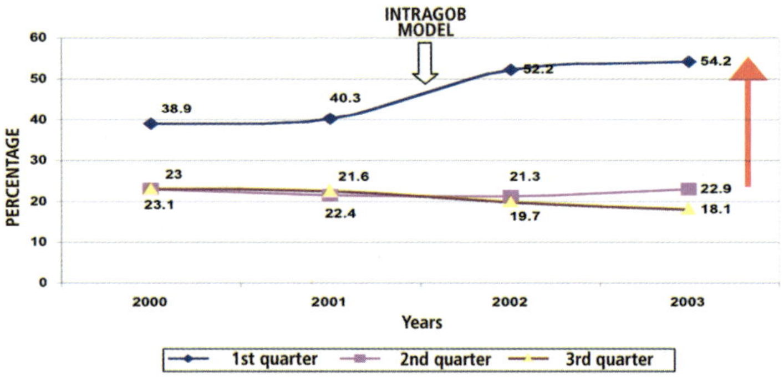

Petroleos Mexicanos (PEMEX)

Coastal Exploration Resource, Southwestern Marine Region

Background

On August 21, 2002, the Sub-directorate of the Southwestern Marine Region, with its group of managers, determined the participation of five Manager's Offices/Resources of the region and the Sub-directorate as such to reinforce a culture of quality in the Southwestern Marine Region.

For the Coastal Exploration Resource it represented a challenge which was taken up by all the personnel, since they were fully aware that the management system certified in 2001 included many of the criteria of the INTRAGOB model.

The systems' approach was based on the practice that was being developed since a few years ago and that was giving the results planned until it was considered the best Exploration Resource at national level and in the top 10 at international level (source: Energy Information Administration. Major profiles. Company Annual Reports).

The manner in which the Resource's systems were documented, but mainly the clarity of its exploration processes model, which indicated systems and criteria, resulting in a significant incorporation of reserves, was the key for the assessors to understand the abstract activities carried out on interpreting and modeling geological areas.

The key of the exploration processes model was breaking the paradigm of the traditional value chain model, which was linear, for it considered the cycles in which processes interacted with information and operative systems, among others.

Elements of the Coastal Exploration Resource System

Traditionally, the exploration process is conceived as a linear (substantive areas) and parallel (support areas) chain.

The new model takes into account focusing on the customer, planning, leadership, human resources, management and control of information, interrelation with the communities and also the result offered to customers; furthermore, it considers analysis of the information generated in the model, review by the administration of the functioning of the system and model, customer feedback and continuous improvement.

The model should include ingredients that make the personnel feel a sense of belonging —*where am I and how do I participate;* to that end the model was rescaled to achieve continuous improvement by means of feedback and interaction of all the elements participating in it, but also favoring that the model should not distance itself from the substantive proposals of the total quality models; it was necessary to reach alignment between its own model and the demands of the basic models.

A factor was added in the development of the management system which is not always considered, that is, the system's process of

Despite the ups and downs in budget allocation, reserves have been incorporated even without the perforation of exploratory wells (1997); the level of customer satisfaction increased with the implementation of the system and the work climate was maintained with an average level of all the parameters measured above 80 percent

maturity. It was considered that in the first steps any system must break the inertia of certain activities carried out by force of habit, but what is important is to believe in the strength to change paradigms and forge a culture of change. Within the Resource the personnel learned to look at the activities as a whole in a different manner, as new challenges, and always seeking opportunities. The task of finding the systems that would make the model viable in accordance with the INTRAGOB Model was also defined; hence systems were designed for each of the criteria without inventing anything, simply by assessing the available *pieces* and how they complied with the INTRAGOB criteria; that made it possible to define the following specific systems that make up the macro-system itself:

Customer Satisfaction. Includes elements such as documented declaration of requirements, measurement of satisfaction, data analysis, preventive and corrective actions, continuous improvement and feedback.

Leadership. Defines values, mission, vision, objectives, policy, strategy, considers strategic and operative planning, empowerment of personnel linked to development of intellectual capital, resulting in teamwork and consequently the forming of high performance groups.

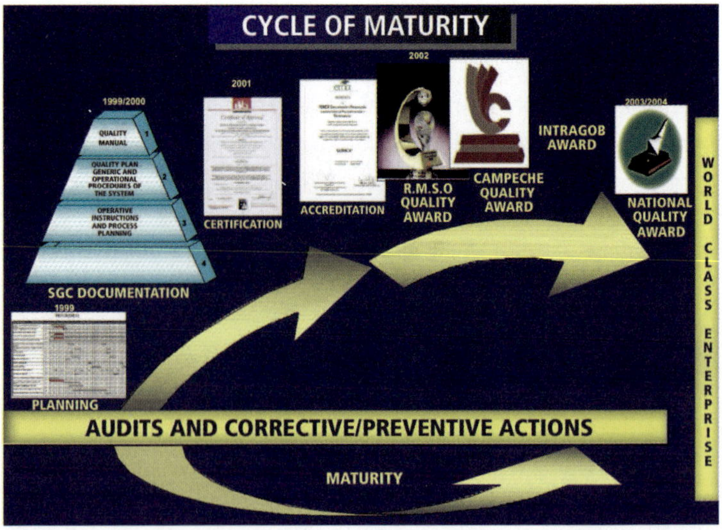

Management of Information and Technology. This is based on assessment of informatics needs over the short, medium and long terms, development of informatics plans and programs to support the part concerning infrastructure, hardware and software, attention to users and maintenance. Both aspects provide support for seismic information processes and for safeguarding and conservation of information, to end in measuring customer (user) satisfaction and provide feedback for the system.

Planning. This system begins with the vision, mission, objectives and policy, since they are aligned with PEMEX Exploration and Production's (PEP) business plan; its own strategies and the planning cycle originate there, and on that basis the quality plans are made, which is the operative part of the system; subsequently the product measuring and follow-up process is carried out.

Benefits

Since its creation, the Resource began to carry out activities aligned with PEMEX Exploration and Production's business plan, aimed at complying with the vision and mission of the Energy Sector. Despite the ups and downs in budget allocation, reserves have been incorporated even without the perforation of exploratory wells (1997); the level of customer satisfaction increased with the implementation of the system and the work climate was maintained with an average level of all the parameters measured above 80 percent and projects continue for improving the system and its subsystems.

It is important to mention that at present PEP is undergoing a period of transition, the consequence of which will be the rescaling of the occupational structure and the redefinition of processes; in other words, the Resource will combine with other Resources to form a Regional Resource.

Ministry of National Defense (SEDENA)

Dental Specialties Unit (UEO)

I. Background

UEO, founded on February 19, 1997, forms part of the Military Health System of the Ministry of National Defense. Its purpose is to provide efficient, timely dental care with quality and warmth, to members of the Mexican Army and Air Force, their beneficiaries and civilians who request it.

The services it provides are the following:

Diagnosis and emergencies: prepares the clinical record, establishes the presumptive diagnosis, deals with emergencies and channels patients to the specialty required.

Dental operation: provides the required care to patients affected only by tooth decay.

Dental pediatrics: cares comprehensively for child patients up to the age of 12.

Orthodontics: carries out the planning, interception and correction of dento-facial anomalies.

Endodontia: provides treatment corresponding to teeth with diseases of the pulp.

Periodontics: treats diseases affecting the tissues that support the teeth.

Prosthodontics: rehabilitates the chewing function by means of the placement of fixed or removable prostheses as well as on implants; it also returns the aesthetic aspect and self-esteem to patients who have lost some or all of their teeth.

Mouth surgery: carries out the required surgical treatments on patients with acute or irreversible dental ailments or processes.

Dental laboratory: prepares fixed and removable prostheses.

Research and teaching: programs training and research activities.

In order to contribute to the Federal Executive's efforts, the Ministry of National Defense participates in the Innovation and Quality Model through the implementation of the INTRAGOB Quality Model in its medical, dental and hospital facilities.

Interpersonal relations represented a challenge by having to combine the military and ranking line of command with a democratic and participatory leadership, as the model stipulates

II. Problems Arising during the Implementation of the INTRAGOB Model

The main problems that had to be faced by both supervisory personnel and criteria leaders in achieving first the approach, and then the implementation of the INTRAGOB Quality Model in the Dental Specialties Unit, were the following:

1. Perform an arduous task of training, in order to change the paradigms and the way of thinking and acting in the Unit's staff, without neglecting the commitment to the dental care provided to patients, the Dental Specialties Unit's reason for being and existing.
2. Another challenge was to interrelate a system—the product of a Quality Model—created for organizations and adapt it to the system with which the Armed Forces are accustomed to administering their health care facilities; the problem was the approach and intellectual development of the culture of quality in harmonious interaction with military culture and professional technical culture.
3. Another important aspect of the problems encountered was that the military administration focuses on complying with tasks by giving responsibilities according to rank; the difficulty in locating and designing processes and systems required special training, both for the criteria leaders and for those responsible for each process. It was necessary to make a conceptual analysis of systems, subsystems, processes and sub-processes in order to learn not only to identify existing ones and design those needed, but also to document them, show them on charts, assess them, compare them and improve them; an analysis that had to include the interaction between them in a comprehensive manner; this was perhaps the greatest challenge to overcome.

The strategies that facilitate complying with the Mission were established by motivating personnel on implementing its policies, goals and strategies, supported by the military and professional values and principles with which the day-to-day work of the Dental Specialties Unit is carried out

4. Military administration traditionally focuses on carrying out activities in the best possible way, by optimizing existing resources. Learning to measure production, productivity and the real profitability of the resources provided was another situation that was hard to overcome.
5. Interpersonal relations represented a challenge by having to combine the military and ranking line of command with a democratic and participatory leadership, as the model stipulates.

By tradition, the patient has been the most important person in military health care facilities, but patient satisfaction was registered only through the few complaints recorded. Creating a customer attention system that would make it possible to know not only their satisfaction by means of surveys but also their expectations on making use of the Unit, was essential.

In addition to these actions, approval studies were made after patients' discharge by means of monitoring by telephone, and furthermore, measurement of these results was performed by statistical methods and they were disseminated among the senior management and process owners, in order to carry out actions of redesign and continuous improvement as soon as possible, based on the opinions expressed by the patients.

This represented one of the main value generators for patients of the Dental Specialties Unit. The communion of knowledge and performance of functions in the whole allows the development of a culture known as military doctrine, which combines the principles, values, virtues, beliefs, attitudes, standards and habits that characterize the Army and Air Force. Each individual's attitude stemming from military culture integrated into his or her life facilitates pertinent changes for improvement.

III. Implementation

Participating in the implementation of the INTRAGOB Quality Model somehow represented a change of paradigms since interpersonal relations were a challenge by having to combine the military and ranking line of command with a democratic and participatory leadership, as the model stipulates. Without sidestepping the commitment to dental care for patients, the organization's development was adapted to systems and processes consistent with the INTRAGOB Model.

The main problems were due to the lack of understanding and correct interpretation of the referential meaning of each of the criteria that comprise the Model; it was necessary to carry out an analysis of the conceptualization of the aspects that compose the Model, such as systems, subsystems, processes and sub-processes, and to that end a self-diagnosis was made which determined the Unit's own system, which took into account the design of processes and their indicators, measurement, analysis of results, continuous improvement, referential comparison with best practices and innovation. That made it possible to detect areas of strength and of opportunity; the latter were modified and improved in order to guarantee customer satisfaction and meet their expectations detected.

The implementation gradually permeated all the Unit's structures and levels by means of training and dissemination of the Model through workshops, lectures and printed matter in order to ensure that all the participants should share the desired culture of quality and mainly that the patients (customers) should perceive that way of life in which all the members were involved.

Communication increased by modifying processes to assure the reliability and efficiency that provides feedback to all the interest groups, and also interaction between the medical information system and the administrative system, which make up communication in general, was achieved.

The strategic planning that ensures the permanence of the organization, as well as its development, made it possible, based on participatory leadership, to implement and further systems, methods and practices to improve this leadership and promotion to increase the principles and values of quality, integrity and transparency, translated into codes of conduct shared by all the members of the organization. The strategies that facilitate complying with the Mission were established by motivating personnel on implementing its policies, goals and strategies, supported by the military and professional values and principles with which the day-to-day work of the Dental Specialties Unit is carried out. The fulfillment of goals has facilitated coordination of the supervisory group's decisions and provided measures to assess organizational performance, seeking prevention in oral health and to project a model of customer satisfaction by means of comprehensive attention with processes that cost less and that can be implemented throughout the public health system giving projection to the military health system.

The principles, values and standards applied in the military model are compatible with the principles and values of the INTRAGOB Model, which enabled administrative management to be adapted without difficulty, due to the type of organization, discipline, order and unity of doctrine that prevails, which made it easier to instill the culture of quality.

Ongoing management of processes as a culture of continuous improvement will make it possible to provide quality services to all patients (customers) with sustained development through quality assurance.

IV. Results

The implementation of the INTRAGOB Quality Model has made possible the following results, among others:

- Redefining the Vision, Mission, Principles and Values in accordance with the established guidelines.
- Having documented and detailed results for each of the criteria.
- Improving the quality of the service provided, bearing in mind patients' expectations and their needs with regard to attention, guidance, communication and complaints, through surveys, information modules and complaints and suggestions mailboxes.
- Developing comprehensive and strategic planning that takes into account the implementation of systems, methods and practices to improve the established processes and results.
- Combining military principles, values and standards with those of

the Quality Model, developing and consolidating the established culture of quality.

DISAGREEMENTS 2000-2003		
YEAR	COMPLAINTS RECEIVED	COMPLAINTS RESOLVED
EXTERNAL AUDIT MAILBOX		
2000	0	0
2001	1	1
2002	0	0
2003	0	0
VERBAL COMPLAINTS		
2000	0	0
2001	5	5
2002	5	3
2003	2	2
OPEN OPINION		
2000	18	18
2001	16	16
2002	14	14
2003	7	7
TOTAL	68	66

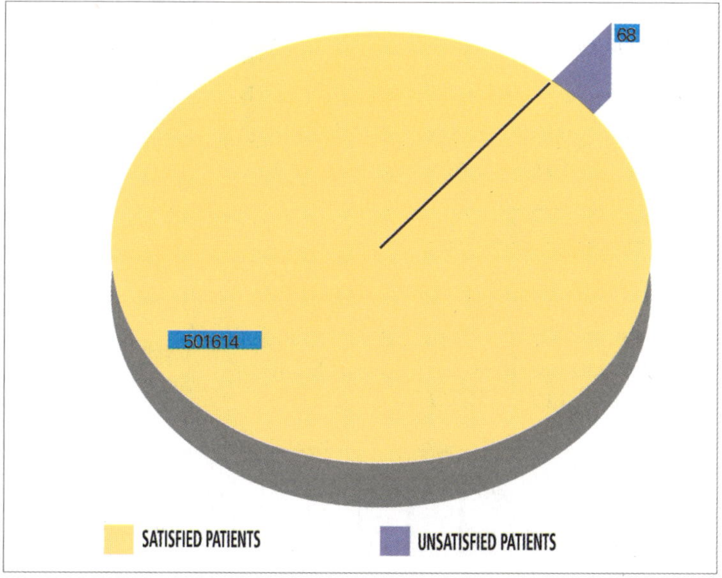

The Dental Specialties Unit is recognized nationally and internationally as a quality institutional attention center, reliable, efficient and with decent treatment, in which the personnel who compose it have a strong sense of belonging to the Institution

Knowledge and application of the principles and values in UEO personnel increased by 42 percent in 2003 over 2001.

- Optimization of time and human, material, technical and financial resources.
- Certification of the totality of professional personnel before their respective Councils.
- Strengthening the development of continuous training programs by means of courses, workshops and seminars that enable medical personnel to reinforce their skills so as to care for patients with quality and warmth, as well as to reaffirm knowledge of their specialties.

Specialist Dental Surgeons Certified in the UEO

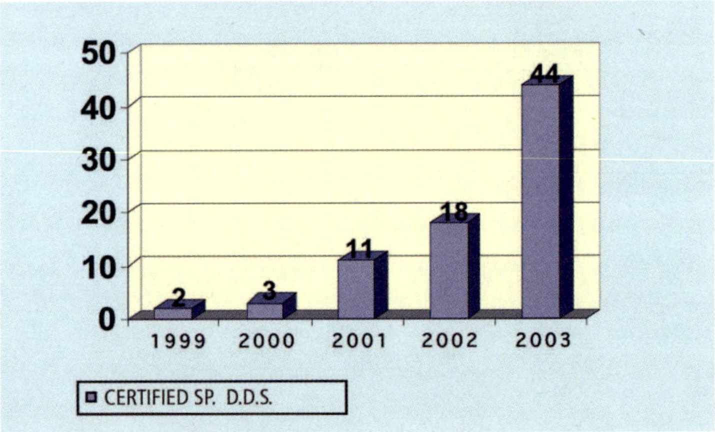

Percentage of Processes and Procedures of the Dental Specialties Unit Designed According to ISO 9000-2000 in 2003

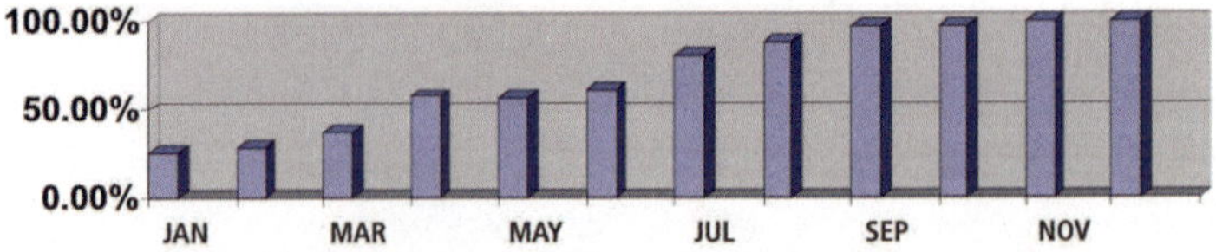

- Reorientation of actions to satisfy and exceed oral health expectations.
- Introduction of the telephone appointments service.
- Permanent setting for quality, directly related to savings, productivity and attainment of objectives, through a framework of transparency and integrity.

Securing of the 2003 INTRAGOB Award

The Dental Specialties Unit is taking shape to become consolidated as a comprehensive dental care unit, mainly oriented toward prevention, providing an effective service with respect, equality, transparency, honesty, integrity and impartiality, and with leading-edge technology. It is recognized nationally and internationally as a quality institutional attention center, reliable, efficient and with decent treatment, in which the personnel who compose it have a strong sense of belonging to the Institution.

Mining Development Trust (FIFOMI)

Problems Encountered

Situation in 2000

The administration that came in as of December 1, 2000 proceeded to establish a diagnosis that would show the situation in which the Trust operated, and the results were as follows:

FIFOMI figures to 2000:

- Assets of 2,874,355 pesos.
- Human Resources with 242 full-time jobs.
- 34 percent of these working in credit and administration.
- 14 regional offices.

Placement of 453 million pesos a year.

- 33 percent of overdue portfolio.
- 44 companies catered to with credit in the year.

With the following red lights:

- Very high percentage of overdue portfolio.
- Very low credit operation.
- Poor perception of the mining sector in the financial system.
- Inappropriate structure, functions and working environment.
- Deficient operation of Regional Offices.
- Budget for growth.
- High number of relevant observations determined by the Internal Control Organ.
- Decree of the Expenditures Budget of the Federation, which did not permit operation of first-floor credits.

Implementation of the System

In order to correct this situation the following actions were carried out:

Definition of the course:

- The first Comprehensive Strategic Plan for the Institution was prepared.
- The Mission, Vision, Values, Objectives, Strategies, Programs and Indicators were established, aimed at promoting the development of the mining sector and its chain of production at national level.
- **Establish a Quality Management System based on Standard ISO 9001:2000.**

Actions to be Carried out

Due to FIFOMI's requirements it was deemed appropriate to carry out a long-term program aimed at quality. However, to take care of the process it was essential to begin by the senior management group, since it was responsible for the result of implementation of the system in FIFOMI.

Based on the above the proposal known as Program of Education for Quality was presented.

Program of Education for Quality

Contents of each stage:

A. Seminar for directors: Quality 101
   1. The reasons for quality systems.
   2. Organization as a system.
   3. Quality 101.
   4. The responsibility of the director in the process of implementation and management of quality.

Product: Commitments to performance of each of the members of the senior management group.

B. Awareness building for quality
   1. Conceptual scheme and reality.
   2. Sphere of duties and behaviors.
   3. Alternatives for solution.
   4. Motivation for quality.

Product: Commitments to performance referring to disposition and to assimilating the quality scheme.

C. Leadership for quality (seminar for command levels)
   1. Management and what is vital.
   2. Leadership.
   3. Sources of influence.
   4. Personnel management and guidance.

Product: Commitments to performance to exercise the leadership styles appropriate to the maturity of each collaborator.

D. High performance teams
   1. Individual differences.

2. The working group.
3. Work team.
4. Quality-oriented high performance teams.

Product: Commitments to performance aimed at working in quality-oriented teams in each area of the organization.

E. Analysis of problems and decision-making
   1. Difficulties in implementing quality.
   2. The problem.
   3. Analysis of problems through the team.
   4. Administration of resolution projects.

Product: Commitments to performance to solve problems in quality implementation, in keeping with the established project.

Resulting products:

- Prior, final and follow-up assessment of knowledge.
- Assessment of application in the work sphere.
- Certified throughout the process.
- Performance results linked to indicators.
- Progress reports for each stage.
- Behavior oriented to customer satisfaction.
- Work based on securing of indicators.

Implementation of the Quality Management System under Standard ISO 9001:2000

A) Strategic Planning: It is verified that the objectives of Strategic Planning are aligned and the Quality policy and objectives are created, which are duties under the Standard.
   - Quality Policy.
   - Process Mapping.
   - Quality Objectives.

B) Document Design. All the documents to be put together and controlled in the Quality Management System were designed.
C) Dissemination Plan.
   - Internal training.
   - Talks.
   - Orientation.
D) Preparation of Documents.
E) Preparation of Registers.
F) Drafting of the Quality Manual.
   - Establishment of the Quality Committee.
G) Prepare Measurement of Customer Satisfaction.
H) Measuring of Competences.
I) Measuring Control Points.
J) SAM Format. This format was prepared to show corrective actions, preventive actions or agreement by customers, and actions of improvement.
K) Carry out Internal Audits.
L) Review by Senior Management.
M) Actions of Improvement.
N) Pre-audit.
O) **Certification Audit.** This was carried out in November 2002.

Reason for the Implementation of the System

It was decided to implement this system because ISO 9000:2000 is an outstanding tool to identify, measure, control and follow up on any type of organization at world level.

General results and impact on citizens:

- Clarity in the activities to be supported, for which purpose they were published in the Official Gazette of the Federation.
- Discretionary authority in extending credits came to an end.
- The process was streamlined.
- Eligibility of companies to be supported became transparent.
- The number of financial intermediaries rose from **4** to **70**.

- The number of companies dealt with increased.
- The Institution's portfolio risk diminished.
- New amortization schemes.
    - Growing payments of capital.
    - Decreasing capital.
    - Equal and consecutive.
    - Advance payments at the customer's choice.
    - Adjust charge-offs to the company's capacity.
- Simplification of procedures.
    - Overall discount line.
    - Reduce time frames in credit operations.
    - Greater participation by banks.
    - Correct discount operation processes.
    - Reduce response times from 38 requirements to 7.
    - Authorization and deposit in two hours in automatic discount operations carried out by banks for up to one million dollars.
- New rate schemes.
    - Fixed rate.
    - Variable rate with ceiling guaranteed.
- New types of credit.
    - Clean credit.
    - Current account.
- Increase in placement.
    - From 453 million placed in 2000 to 2 billion in 2003.
    - The aim is to place 3.4 billion in 2004.
- Attention to overdue portfolio.
    - Create the rules and bases for remissions.
    - Develop programs of reduction for the unions portfolio and the extinct Mining Development Commission (COFOMI).
    - Reactivate 40 proposals from earlier years.
    - 240.8 million pesos were recovered in 65 proposals dealt with.
    - Overdue portfolio of 755 million in 2001 to 579 in 2003.
- Companies catered to with credit.
    - From 44 in 2000 to 360 in 2003.

- Evolution of Assets.
  - From 2.87 billion in 2000 to 3.6 billion in 2003.
- Technical assistance.
  - In 2003 technical assistance was provided to 1,162 companies in small-scale mining and the minerals chain, representing an increase of 1,056 percent over the year 2000.
  - Reactivation of mining districts.
  - Parral, Chihuahua.
  - San Javier, Sonora.
  - San Ignacio, Sinaloa.
  - Zacatecas District.
- Exploration Program.
  - Projects defined in Parral, Chihuahua; Zacatecas, Zacatecas; Topia and Mapimi, Durango; San Ignacio, Sinaloa, and San Javier, Sonora.
- Training.
  - The institution used to give courses throughout the country with 6 instructors based in Mexico City. Now it is an institution that promotes comprehensive training, with 53 promoters, the result of alliances.
  - The number of courses given rose from 15 in 2000 to 165 in 2003.
  - In 2003 training was provided to 3,551 companies; more than 12 times the number of companies assisted during 2000.
- New image.
  - New logo with a greater number of graphic features.
  - Greater presence in fairs, forums, exhibitions, tours and events related to the minerals chain.
  - With all of this, FIFOMI carried out financing, technical assistance and training activities in 30 states in the country and from 341 companies attended in 2000, the number rose to 5,080 in 2003.
- Human Resources.
  - Reduction of posts from 242 to 188.
  - 72 hours of training in 2003 as against 40 in 2000.

Like many other organizations, LICONSA faced the dilemma of whether or not to join the limited group of companies that display world-class rank

- Job description and profiles by labor competences.
- Development of internal auditors.
- Winners of the 2003 INTRAGOB Award.
  - Feedback from the award.
  - Considerable improvements to our system.
- Follow-up audits without a single *not in agreement*.

Ministry of Social Development (SEDESOL)

LICONSA

Northern Metropolitan Directorate (DMN)

1. Background

LICONSA is an enterprise established in 1945 whose prime task has been to support the most disadvantaged Mexicans through the production, distribution and marketing of high quality milk at subsidized prices, as an agent that contributes to the forming of human capital. LICONSA'S target population is made up of all the country's economically vulnerable communities. LICONSA is a key instrument in the social policy of combating poverty furthered by the Government of the Republic. Throughout its 50 years of existence, it has been the means whereby the government has made it possible for various generations, especially during childhood, to complement their nutrition by drinking milk every day. Its Subsidized Milk Supply Program reaches more than 5,178,000 beneficiaries throughout the country, through 9,220 sales outlets, and its production is over 3,305,000 liters a day.

DMN is a work center that operates one of the 10 industrial milk production plants that belong to the LICONSA family. Its mission is to produce, distribute and market the product in the best conditions of quality, quantity, timeliness and at the lowest cost, to cater to the beneficiary population in its area of influence. Its main industrial activity consists of re-hydrating powdered milk, reconstituting it to obtain as the final product a liquid fortified milk, with simple concentration and characteristics similar to those of fresh, pasteurized, homogenized milk. It also acquires for pasteurization, in lower percentages, fresh milk from various national producers from the center and north of the country.

Its Subsidized Milk Supply Program reaches more than 5,178,000 beneficiaries throughout the country, through 9,220 sales outlets, and its production is over 3,305,000 liters a day

The DMN produces an average of 1,080,000 liters of milk a day. This production supplies 547 dairies in five boroughs of the Federal District and 36 municipalities in the State of Mexico, benefiting slightly more than 768,800 families made up of almost 1,223,000 people in the most vulnerable population segments. It also supplies powdered milk to 15 social welfare homes and two shelters of the National Institute for Older Adults (INAPAM).

2. Problems Encountered

Although the DMN complied satisfactorily and regularly with the requirements stemming from its mission, the fact is that in the daily course of activities the reliability and predictability provided by methodological and systemic practice had been replaced by routine based on the tenure of operative personnel (experience), the absence of changes in the production infrastructure (technological obsolescence) and by certain other factors of a behavioral nature that respond to LICONSA'S internal idiosyncrasy.

In addition to the foregoing, the growing competitiveness currently faced by Mexican enterprise, both in the industrial and in the services spheres, emerged as an engine that gave impetus to the search for more and better practices of creativity, innovation and development of continuous improvement schemes. Like many other organizations, LICONSA faced the dilemma of whether or not to join the limited group of companies that display world-class rank. Undoubtedly this has not been an easy challenge, for it has meant breaking away from traditional development schemes in which the adoption of a genuine culture of total quality is motivated, a fact that has contributed to achieving the governmental expectation of *bringing Mexico up to date and into the vanguard.*

In communities in which LICONSA Milk is present, children are healthier and better developed

Supported by its nature as an eminently social enterprise, LICONSA assumed the commitment to operate in an efficient, effective, transparent and modern manner, always in favor of those who most need its presence. To that end, first it had to identify and acknowledge the existence of different fields of opportunity for improvement, so that in a second step the modernization strategy would be created that would set us on the desired path.

The following feature among the aspects identified:

a) Raising the nutritional contribution provided by consumption of LICONSA Milk to its beneficiaries, thus ratifying the institutional commitment to the development of Mexican children.
b) Taking the benefits of LICONSA Milk to a larger number of Mexicans who need it.
c) Supporting the development of national milk producers to motivate the growth of the domestic market, thus contributing to the impetus given by the Federal Government to the livestock sector.
d) Supporting Mexican families' finances by not increasing the price of LICONSA Milk, a premise upheld by the internal reorganization of its finances.
e) Making LICONSA 's register of beneficiaries an up-to-date and reliable instrument.
f) Contributing to the creation of a sustainable ecological environment.
g) Making LICONSA a range of possibilities within the new, overall and integrating strategy of the social policy established by the Federal Government through different programs oriented to the human and social development of the population in conditions of extreme poverty.
h) Making quality a habit associated with its work culture, through the modernization of its productive and administrative infrastructure, avoiding obsolescence and technological lags.

3. Development Strategies Undertaken

Each of the areas of opportunity described above, respectively, observed application of the actions pointed out below:

a) In collaboration with the System for Integral Family Development (DIF) of the State of Mexico, in 2001 a "Study of Weight and Height, School Performance and Impact on Family Finances" was carried out on a significant sample of the beneficiary population to know their nutritional condition. The result made it possible to confirm that in communities in which LICONSA Milk is present, children are healthier and better developed.

   In response to the problem of malnutrition faced today by children in the communities with the highest poverty rates, LICONSA Milk was enriched with qualities that are added to the nutritional values of their traditional milk.

b) President Vicente Fox's administration has distinguished itself by the high priority placed on social programs. The significant increase in LICONSA's register of beneficiaries shows the determined support currently given to the Subsidized Milk Supply Program. Thus, in addition to the requests for opening new sales outlets received from different social agencies, the DMN has proposed the expansion of the social program's coverage.

c) Being deficient in milk production, Mexico turns to international markets to supply its internal demand. Receiving milk of domestic origin translates into support provided by the Federal Government through LICONSA to the country's cattle raisers in order to consolidate them as a highly productive sector.

d) The fight against poverty through transparent and efficient application of social programs has become one of the Federal Government's priorities, which the DMN has taken up, guaranteeing the viability of its Subsidized Milk Program by means of strict application of budgetary discipline.

e) In order to have a current, standardized, reliable and transparent register of the population of beneficiaries of the Subsidized Milk Supply Program, the DMN implemented an ambitious Program of Updating and Screening of the Register of Beneficiaries which

Everyday, more than 3,000 quality control analyses and assessments are conducted on raw materials, on the process and on the end product, both at the plant and at sales outlets, providing certainty to consumers

began in 2002 with the application of the New Information Document and concluded in the first moths of 2004.

f) One of the most important commitments assumed has been **contributing to the preservation of the environment** with the definition of strategies resulting in the least possible impact of production processes on the environment, both local and regional. Even though this producing unit is not considered among the companies with high environmental risk, voluntary enrollment into the National Program of Environmental Audits (PNAA), established by the Office of the Federal Attorney for Environmental Protection (PROFEPA) was decided on.

g) **LICONSA's institutional work has been supported by the new global and integrating strategy of the social policy that the government of the Republic has established through its program *Contigo es Posible* (With you, it is possible).**

Other programs corresponding to the Federal Government's social policy in which LICONSA participates by contributing to better nutrition for the population are **Oportunidades** (Opportunities), **Arranque Parejo en la Vida** (Equal Start in Life) and the **Food and Nutrition Network.**

h) In order to favor the incorporation of the DMN of LICONSA into an ongoing process of modernization, both technical and administrative, in recent years it has maintained a course toward continuous development. To that end, it has made significant investments in infrastructure and productive equipment, in order to have cutting-edge technology in its processes to enable it to continue to achieve the highest quality parameters in its product.

Likewise, it has developed a philosophy of service with quality, oriented to meeting the legitimate needs of the population it serves. In this regard, it has created systems, processes and work methods based on the Quality Model approach, obtaining diverse awards in the national and international spheres.

Even so, the population segment it serves has risen from 4.2 million beneficiaries in the year 2000, to 5.2 million at present

4. Development Strategies Undertaken

a) For the DMN it has always been vitally important to keep its image well-established among consumers. Therefore, everyday, more than 3,000 quality control analyses and assessments are conducted on raw materials, on the process and on the end product, both at the plant and at sales outlets, providing certainty to consumers.

LICONSA Fortified Milk has proved to be a means not only to combat anemia and malnutrition in children, but also to favor their physical and mental development, which translates into a society with healthier children and with better school performance.

b) Due to various factors afflicting the world economy today, the parastate enterprise faces the challenge of operating with greater needs and increasingly scarce resources. Even so, the population segment it serves has risen from 4.2 million beneficiaries in the year 2000, to 5.2 million at present.

In October 2003, the DMN signed up beneficiary number "5 million" of LICONSA. So far in President Vicente Fox's administration, the number of beneficiaries has increased by 24 percent.

To know its customers' needs and expectations, the DMN systematically gathers, day after day, through its social promotion efforts, opinions on the product and the services provided. With these practices it has been possible to define certain requirements for operation that have served to improve the service provided as regards warmth, attention time, timeliness in service and response, among other mechanisms.

Furthermore, to provide guidance, advice and immediate response to the concerns of its beneficiaries and society in general, the DMN has an attention scheme based on the work of almost 100 social workers who are the permanent contact with its beneficiaries by visiting daily the dairies that make up the Program's sales network.

Through the screening process of its Register of Beneficiaries, the DMN succeeded in updating a total of 768,962 entries, reaching a high degree of precision in identification of the families in conditions of extreme poverty it caters to, providing greater certainty that its support reaches those who most need it

In addition, all the sales outlets have mailboxes that make it possible to gather the comments, complaints and suggestions of consumers, as well as having a news display of notices and posters placed at the disposal of the citizenry in general, and toll-free telephone numbers in which they can channel their concerns.

To guarantee the transparency of the Subsidized Milk Supply Program, in each dairy there is a committee of beneficiaries made up of members of the population served, who, without financial remuneration, carry out activities of a true controller's office.

c) The DMN's main suppliers are the providers of the two most important raw materials, which are powdered skimmed milk and vegetable fat. Seventy-five percent of the net operating cost is absorbed by these inputs. Powdered skimmed milk is a raw material, which is almost entirely imported. At present, we are the main purchaser of powdered milk worldwide; therefore the efforts it makes in favor of obtaining domestic milk give a new dimension to the efforts made in this regard.
d) In the ongoing search for achieving a healthy balance in its finances, LICONSA has established an appropriate balance between its operating costs and sale prices.

In the year 2000 it achieved direct profits for its products for the first time in its history. In this context, the DMN has played a preponderant role, as since that time it has maintained significant profit levels that have made it possible to support the operation of other smaller social programs belonging to the parastate enterprise. This is how it has been possible to eliminate operating subsidies that come from the public treasury, thus contributing decisively to the creation of a Government that Costs Less.

In this regard, the Federal Government's commitment has been to maintain the **price of milk at 3.50 pesos a liter** in the medium and long terms, gradually increasing its proportion with respect to commercial milks, with all due respect for its quality, in addition to continuing to add more and better elements to the product that also provide more and better benefits to the population served.

Referential Comparison of the Price of Liquid Milk in the Market

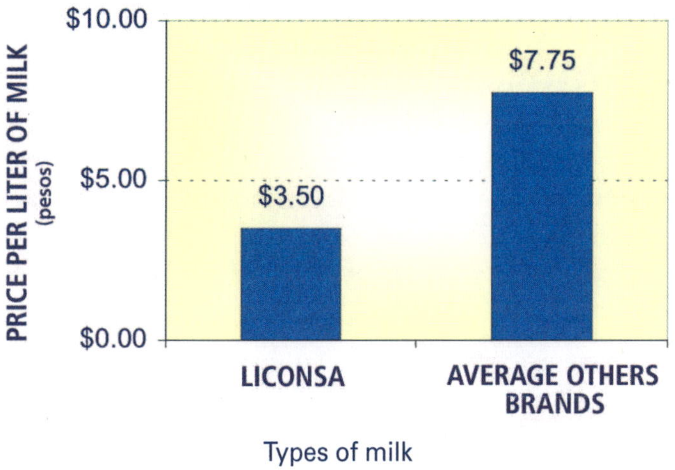

In its next effort, the DMN attained International Certification ISO 9001:2000 in regard to quality, during the course of the second half of 2002, succeeding in developing the full Model in a record time of six months. In 2003 the efforts in this field continued to bear fruit by obtaining the INTRAGOB Award

In 2004 LICONSA will sell around one billion liters of milk, and this is a highly important economic transfer for the low-income population. September 1, 2004 **marked 39 months since the last authorized increase in the price of LICONSA Milk.**

e) Through the screening process of its Register of Beneficiaries, the DMN succeeded in updating a total of 768,962 entries, reaching a high degree of precision in identification of the families in conditions of extreme poverty it caters to, providing greater certainty that its support reaches those who most need it.

f) With regard to the environment, the DMN has provided an effective response to the principle of Respect for the Environment contained in its Quality Model, but above all, in so doing it is contributing to healthier **sustainable development.** This action supports the provisions of the line of action of Quality Government.

g) The country's social dynamics have given rise to the adaptation of the overall strategy to the growing needs of LICONSA's target population, with the aim of fully complying with the institutional mandate of taking the benefit of the Subsidized Milk Supply Program to those who most need it.

In this regard, the results of the National Nutrition Survey issued in 1999 supported not only the need to fortify milk, but also to consider the nutritional needs of other vulnerable population groups.

h) For the DMN quality is not a novel matter, for it has succeeded in moving forward along that path with firm, determined steps. Suffice it to point out that as of the year 2001 its Quality Control Laboratory gained the title of **"Test Laboratory"** from **the Mexican Accreditation Entity,** and in 2002 it obtained **Approval as "Test Laboratory"** from **the National Public Health Laboratory of the Ministry of Health.**

In its next effort, the DMN attained **International Certification ISO 9001:2000** in regard to quality, during the course of the second half of 2002, succeeding in developing the full Model in a record time of six months.

In 2003 the efforts in this field continued to bear fruit by obtaining the **INTRAGOB Award.**

In 2004, the pace and perseverance of quality tasks were projected at international level, obtaining the **Ibero-American Award in Honor of Educational Excellence,** in the category of institutions not devoted to education, in honor of the contribution and impetus it gives in favor of a culture of service with quality. Thus also, and based on the Quality Model, in 2004 the DMN was declared a **finalist** in the participation scheme of the **National Quality Award**.

Office of the Attorney General of the Republic (PGR)

Specialized Inspector's Office for Attention to Electoral Offenses (FEPADE)

The FEPADE was created by presidential decree on July 19, 1994. Its origin is based on the citizen political agreement contained in the Pact for Peace, Democracy and Justice, signed by the political parties with the aim of knowing about, integrating, resolving and sanctioning criminal conduct in connection with federal electoral matters and the National Citizens' Register. In August 1996 it was conferred the rank of Specialized and its technical autonomy was ratified.

In the 2001/2006 Federal Public Administration, the introduction of Quality Models in all administrative units is a vision supported by citizen demands and embodied in the 2001/2006 National Development Plan (PND). Moreover, the National Law Enforcement Program establishes the need to count on an immediate reaction unit, with public servants committed to justice, equity, transparency, efficiency and juridical effectiveness, as well as to provide citizens with high quality in the delivery of the service.

Within this conceptual framework, in 2001 a comprehensive diagnosis of the Institution was carried out in order to assess the regulatory, substantive, organic and administrative aspects, as well as the institutional and social impact of the Inspector's Office.

An analysis of this diagnosis led to the development of a specific system of strategic and operative planning which, with the definition of objectives, strategic lines, processes and projects, and the firm conviction of establishing a culture of quality in the service, made it possible to reappraise the mission, and the processes and projects to fulfill it were established.

At the same time the mapping of operative procedures was carried out to detect the ones with the greatest value and the ones that were substantive in the work of the Inspector's Office. Thus it was decided to seek the certification of 31 of them, which range from reception of the complaint of criminal conduct in federal electoral matters to the penal lawsuit as such, including all the stages of integration of the preliminary investigation.

On January 21, 2002, the internationally renowned British Standards Institute (BSI) awarded the FEPADE **the certificate with registration number FS 61750** under International Standard ISO 9001:2000.

Two years after the introduction of the Quality Management System, in January 2004, BSI carried out the "re-certification audit" to the Inspector's Office's substantive processes, **and certification was confirmed.**

The Quality Management System implemented, by representing a consensus on good management practices whose purpose has been to ensure that FEPADE systematically delivers services that satisfy customers' quality requirements, has been integrated into a Total Quality Model, with evident results in citizens' response, who went to the polls in the 2003 federal electoral process with greater credibility and confidence, reporting all the offenses committed; all of them met with a timely response.

The essence of the implementation of a Quality Model is a systemic, holistic approach to maintaining and invigorating the path to total quality in the face of the new challenges of increasing the competitiveness of the FEPADE. To that end, we have developed systems that make it possible to determine customers' expectations and needs, and measure satisfaction levels, leadership, values, staff development and intellectual capital, training, of information and technology management, strategic and operative planning, process management and improvement, and impact on society, which has enabled greater value to be created in service to customers, to society, to public servants and to the Institution itself.

Today the capacity to innovate of all the personnel has been strengthened by contributing ideas to improve the organization; this activity is supported by the promotion of ethical values to create a healthy environment in which the different actors coexist in harmony. The high performance of work teams is the result of systems and processes designed to respond to the needs of interest groups in order to create value.

An annual program of review of strategic and operative planning is under way, based on the opinion of the interested parties, the processes, the opinion of internal customers and considerations of the environment. Through a specific system the strategic objectives and lines are established, linkage with processes and projects is carried out, budget needs are determined and indicators and goals are identified that make it possible to carry out the follow up which, by means of monitoring and internal and external quality audits, naturally establish cycles of improvement.

In FEPADE it has been possible to overcome the traditional manner of identifying strengths and weaknesses through the use of the

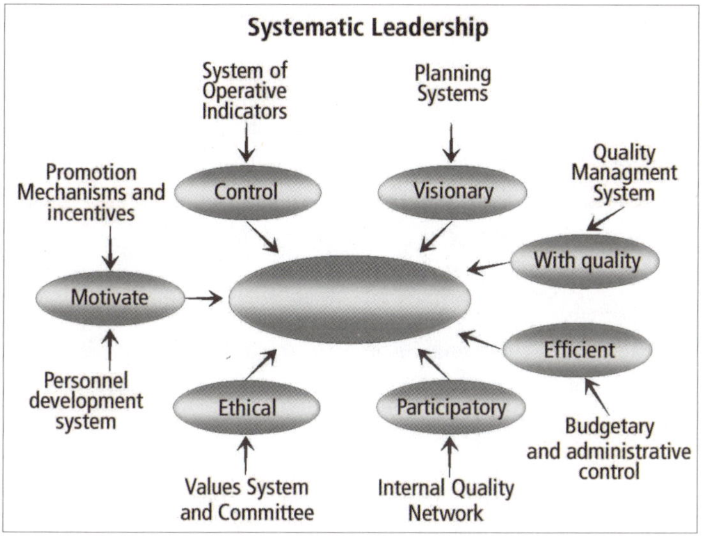

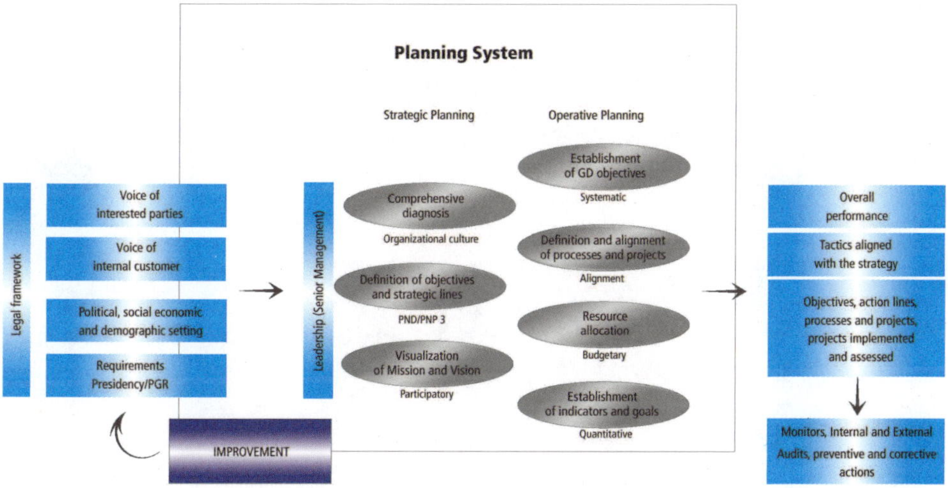

organizational culture tool for more precise identification of control mechanisms, symbols and language, rituals and routines, values, cultural and technological aspects, etc.

Since in 2001 it was an entity that was unknown to the units of the Office of the Attorney General of the Republic and to the immense majority of citizens, the experience of the Inspector's Office with regard to quality began with efforts to establish a culture of accusation and crime prevention and provide a service with quality supported by the Values System; this system involves the appropriation of a Code of Values defined by the Institution's personnel by agreement. A committee elected democratically by the public servants of the Inspector's Office oversees these ethical values. An Internal Quality Network was also established, involving participatory and committed leadership. The organizational and intellectual-capital development that listens to the voice of clients and processes has resulted in:

- Real positioning of credibility and confidence in the citizenry.
- National and international recognition in the communications media.
- Recognition by obtaining the **2003 INTRAGOB Award**.

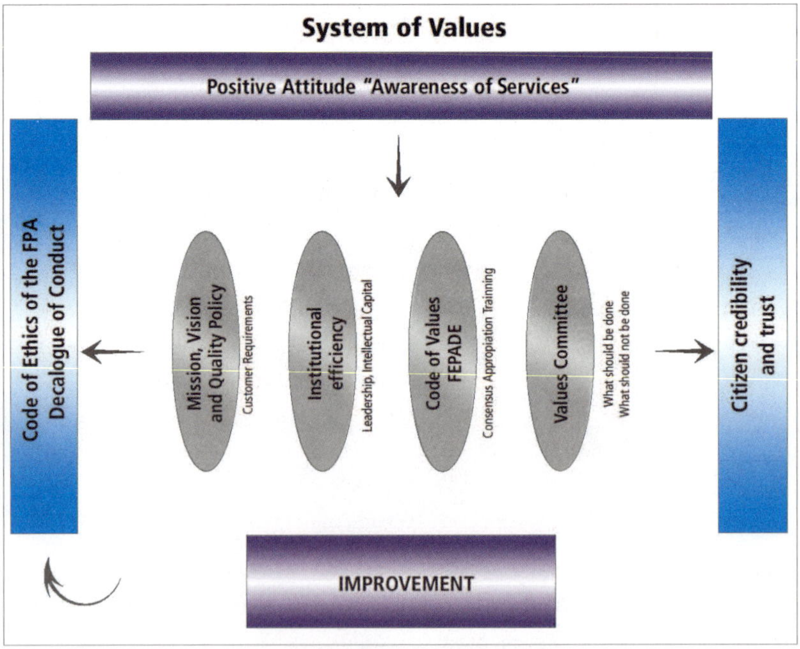

Customer System

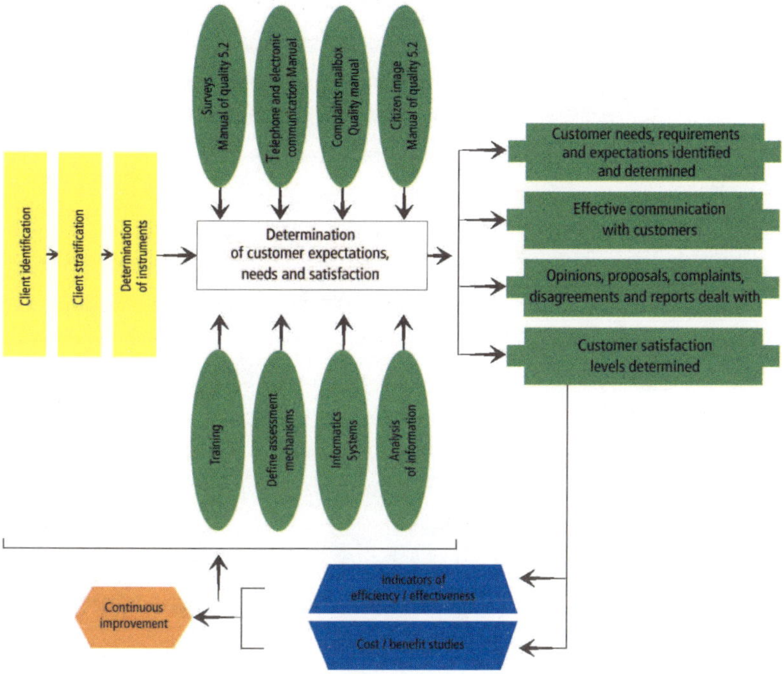

The importance of the human factor in organizations has no parallel, since it generates the products and services and makes them a reality. From 2001 to mid-2004, FEPADE carried out 5 surveys of organizational climate which in 12 segments made a 180-degree assessment of the conditions and characteristics of labor relations and, directly, of the organizational environment.

At present the Inspector's Office is an organization that performs under a scheme geared to satisfying its customers' needs and expectations; to that end, by identifying, stratifying and determining its critical characteristics and applying surveys, it has succeeded in gathering customers' requirements. Among these requirements is the need for law enforcement to be carried out promptly and expeditiously, and to achieve this, actions were carried out in connection with starting times and preparation and determination of investigations in federal electoral penal matters.

> Prior to implementing the Quality Model, the terms for the beginning of complaints were extremely long; at present, more than 85 percent are started in two days. Bearing in mind their complexity and social or political impact, it would not be possible to reach 100 percent, and therefore a challenging goal of 96 percent has been imposed.

Likewise, before introducing the Quality Model, the activity of the Agent of the Office of the Federal Public Prosecutor to investigate, reach the historical truth and act with equity and impartiality was nine months on average; at present 81 percent is carried out in an average of six months. This measurement can only be made when processes are identified, made more efficient and periodically audited.

The chain of processes of preliminary investigations determines very clear actions that are subject to measurement after the last proceeding carried out, which virtually closes the stage of preparation of the file. Consequently the corresponding reports should be issued.

> In 2003, 97 percent of inquiries were ruled on in ten working days, a time in which the validity or not of the exercise of penal action was determined, or else the lack of jurisdiction, reserve. The challenge for 2004 is to reach 100 percent, by virtue of improvements in the process and teamwork carried out by the General Directorates of Preliminary Investigations and Juridical, both in matters of Electoral Offenses.

The factors that have been decisive in attaining the objectives are:

- Effective leadership.
- Establishment of an Internal Communication and Execution Network.
- Specific training in total quality.
- Creation of a small quality group that coordinates and multiplies.
- Availability of the minimum resources necessary.

- Implementation of systems, processes and projects adapted to Mexico for the administrative unit.
- Establishment of internal and external quality circles, promoting continuous improvement, innovation and analysis of referential comparison.

The administration of electoral penal justice is carried out by increasingly informed, increasingly transparent and increasingly committed public servants. International quality standards such as ISO 9000 and the implementation of a total quality model have provided a reference framework for the efficient, effective and professional execution of activities, understanding systems and processes not only as cause-effect, but as a tool that promotes and motivates the development of the organization and individual and collective advancement; also as a way of acting that creates added value both for customers and for the Institution's personnel and society as a whole.

"Our actions look after your elections"

Mexican Social Security Institute (IMSS)

Family Medicine Unit No. 26

Health is a value in society and a prime commitment of social well-being. The IMSS is an organization that envisages in its Vision being the best social security institution in the country, because it is sensitive to users' opinions and offers flexible world-class services that meet comprehensive health needs.

The First Level of Attention in the Unit covers 85 percent of overall daily demand through the Family Medical Attention System, which generates responses for users with the Health-Sickness approach through specific service areas.

An organization's quality begins from the moment it is designed, continues with day-to-day work and becomes crystallized in its results.

The Family Medicine Unit (UMF), in accordance with the provisions of the IMSS' Integral Quality Plan, has an Integral Quality Model known as MIC-26, which focuses its strategies on giving added value to the services it provides its beneficiaries and intermediate customers; the implementation of the model is supported by the Strategic Plan (1997/2002) and by the Unit's 2003/2008 Strategic Plan, whose interdependent elements (including MIC-26 and key and support processes) have been established, declared and applied since it began in 2001 to date.

As of October 1996, in a farsighted manner, it began the mobilization toward service-oriented quality by means of activities, plans and programs channeled by a vision of the future: "Being the Best Unit, the one that provides the Best Services with the Best Personnel."

The globalizing element of the Model used is Strategic and Operative Planning, the purpose of which is to consolidate the Mission and Vision. The substantive elements of the Strategic Plan were built in production workshops with a group of workers representing all the service areas, answering the following questions:

Identification: Who is the Unit?

The Family Medicine Unit No. 26, belonging to the First Level of Care of the IMSS, in Monterrey, Nuevo Leon, is a medical institution that provides healthcare, administrative and educational services to the beneficiary and non-beneficiary population living in 80 neighborhoods that make up its area of influence.

Interest groups: Who Are our Customers?

The beneficiary population (end customers), population at large (potential customers), employers of affiliated companies, representatives of labor union organizations, schools located in the area of influence, day-care centers, second and third-level hospitals, higher education centers, delegation regulatory coordination offices, delegation consultative council.

Products or Services: What Are the Products and Services?
The services it provides are:

- Health care:
  a. **Medical:** family medicine outpatient visit, emergencies, occupational health, clinical laboratory, community health, reproductive and mother-and-child health, and radio diagnosis.

  b. **Paramedics:** nursing, social work, nutrition, psychology, attention and guidance for beneficiaries, financial and social benefits.
- Administrative:
  Resolution in pension procedures, procedure for assistance with funeral and marriage dowry expenses, registration of those insured and beneficiaries, certification of validity in the social security regime, certification in payment of subsidies, reports on service productivity, reports on advance of programs to delegation regulations.
- Educational:
  Education and training of human resources for health; training in general.

  The answer obtained by consensus, in addition to identifying the needs of its groups of influence, made it possible to prepare and declare the following statement in October 1996: "Mission of Family Medicine Unit No. 26 of the IMSS: Provide health services with professionalism, quality and warmth to our beneficiaries. *Your health is our satisfaction*".

In order to identify the long-term vision more clearly, the senior management and employees answered the following questionnaire in a workshop:

What Do the Unit's main interest groups Require?

Interest Groups	Needs (Critical Elements)
Beneficiaries	Timely and resolvent medical attention
Population at large	Application of vaccines and timely detection of illnesses
Employers of affiliated companies	Eliminate long waiting times
Labor union representatives	Expeditious procedures
Schools actions to foster	Health
Day-care centers	Entry examination and epidemiological studies
1st and 2nd level hospitals	Justified transfer of patients
Universities	Development of abilities and skills
Regulatory authorities	Progress report on goals and increasing resolvent capacity
Delegation consultative council	Service quality and operative efficiency

How has the Unit responded to these requirements in the past? As an element of the IMSS macro-system, and since its creation (October 6, 1980), the Unit has developed plans and programs aimed at both beneficiaries and the population in general, in keeping with the demand for attention in health and sickness. As of 1995 it incorporated innovative proposals aimed at service quality, in accordance with the suggestions expressed by patients and government, labor and employer representatives by means of opinion forums and quick surveys, in addition to carrying out a situation diagnosis of the Unit. The diagnosis underscored the need to reduce service delivery time; moreover, patients made the petition to receive information on their ailments or those of their relatives. As of 1996 planning has been oriented toward Quality Management, implementing the planned change by means of MIC-26.

The main elements in planning design are the critical factors identified by interest groups, and this is what nourishes the system and facilitates administration of the service provided.

The progress of the Strategic Plan is measured annually. The results are incorporated weekly and monthly by measuring the satisfaction of the end user, known by means of the suggestions box, exit polls by processes, questionnaires, interviews and reception of complaints and/or suggestions.

Which aspects of the Unit, administration and labor relations foster efficiency in its tasks and which do not?
There is a diagnosis which is updated periodically and makes it possible to establish current and probable scenarios within the field of forces that further or limit the process of implementation of the Integral Quality Model (MIC-26), which facilitates selection and reorientation of orientation strategies.

How does the UMF 26 see itself in five years' time?
Carrying out its work focusing on Total Quality.

What strategic actions can be carried out for the better functioning of the Unit in the medium and long terms?
Those aimed at consolidating attainment of the Vision with the application of high-performance work systems that facilitate the service chain, development of personnel supported by the practice of values and principles, focus on the customer and ongoing training oriented to achieving a change through culture toward quality, and that everything results in the satisfaction of the customer and the service provider.

With the foregoing answers, and considering the capacity for change, the current and desired scenarios are compared in order to build the future scenario.

Vision of Family Medicine Unit No. 26

The best Unit that provides the best services with the best personnel.
Which implies:

Achieving harmonious interaction between users and providers of the service, in benefit of their comprehensive health, demonstrable by:

Continuous improvement of processes that increase operative efficiency, service quality and satisfaction of users and providers of the service.

- **Service:** The magic of being useful.
- **Makeup:** Forming work teams.
- **Commitment:** Complying with the Vision.

And as **Principles:** Orientation to the customer, continuous improvement of processes, teamwork, professionalism.

The deployment of the Vision is carried out with the establishment of specific strategies described in the Operative Program of Continuous Improvement, which, in addition to the corresponding objectives and goals, enables plans to be put into practice.

> **Strategic objectives:** 1.- Reducing waiting time to 30 minutes in outpatient visits, 2.- Reducing waiting time to 15 minutes in the Emergencies service, 3.- Increase workers in Quality practices by 100 percent, 4.- Develop four improvement projects aimed at improving the satisfaction of users and providers, 5.- Compliance with the Unit's Academic Program of more than 90 percent.
> Note: These objectives are planned to be carried out annually.

Indicators: 1. Percentage of waiting time in outpatient visits, 2. Percentage of waiting time for attention in Emergencies, 3. Percentage of workers participating in quality practices, 4. Improvement projects carried out, 5. Programmed improvement projects, 6. Number of courses given, 7. Number of courses programmed.

Benchmarking

The referential process has been carried out internally with other units of the system, but the Unit has also served as a reference for other IMSS and international Units, such as that of Ohio University, among others.

Conclusions and Recommendations

"Conserving what has been gained and aspiring for more."
With the enthusiastic, committed participation of all those who work in the Unit and recognizing efforts and renewing commitments, we share with customers —users— citizens the perspective of prevention to contain diseases and to keep a community and its social environment as healthy as possible.

What has been achieved?

> IIMSS Quality Award, 2003 INTRAGOB Award, Certification as a first-level outpatient establishment by the Ministry of Health 2003, implementation of the electronic medical record, electronic Information System that feeds the Data-Mart System, but above all cohesion and improvement of the labor climate, as well as maintenance and continuous improvement of the MIC-26 work model, **because the staff and the users are the most important element for development and continuance as a Health Care Unit.**

Since 2000 the PREVENIMSS strategy has a *preventive approach* rather than a curative one. It was created because chronic-degenerative diseases have been predominating, and therefore now the fundamental occupation is giving *quality to life*. Due to the foregoing, many of the actions go outward from the Unit, with companies, schools, day-care centers, churches, libraries and other institutions in its area of influence; thus there has been compliance with the criteria of the INTRAGOB Award, a management model similar to the IMSS Quality Award, systems that have been implemented in Unit No. 26 to achieve the Mission and Vision.

The following tables summarize some of the procedural activities systematized with the achievement attained, always in continuous improvement.

Functioning of the Strategic Planning System

Item	Goal	2000	2001	2002	2003	Achievement	Strategy
Average of prior appointment in family med	85% 90%	75	85	92	96		Verbal and written dissemination of the benefits of prior or programmed appointment for users and providers
Average of waiting time in FM	30 min	21.31	18.54	18.73	17		Success in prior appointment
Average of waiting time in emergencies	15 min	12.23	9.48	12.93	14.3		Dissemination to users and service providers of optimum use
% supply received of medicines	95%	86.45	84.83	92.62	99.2		Dissemination of Dx-Tx clinical guides and basic table of medicines
% consistency Cl- Dx- Tx	95%	93.18	96.6	98.26	99		Adherence to Dx-Tx clinical Guides and operative and documentary supervision
% of reference to second level	2 to 4	4.64	4.69	2.98	4		Adherence to reference guides
% user satisfaction	80%	85	93	90	93.19		Application and analysis of exit and telephone polls
% satisfaction of service provider	85%	86	91	94	95		Analysis of results of surveys applied and listen to proposals for service improvement and training needs
% non-programmed absenteeism	7	6.2	3.85	4.2	4.7		Replacement of worker by worker and motivation and labor recognition

PREVENIMSS to the Company 2000/2003

Companies visited	2000	2001	2002	2003
	34	29	26	10
Actions carried out	10,622	12,250	11,330	15,665
Persons benefited	3,035	3,500	2,914	3,200

PREVENIMSS in the Community

Item	2000	2001	2002	2003
Courses	14	16	22	24
Persons attending	7,320	8,366	10,909	12,500
campaigns	22	25	30	20
Talks	47	50	60	72
Self-help groups	11	12	14	14
Total of pers. benef.	9,501	10,697	12,844	15,650

Activities carried out PREVENIMSS at school

Level	No.	Visits	Programmed School Population	Population Attended
Preschool	30	36	1,089	100%
Primary	27	31	2,363	100%
Secondary	12	16	5,133	100%

PREVENIMSS at school

Actions	2001	2002	2002	2002	2003	2003
School	Juan Gza.	Juan Gza. Fdz.	Nicolas Bravo Gza.	Luis G. Urbina	Sofia Alvarez	Sec. Tec. No. 38
Preventive	3,963	7,070	7,840	1,200	1,600	1,770
Odontograms	342	707	784	120	164	175
Preventive dentistry	1,368	2,121	2,352	360	429	525
References to institutions	217	707	784	120	54	60
Appraisal of nutritional state	342	652	556	105	164	175
Inter-Institutional coordination	14	25	25	15	18	20
Education for health	44	75	70	36	20	24
Forming of health committees	4	6	4	4	3	4
Total	6,294	11,363	12,415	1,960	2,452	2,753

Effectiveness of Coverage in Preventive Medical Programs (Coverage %)

	Goal	2000	2001	2002	2003
Diabetes mellitus	100	103.7	106	100	98
Arterial hypertension	100	103.4	120.9	100.5	94
Cervico-uterine cancer	95	97.6	93.8	98	94
PTB	95	97.6	93.8	91	88
Breast cancer	100	106	117.1	93.3	98

Coverage of schemes in the Universal Vaccination System (Coverage %)

	Goal	1999	2000	2001	2002	2003
Basic vaccination in < 1 year	90	97.6	94.6	91.5	98.9	99.8
Basic schemes 1–4 years	51	99.9	99.6	99.4	99.8	99.9
Pregnant women	63	45	77.8	99.3	100	

Level of efficiency in the Management of Hazardous Biological-Infectious Wastes

Year	Manifests Prepared	Manifests with Inconsistencies
2000	850	1
2001	780	0
2002	847	0
2003	517	0

Effectiveness of Preventive Activities for the control of outbreaks of dengue fever

	1999	2000	2001	2002	2003	Rate N.L. of Dengue Fever 2003
Number of cases	405	20	0	0	0	0.2

Leon Technological Institute

Educational Exposition

Presentation

The Leon Technological Institute was founded in 1972 as a technical education institution at the senior high school level. Since then it has offered academic programs whose educational contents take into account aspects of quality.

In its early days, the career of quality control technician allowed teaching staff to become specialized in the country and abroad in specific quality-related aspects; and since 1975, the year in which the industrial engineering career began, staff and pupils are trained continuously in the subject of quality.

In recent years the subject of quality has penetrated all the educational programs at degree and postgraduate levels offered at the Institute, and it became a topic of special interest to take it to the level of good administrative practice. It was inconsistent that having expert academic staff in the subject, and having a large number of successful references in the world, as well as being a proposal for the nation, the opportunity to apply it in the Institution should be wasted.

Background

In 1996, a year in which Vicente Fox was Governor of the state of Guanajuato, important decisions were taken in the Institute for the implementation of quality models. During the first quarter of that year two important events took place in relation to quality. The first was the establishment of the Guanajuato Institution for Quality, of which the Technological Institute is a founder member, and the second was the setting in motion of a model for quality in the National System of Technological Institutes, of which it is a part.

In the summer of 1996, the Leon Technological Institute found itself involved in a heated debate on the institute's course in relation to its medium-term future. The crux of the debate was its level of quality with regard to its students, its staff, its infrastructure, its educational programs and other important topics.

All the Institute's workers participated in the debate; there were those who envisaged a difficult, adverse, almost unattainable panorama with regard to quality, and those who envisaged a possible and attainable horizon in the medium term.

Being a Technological Institute of more than 20 years' standing and being in a large and important city located in a state with an educational lag, it was decided that two important projects could be foremost in the second half of the nineties: increasing enrollment and improving the quality of educational services.

Those who opposed increasing enrollment argued that it was more responsible and effective to deal with small groups than large groups. Those who were in favor argued that in education quantity is also quality—specifically, quality of life. It was decided to undertake the adventure of providing services with an approach centering on coverage, raising its quality for the satisfaction of students and other related interest groups.

Implementation

In a meeting of the Board of Directors of the National System of Technological Institutes held in March 1996 in Queretaro, a pact for quality was made, committing all the system's institutions to launching an institutional quality program.

As a result of this pact, and with the exercise carried out in the summer of that year, the Institute became a pioneer in the educational system in the introduction of quality programs. The methodology for the introduction of the program included the following phases:

- Awareness building for quality.
- Education and training.
- Establishment of work teams.
- Project planning.
- Deployment, assessment and follow-up.

An institutional review revealed problems in different aspects and a series of continuous activities was undertaken to overcome them, with the goal of raising quality and user satisfaction within a period of five years.

The Institution's administration decided that the key to success lay in management by projects, while putting the work in order to focus on process improvement.

In the education and training phase support from experienced personnel was sought and the process of learning and adopting began.

Formal training was undertaken to learn about quality and human development in the awareness that personnel trained in these areas would lead to better quality.

The training, which is now continuous, is structured into professional training, teaching development and human development. It was not until implementation of the Federal Government's INTRAGOB Model that formal assessment was resumed on the basis of quality models. The application of this Model renewed the commitment of the National System of Technological Institutes, which, in a Board meeting held in San Juan del Rio, Queretaro, pledged to adopt the principles of the Good Government Agenda of the Presidency of the Republic, in addition to applying the principles of the models of the National Quality Award and the INTRAGOB Award.

Work was adjusted based on processes and by projects in accordance with the Presidential Agenda for Good Government, considering gains in each point of the agenda and focusing them as shown in the on the following page.

Furthermore, the development of a culture based on external assessment was initiated, and since 2002 three assessments have been carried out based on the Model of the National Quality Award, two assessments with reference to the INTRAGOB Model and one assessment within the purview of the Recognition for Quality of the Ministry of Public Education (SEP).

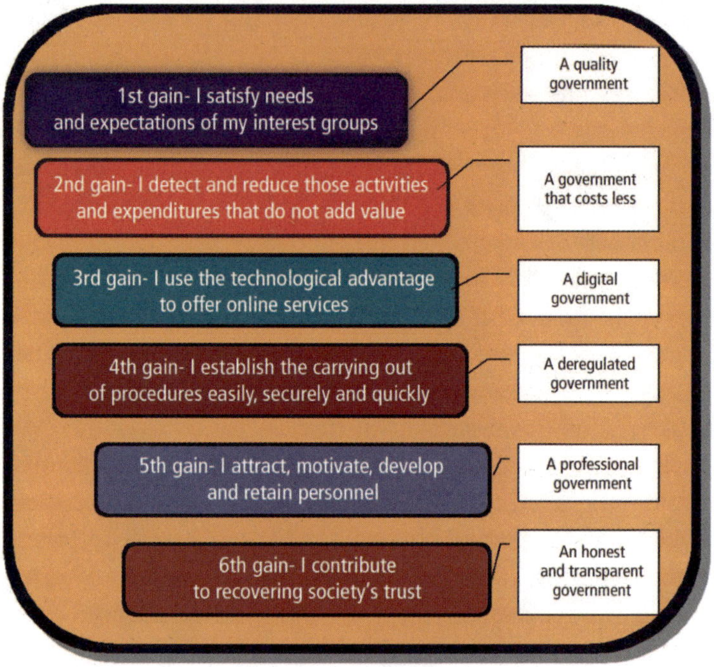

Results

The Leon Technological Institute won the Guanajuato Award for Quality in 1997, the first year in which it was awarded. Its main strength was the approach focusing on coverage and quality, central elements of the country's education agenda.

From 1997 to 2001 the work centered on implementing improvement projects, aiming to order the work so as to move from administering activities and functions to process-centered work.

As of 2001 the approach has centered on bettering the quality of educational programs, process certification and system maturity.

In 2003 the Institute was distinguished with the INTRAGOB Award and with the Recognition for Quality of the SEP, confirming that it was on the right path. Some results have been the optimization of installed capacity, increase in the awarding of degrees, control of the failure and dropout rates, increase in earnings, and participation by students in infrastructure projects.

Today the Institute has three strategic elements: coverage, quality and integration with systems of interest. In the continuous learning process five basic ideas are applied:

- Systems approach.
- Quality tools.
- Approach aimed at students.
- Leadership of the administration.
- People's participation.

Work teams continue to be formed to develop ideas as a strategy for working on specific projects. The soundness of the approach and the work culture has gained the confidence of different educational systems for having organized the XLVI National Sporting Event, the XIX National Arts and Culture Festival, the V National Encounter of Military Escorts and Bands, the XXV National Engineering Conference, three National Human Development and Creativity Congresses and having been designated to organize the VII National Quality Congress in October 2004.

3. Agencies and Entities with ISO 9000 in all Areas

Introduction

ISO 9000:2000 Standards

The governmental agencies and entities that have achieved and continue to maintain ISO 9000 certification in all areas are setting an example to follow in this field, given the teamwork, effort, discipline and methodological rigorousness required to meet this goal.

ISO 9001 Requirements

The ISO 9001 International Standard specifies the prerequisites that a quality system must fulfill when it is necessary to demonstrate the ability of a supplier to design and supply products that comply with standards. The list of those 20 prerequisites or directives evaluated is as follows:

1) **Senior Management Responsibility**

- Quality policy
- Organization
- Responsibility and authority
- Resources
- Senior management representation
- Senior management review

2) **Quality System**

- General requirements
- Procedures
- Planning for quality

3) **Contract Review**

- Review
- Modification of contracts
- Registers

4) **Design Control**

- Design and development planning
- Organizational and technical interfaces
- Inputs
- Outputs
- Design review
- Design verification
- Design validation
- Control of changes

5) **Documentation and Data Control**

- Approval and distribution of documents and data
- Changes in documents and data

6) **Procurement**

- Evaluation of subcontractors
- Purchasing data
- Verification of products purchased
- Verification by the purchaser at the supplier's place of business
- Verification by the customer of the products subcontracted by the supplier

7) **Control of Products Supplied by Customers**
8) **Product Detection and Monitoring**
9) **Process Control**
10) **Inspection and Confirmation**
- In receiving
- In process
- Final
- Inspection and confirmation records

11) **Control of Inspection, Measurement and Confirmation Equipment**
- Control procedures

12) **Inspection and Confirmation Status**
13) **Control of Nonconforming Products**
- Review and treatment

14) **Corrective and Preventive Intervention**
15) **Handling, Storage, Packaging, Conservation and Provision**
16) **Control of Quality Records**
17) **Internal Quality Audits**
18) **Training**
19) **Post-Sale Service**
20) **Statistical Methods**
- Identification of need
- Procedures

Federal Electricity Commission (CFE)

Total Quality Process

Various areas of the CFE have received INNOVA recognition awards, as was the case for the *Virtual Service Center*, and the INTRAGOB Award was granted to the *Online Services* of the Commercial Management Office, as well as to the Eastern Control Area, the South Central Distribution Division, the Temascal Transmission and Transformation Sub-area, the Materials and Equipment Testing Laboratory, the West Central Division, and the Jalapa Transmission and Transformation Sub-area.

However, we have chosen to describe here the organization's Total Quality Process.

1. Institutional Program for Total Quality

The Public Electric Power Service involves:

- Knowing exactly what CFE customers need
- Positioning the electricity sector as a promoter and engine of national development

- Consolidating and maintaining short, medium and long range planning horizons that take into account the following aspects:

  - Service quality
  - Reliability and rates
  - Productivity, efficiency and competitiveness
  - Modernization and innovation (processes and services)
  - Intellectual capital and high-performance personnel
  - Sector outlook

In order to create the proper environment for achieving the development and implementation of the Formal Total Quality Process throughout the Institution, as well as to make specialized Quality Systems personnel available, the following resources and workshops were developed:

- Management using Total Quality
- Customer-Supplier Chains
- Quality Assurance Systems Training
- The Path to Quality
- Statistical Process Control
- Administrative Tools
- Tools for Improving Quality
- Training for Quality Assurance System Auditors

- Formulation of Quality Assurance System Manuals and Procedures
- Survey Design

Some actions and programs were also identified that the CFE already had in progress, and others were established for each module in order to integrate them as systematic elements in the Total Quality Process:

Customer Satisfaction Module
- CFE Commercial System
- Facilities Rehabilitation and Modernization
- CFE Information Systems
- Reduction in Downtime per User (TIU)

Leadership Module
- Managerial Cadre Development Program
- Motivation, Attitudes and Leadership Program

Information and Analysis Module
- Dissemination of Institutional Goals and Objectives (Strategic Plan)
- CFE Retrospective and Prospective Information System
- Benchmarking
- Modernization of the Informatics Network and Telecommunications

Human Resources Module
- Institutional Program of Motivational Communication (PICOM)
- Motivation, Attitudes and Leadership Program
- Compensation and Productivity-based Incentives System
- Programmatic Structure for Training and Development
- Creating a Culture of Quality (Vocation for Service)
- Qualification and Certification of Personnel

Strategic Planning for Quality Module
- CFE Strategic Planning
- Strategic and Operations Planning for Each area

- Definition of Service Quality Objectives, Strategies and Goals for Each Area

Quality Administration, Environmental Protection and Industrial Safety Module

- Formulation of the CFE L0000-42 "Requirements of the CFE Quality Assurance System" Specifications
- Formulation of the CFE L0000-57 "Industrial Safety System" Specifications
- Formulation of the CFE L0000-58 "Environmental Management System" Specifications
- Approval of the CFE Corporate Quality Assurance Manual
- Formulation of the Procedure for Qualifying and Certifying Quality Assurance Auditors
- Conduct of Quality Audits in the Various Work Centers
- Quality Audits of Central Offices to Verify "Turnkey" Projects (Supplier-leader, Electrical-Mechanical Assembly, Storage and Entry into Service)
- CFE Supply Quality Assurance Program

Environmental Impacts Module

- Creation of Social Development and Environmental Protection Offices
- Development of a Culture of Conservation and Efficient Energy Use
- Evaluation, Preservation and Environmental Cleanup Programs
- Respect for Communities
- Facilities Rehabilitation and Modernization
- CFE Contributions to Developing a Culture of Quality in Mexico Through:
  a) Supplier Development
  b) Standards Formulation
  c) Support and Assistance to Governmental Agencies
  d) Collaboration with Educational and Research Institutions

Results Module

- Creation of Results Centers
- CFE Management Indicators
- Performance Assessment
- Work Climate
- First Institutional Meeting on Total Quality
- Regional Meetings on Total Quality (some CFE areas)

CFE 1997 Total Quality Model

Based on the identification of opportunities for improvement, in the arena covered by the CFE Strategic Planning Module—and particularly as regards Strategic Planning for Quality—changes were made in the module's content and the "Strategic Plan for Quality at CFE" was updated.

CFE 1998 Total Quality Model

On the basis of analysis of international Quality Assurance standards (ISO 9000), Environmental Management (ISO 14001) and Management of Occupational Safety (BS8800), as well as compatibility among these standards and worldwide trends, the Unified System of Quality Management, Environmental Protection, Industrial Safety and Process Improvement was incorporated.

CFE 1999 Total Quality Model

The Human Resources Module was given a new orientation to emphasize personnel development with a focus on quality. In addition, the scope of the Information and Analysis Module was expanded to integrate the Information Management System. Furthermore, emphasis was placed on actions geared toward improving technical and administrative processes.

CFE 2000 Total Quality Model

Owing to the progress achieved by the various areas in their quality processes, CFE determined that it was advantageous to link the Institutional Total Quality Program with the CFE Modernization Program beginning in 2000. This Model is shown in the following page:

Institutional Total Quality Program 2000

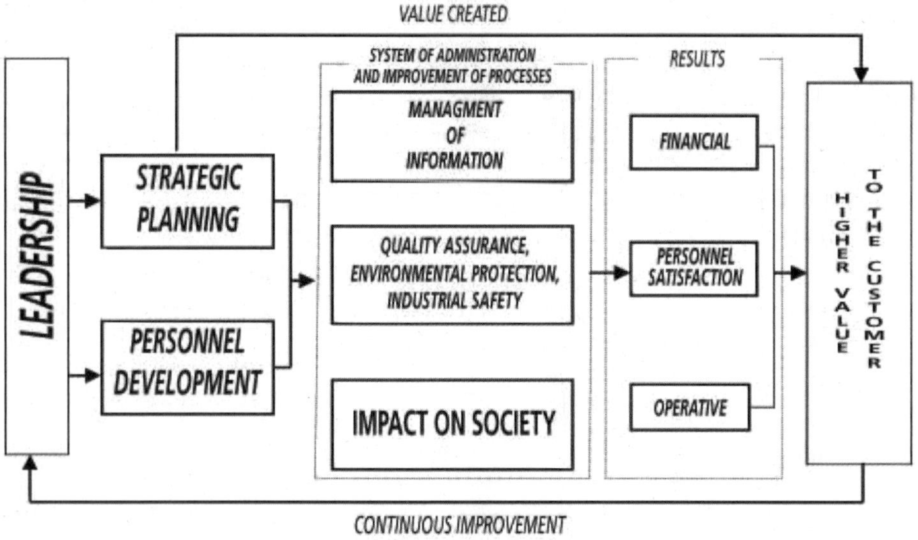

After the CFE's Internal Control Office had analyzed the purposes of the Institutional Total Quality Program and owing to their compatibility because of their focus on preventive action and continuous improvement in the quality of internal services and electric energy services, on August 11, 2000, the CFE decided to integrate the Services Improvement Program and the Program for Transparency in Public Management with the Quality Improvement Program's coordinators and to incorporate the activities assigned to them into their work programs.

CFE 2001 Total Quality Model

In light of the evaluation of the CFE's Total Quality Process and the progress and trends in the environment toward the development of regimes for information, innovation and intellectual capital as fundamental elements on which world-class organizations base their strategies for competitiveness, the CFE Total Quality Model (Management by

Quality and Competitiveness) was modified by incorporating the Management System for Intellectual Capital and Competitive Technological Intelligence.

Model for Management by Quality and Competitiveness

In 2003 and in order to consolidate the implementation of the guidelines for Quality, Modernization and Competitiveness, CFE proceeded to again update the Institutional Quality Program, which will evolve substantially in order to promote the Institution in order to position it as a highly competitive organization. Thus, today they are evolving into an ***Institutional Quality and Competitiveness Program***.

The substantive objective of **the *Institutional Quality and Competitiveness Program*** is to increase productivity and competitiveness with the participation of all work centers. For this purpose, the following activities are emphasized:

- Implementation of the Comprehensive System for Quality Management, Environmental Protection and Industrial Security;

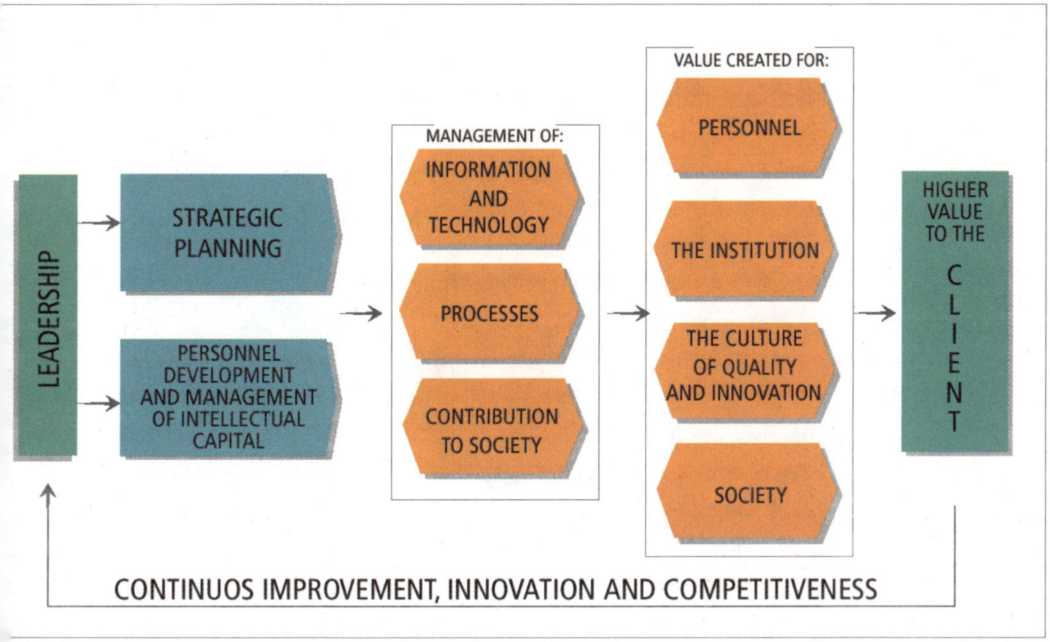

- Development of personnel and consolidation of Intellectual Capital Management;
- Implementation of the Technological Management Model and the promotion of development and implementation of projects for innovation and technological development;
- Use of indicators to measure the performance of service and of work centers; and
- Maintenance of strategies for continuous improvement, innovation and technological development.

In this new stage it is important to stress the active and determined participation of all personnel and the impetus given to development of technology and intellectual capital as the fundamental cornerstones of modernization and innovation in the Institution's processes and services.

2. Certification of the Management System for Quality, Environmental Protection and Industrial Safety

Within the framework of the CFE Institutional Total Quality Program, March 19, 1992 marked the beginning of the strategy to promote the Quality Assurance System with a view to guaranteeing the quality of facilities, processes and electric energy service, and to demonstrating to society that its operations are reliable.

To this end, in May 1993, the Corporate Quality Assurance Manual was issued, which outlines the CFE's Assurance policies. This document has been through four cycles of improvement.

The fourth revision of the Corporate Manual incorporated the processes of Environmental Protection and Industrial Safety. This enabled the CFE to have a Comprehensive System for more effective administration, while it is maintaining its focus and the principle of quality through continuous improvement.

During 2002, the fifth and last revision of the Corporate Manual of the Quality Management, Environmental Protection and Industrial Security System was made in order to incorporate the elements of the

ISO 9001:2000 Standard and thus bring up to date the directives for development of systems in the Institution's work centers.

The certification of Quality Systems officially began in 1997. Ten work centers were the first to receive certification, and later commitments were established for the 1998/2003 period. These commitments were met and exceeded as shown below:

Year	1997	1998	1999	2000	2001	2002	2003
Certified Centers	10	42	50	82	74	40	150

In 2003, the CFE made the commitment to certify the main work centers and its high-impact processes, which were: Generation, Distribution, Construction, Transmission, Control, Administration, Financial, Programming and Technical, achieving 100 percent certification, and more of the 353 centers previously identified in accordance with the ISO 9001:2000 international standard.

In 1998 three generation centers obtained ISO 14001 certification, and there has been a noteworthy increase in subsequent years:

Year	1998	1999	2000	2001	2002	2003	2004
No. of Centers	3	9	13	5	25	68	4

As regards Workplace Safety and Health, it is noteworthy that the first organization to obtain the corresponding certification at the national level was a CFE work area—the Equipment and Materials Testing Laboratory: (LAMEM). Since 2001, 32 work centers have obtained certification, as shown below:

Year	2001	2002	2003
No. of Centers	1	11	20

Work centers qualify and certify their auditing personnel for systems of quality, environmental protection and industrial safety, and they are also certified in systems in accordance with the NMXCC-9001-2000, NMX-SAA-001-200 AND NMX-SAST-001-IMNC-2000 standards.

2.1 Institutional Meetings on Total Quality

Beginning in 1994, the CFE adopted a strategy of holding Institutional Meetings on Quality with a view to sharing among the various areas of our Institution the experiences, results, systems, success stories, and best practices with regard to Quality, Environmental Protection, Workplace Safety and Health, Labor Competitiveness, Leadership, Customer Service, Strategic Planning, Process Improvement, Information Technologies, Intellectual Capital, Continuous Improvement, Auditing, and Technological Innovation and Development, among other subjects.

Total Quality Program results have been described at nine ***Institutional Meetings on Total Quality*** held in the cities of Veracruz, Manzanillo, Merida (twice), Monterrey, Acapulco, and Mexico City (three times).

2.2 CFE Quality Award

In 1996 the CFE Quality Award was created with the goal of promoting and recognizing those work centers using best practices in implementing their Total Quality Process.

Year	No. of Winners
1996	2
1997	4
1998	3
1999	3
2000	5
2001	5
2002	3
2003	7

2.3 CFE Award for Innovation and Technological Development

This award seeks to encourage individuals and work groups that use the best practices and the technological development associated with improvement and the creation of value in processes and services that impact customer satisfaction and the management indicators that the CFE uses within the context of the Institutional Program for Quality and Competitiveness. In 2003, the General Directorate issued the first CFE Award for Innovation and Technological Development. At that time, 11 centers received the award, which was presented during the Institutional Meeting on Quality held November 2 to 6, 2003, in Mexico City.

2.4 Assessment of the Total Quality Process

As part of continuous improvement, in 2000 the CFE instituted the strategy of assessing the level of maturity (implementation on the basis of 1,000 points) of its Total Quality Process. At that time, a score of 232

Implementation Points

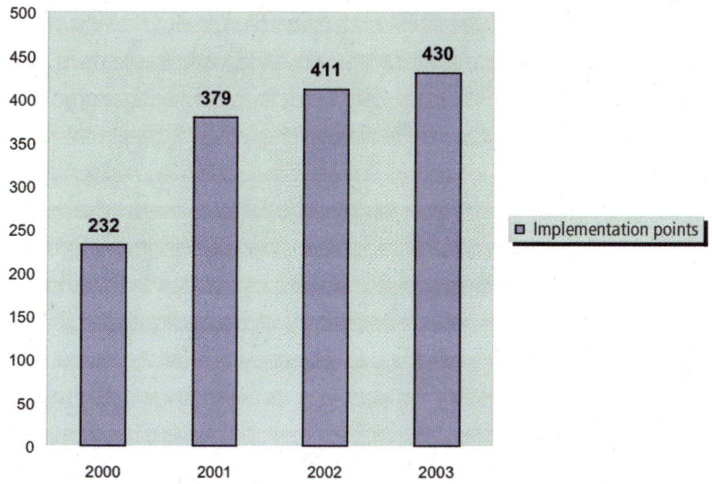

points was obtained and existing areas of opportunity were identified for each of the modules. This enabled various work centers to set up the actions necessary for promoting their implementation on a continuous and ongoing basis. These assessments have been conducted year after year as is shown on the previous page.

2.5 Institutional Metrology System

IN 1994, the CFE Institutional Metrology System (SIMCFE) was launched with the goal of providing metrology services to all work centers that needed them, giving them assistance, training and assurance in measurement that enabled them to improve the knowledge they already had about metrics. Another basic goal was to strengthen those substantive processes in order to operate at high levels of reliability, maintainability and availability.

The SIMCFE grew out of the desires of a group of people who wanted to unify the measurement methods used in the CFE. Its original name, the Institutional Calibration and Standarization System (SICH) makes this clear. The name was later changed to the Metrological System for the Electric Power Sector (SIMESE), which sought to involve the entire electric power sector. Its name is now CFE Institutional Metrology System, which has the form we know today.

Although they have achieved conformance at different times, there are now 16 laboratories in compliance with the System, and others are remedying *nonconforming items* in order to obtain their full status. Most have appropriate facilities, which they either remodeled or built new.

The models and instruments they use enable them to calibrate the majority of the equipment found within their sphere of activity (20,000 instruments calibrated in 2003).

3. Results

After several years in operation using the strategies set each year, and with the leadership shown and our employees' effort and commitment, the CFE's Quality Process can now report the following results:

Action	Results Achieved
Centers with ISO 9001:2000 Certification (Quality Management Systems)	449 principal centers
Certified High-impact Processes (ISO 9001:2000)	9 processes at 100 percent, which are: Generation, Transmission, Control, Construction, Distribution, Administration, Financial, Programming and Technical
Centers with ISO 14001 standard (Environmental Management Systems) certification	127 centers, which includes 34 General Construction offices
Centers with Mexican Standard NMXSAST-001 (Management System, the first certification for Workplace Safety and Health)	32 centers. The CFE obtained certification of a center at national level
Clean Industry certification	16 generation centers obtained the corresponding certification from the Federal Environmental Protection Attorney's Office
CFE Quality Award	32 areas have earned this award as of 2003
CFE Award for Innovation and Technological Development	11 work centers received this award when it was first granted (2003)
State Quality Awards	From 1998 to date, 30 areas of our Institution have earned various awards granted by the states
INNOVA Recognition Award	3 winners of the award to date

Action	Results Achieved
INTRAGOB Recognition for Quality	6 work centers received this award in 2002, the first year it was awarded, 5 CFE areas have received it.
National Quality Award	4 to date
Level of Maturity of the Total Quality Process	430 implementation points as of 2003

4. Next Steps

Within the framework of the Ninth Institutional Meeting on Total Quality, the Director General established strategies with a view to making the CFE a World-Class Federal Government Entity. These strategies are summarized below:

- To develop and implement six Sigma methodology in order to reduce variability in processes, thereby increasing the Institution's financial indicators.
- To promote technological innovation and development in the processes and services we provide.
- To continue training and educating high-performance personnel who are leaders in their disciplines and processes.
- To maintain and improve work center performance through use of the ISO 9001:2000 Quality Management System.
- To continue work center certification in Environmental Management and Workplace Safety and Health Management Systems consistent with the Mexican NMX-SAA-14001-IMNC-2002 and NMX-SAST-001-IMNC-2000 standards, respectively, for 2004-2006.
- To continue **comprehensive** certification of the Systems for Quality Management, Environmental Protection and Workplace Safety and Health as a single unified system.
- To establish an EMA **accreditation** program for secondary metrology laboratories.

- To begin the development, operation and accreditation of **tertiary metrology laboratories.**

Ministry of Communications and Transportation (SCT)

Continuous Improvement: an Ongoing Process

To meet the Federal Government's objectives and goals, which are set forth in the Presidential Agenda for Good Government, the Ministry of Communications and Transportation is implementing the SCT Quality Model in each of its areas.

This Model aims to meet customer needs and expectations and to favorably impact society, generating information that makes it possible to incorporate continuous improvement.

Among the concepts that comprise the Model are those known as Process Management and Improvement, whose tools are based on the ISO 9001:2000 standard, in which the design, implementation and development of systems for quality is outlined.

For the Ministry of Communications and Transportation to achieve certification in both centralized SCT central offices and SCT Centers, phases were defined that range from securing senior management commitment, to implementing systems for quality management, to using external audits applying international standards to accredit the Institution's services.

Establishing Quality Committees

The SCT formed the Quality Management Committee, which assigns responsibilities to each of its members and is also charged with reporting periodically on progress in this arena.

In order to integrate the various levels of the Ministry, the SCT created a change network made up of the assigned Coordinators, Shared Responsibility Partners and Quality Facilitators, whose levels within the organization correspond to General Directors, Area Directors, Assistant Directors and Department Heads.

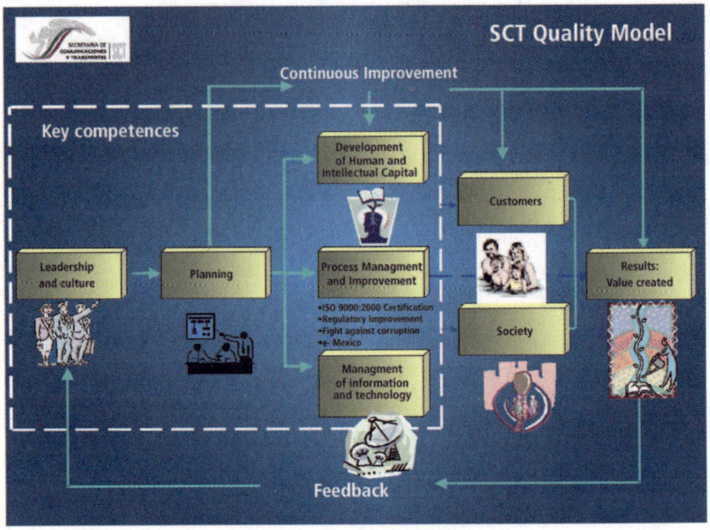

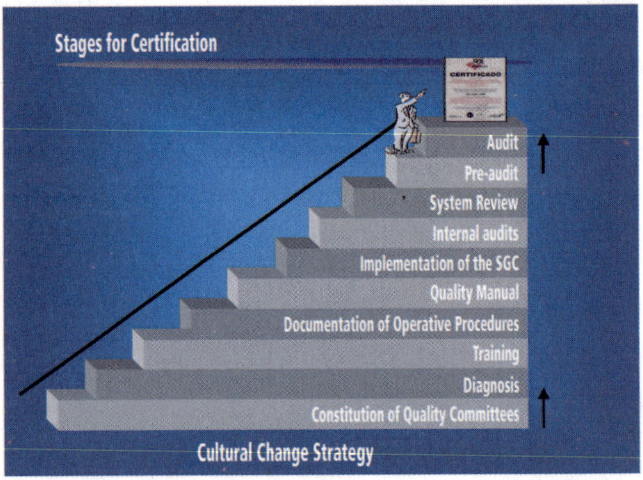

Quality Committees were officially appointed in each of the Ministry's branches, for the Office of the Chief Administrative Officer and Offices of General Coordination and Management, in order to communicate decisions made with regard to quality to the entire organization.

A work plan was drawn up for certification of key processes in centralized Areas and SCT Centers, and Quality Policy and Objectives were also defined.

Analysis

The SCT conducted a study of the existing organizational manuals and subsequently revised their correlation with the functional structure at the appropriate time. Workshops were held to identify the Institution's strengths, weaknesses, opportunities and threats, which, together with drawing up Input-Supplier, Service-Client matrices, identified and mapped the Ministry's processes in a general manner.

As a result, about 250 processes were identified within the Ministry, and high priority was given to those which, because of their high impact on serving the public, would have transparency and profitability as critical for their certification. Therefore, one of the first actions was to select 42 processes, 37 of which were in centralized areas, including the Internal Control Office, and 5 processes that are common to the 31 SCT Centers throughout the country.

Training

To establish a training system that ensures the existence of a highly qualified team for the development and operation of a quality management system, three training blocks were designed, whose content was as follows:

First Block

- Change management and adoption of a new culture of service quality
- Development and implementation of a Quality Management System
- Fundamentals and interpretation of a set of ISO 9000 standards

Second Block

- Elaboration of the documentation required by said standards
- Measurement, analysis and process improvement

Third Block

- Training for internal quality auditors

Operating Documentation and Procedures

The SCT validated the 42 processes identified by the people in charge of the various areas, and general guidelines were established for their documentation. By the same token, normative elements (such as laws, regulations and forms) were identified, their scope was defined and the required procedures were formulated in accordance with the ISO 9000:2000 standard.

With the foregoing, the monitoring and improvement of the Quality System was launched by making a comparison and finding consistency between "what we say is done and what is actually done."

Quality Manual

A revision of the Institutional Quality Manual was done, both for centralized areas and for the SCT Centers. The revised manual is made up of three major sections:

1. Information regarding the Ministry's duties, which gives a brief description of its structure and presents the definition of its mission, vision, policy and quality objectives.

2. Explanation of the structure of the SCT Quality Committee and the functioning of the system at its various levels of activity.

3. Scope of the quality management system. This details the areas in which it is operative and the applicable clauses of the standard for

the system's processes and procedures, as well as the way they interact.

Implementing the Quality Management System

In order to administer the Quality Management System in a comprehensive way, eight institutional procedures were developed, such as Senior Management Review, Internal Audits, Document Control, Records Control, Non conforming Product, Preventive and Corrective Action, Continuous Improvement and Customer Satisfaction Measurement. These procedures apply to the various administrative units involved in the Quality System.

For each of the operational processes, performance indicators and goals were set to measure their effectiveness through the process charts and to contribute achieving the Institution's quality objectives.

Internal Audits

To evaluate the degree of implementation of the SCT Quality System, internal audits were planned on a periodic basis, whose internal objectives were the documented review of processes and the comprehensive review of the system. Furthermore, cross-audits were conducted between the various areas, which made it possible to train more than 300 internal auditors on site and to consolidate the quality management system by identifying preventive and corrective actions and improvement activities.

Pre-Audits and Certification Audits

Certifying organizations were contracted in order to obtain an objective analysis of the Quality Management System and the certification of the 37 processes defined for centralized areas and the five shared processes for the SCT Centers.

This analysis consisted of a documentary review in accordance with compliance with the ISO 9001:2000 standard requirements, which resulted in these certifying organizations agreeing that SCT had a Quality Management System that could be audited.

The Quality Pre-Audit and certification Audit identified a group of *nonconforming items*, which were resolved by presenting to the certifying organizations a Plan of Corrective Actions to obtain certification for the Ministry of Communications and Transportation.

Results Obtained

In completing these steps, the Ministry of Communications and Transportation has received international recognition, and the Ministry has a comprehensive and innovative Quality Management System within the Federal Government.

Similarly, it has been called "the most important Quality Management System in Ibero-America," as reflected in three certificates described as follows:

- Certification at the central level that includes the Office of the Minister, the three Under Ministries of Infrastructure, Communications and Transportation; the Office of the Chief Administrative Officer, and the Coordination Office for Ports and the Merchant Marine.
- Certification under the multi-site Modality, which includes the Coordination Office for Planning and SCT Centers and the 31 SCT Centers throughout Mexico.
- Certification of the SCT Internal Control Office.
  The System in central areas includes a total of 37 certified processes and the participation of about 1,000 public officials, while for SCT Centers there are 5 processes which are common to all, which makes a total of 155 certified processes that directly involve about 3,500 public servants.

Benefits

The benefits of having a Comprehensive Quality Management System are reflected in the greater involvement of the organization in having a system of communications that permeates all levels and fosters teamwork through the quality circles in which employees have a clear role that they fulfill within the System.

Achieving this recognition is a result of the active participation of the SCT Quality Committee, chaired by the Minister, whose members are responsible for improving quality, efficiency and transparency in the services they provide.

> Today certification has been granted for the issuance of licenses for the various modes of transportation, among other processes. For example, in the case of Federal Passenger Transportation licenses, the time required for issuance has been significantly reduced from two days to two hours, which benefits more than 450,000 licensees annually.
>
> Similarly, air traffic control services have been certified. It is worth pointing out that Mexico is the second country worldwide to obtain this certification.

In the near term, the SCT seeks to maintain the system showing improvement in the processes that have been certified, to incorporate new processes that will make it possible to broaden the scope of certification, and to gain the commitment of chambers of commerce and trade associations so that through a variety of agreements the services the Ministry offers can be improved.

> In addition, the following have been certified in sector-specific entities:

Administrative Unit	Processes
Airports and Auxiliary Services (ASA)	1 Process at the Fuel Stations in Merida, Villahermosa and Oaxaca
Federal Toll Highways and Bridges and Related Services (CAPUFE)	15 Processes certified
Integral Port Administrations (API)	5 Processes – Use of port infrastructure – Partial assignments of rights – Provision of port services – Handling – Related services
Trust for National Merchant Marine Personnel Education and Training (FIDENA)	26 Processes in General Offices 17 Processes in Nautical Schools (Tampico, Veracruz and Mazatlan) 6 Processes on the Training Ship.
Mexican Transportation Institute (IMT)	Laboratory Accreditation: Metal Assays and Construction Calibration.
Mexican Air Space Navigation Services (SENEAM)	1 Process for Air Transportation Control Services in the Mexico Area Terminal.

It is important to note that the greatest challenge is not obtaining a certification, but rather taking the responsibility for using these tools and this knowledge to confer dignity on the work of public servants through a work culture based on quality.

Nacional Financiera (NAFIN)

Strategy for Institutional Transformation and Customer Focus

1. Background

One of the main functions of NAFIN is to support Mexico's small and medium-sized businesses by granting credit, acting as a second tier bank. This financing is typically distributed through a network of Bank and Non-bank Financial Intermediaries.

Nacional Financiera seeks to strengthen businesses and their owners through training and technical assistance products and services that further the professional and institutional development of the nation's business activity.

The Institution is also the administrator of resources granted to the various Federal Government entities and agencies so that through its role as a financial agent it can ensure their proper use in sectoral development programs.

By the same token, it contributes to developing and strengthening financial markets, since it operates in markets for foreign exchange, capital and money, as well as their derivatives.

The Institution ran the risk of becoming inoperable, since the minimum level of capitalization required for its operation was 8 percent and in the year 2000 it was at a level of 6.85 percent

2. Problems in 2000

At the beginning of this Administration, an organizational study of the Institution was conducted that made it possible to bring into focus NAFIN's weaknesses with regard to its structure, its strategic focus and its organizational culture which had a negative impact on service provided to its customers and on results.

As a consequence of the foregoing, the following figures were identified:

- Support to businesses fell by 89 percent: in 1994 support was provided to 142,210 businesses, and in the year 2000, to only 15,722.
- The amount of credit extended to the private sector fell by 90 percent, representing a net loss in 2000 of 4.246 billion pesos.
- Recurring losses since 1994, which in the year 2000 generated a net loss of 4.246 billion pesos.

This financial deterioration was caused primarily by the following factors:

- Recurring crises over the past 25 years
- Lack of Strategic Planning
- Absence of a clear mandate and customer focus
- Lack of management autonomy with appropriate administrative entities
- Focus on fulfilling regulatory requirements, generating bureaucracy in processes and their operational inefficiency.

As a direct result of these problems, the Institution ran the risk of becoming inoperable, since the minimum level of capitalization required for its operation was 8 percent and in the year 2000 it was at a level of 6.85 percent.

As part of this Administration's goals, the challenge of serving 400,000 businesses by the year 2006 was set. However, reversing the negative trend in NAFINS's financial condition and addressing the problems identified implied making a clear decision regarding the strategy that should be adopted to reorient the Institution's direction.

3. Strategy for Institutional Transformation

Introduction

The strategy was based on the idea of understanding the needs of small and medium-sized enterprises, and of finding within the international environment the best practices for addressing those needs. These practices were compared and the necessary changes were established within the Institution so that, through a process of innovation and use of the available cutting-edge technologies, they could be implemented in a rational, orderly way consistent with a specific mission: to meet our customers' needs.

> The Strategy for Transformation is defined as the guiding principle that enables us to coordinate all the organization's structural, operational, technological and human elements toward the

> same goal: to meet our customers' needs. Furthermore, the transformation strategy is the means for incorporating into the organization the Good Government Agenda of the Office of the Presidency of Mexico, the INTRAGOB Quality Management Model and the application of quality standards such as ISO 9000.

The Strategy for Transformation addresses each and every one of the elements of quality in the current Federal Administration, as well as those of the Institution itself, creating a synergy between all of these elements, which, in turn, creates a model that is comprehensive and made up of interdependent components (fig. 1).

The Strategy for Transformation is applied to all of the Institution's strategic, human, structural and operational elements, using well-defined steps and with clear results for each of its phases (fig. 2). This approach makes it possible to align these elements of the Institution with the object of our mission: our customers. The clarity of the mis-

Figure 1. Comprehensive Relation of the Strategy

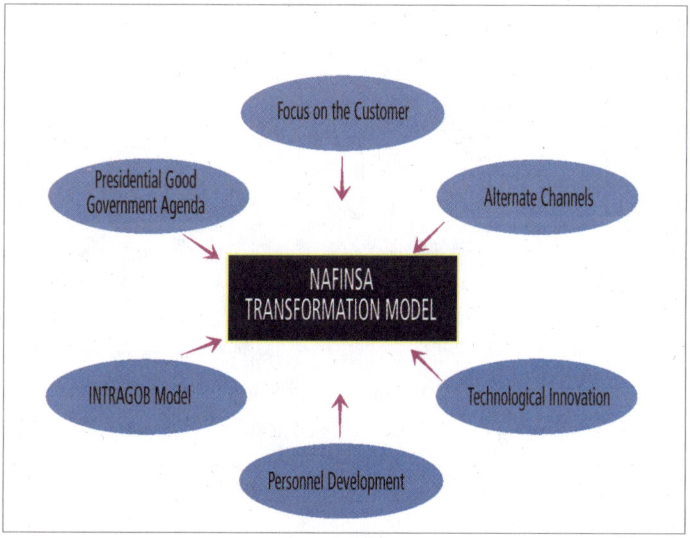

Figure 2. Organizational Alignment

sion enables us to establish consistent courses of action and operations focused on a common purpose for each of the Institution's organizational elements.

The Strategy's Operational Planning

A fundamental part of the strategy is its application to the processes that comprise *Nacional Financiera*'s daily operations. To accomplish this, a comprehensive approach was established that provides for redesigning processes through analysis of the various steps involved in them, aligning the administrative structures to the specific requirements of managing these processes, incorporating quality elements defined in the INTRAGOB Model and the ISO 9000 standard, and the subsequent external certification of these processes. The foregoing ensures that all elements within *Nacional Financiera* are focused on a single goal: meeting the needs of our customers.

4. Results

As a result of implementing the strategy, *Nacional Financiera* has obtained tangible and sustainable benefits. In order to assess its impact on the parameters common to the entire Federal Public Administration, its effects are shown below relative to the strategies of the Presidential Good Government Agenda.

Transparency in Management

The honest and transparent work of *Nacional Financiera*'s public servants is also a subject addressed by the Strategy for Transformation. Thus, committed leadership at all levels of the organization creates a culture of quality that promotes honesty and transparency.

All *Nacional Financiera* employees and officers know and apply the Federal Government Code of Ethics.

Attention to citizen complaints with regard to acts related to corruption at any level is also a very important element for measuring citizen perceptions. Defining the source of complaints, as well as providing the relevant legal monitoring, is the responsibility of the Internal Control Office (OIC). In order to ensure the correct functioning of OIC activities, the Institution decided to also certify the OIC under ISO 9001:2000 standards and, in turn, its process forms part of the systems of our INTRAGOB Model.

Throughout the current Administration, no complaints of corruption have been received through the channels provided by the OIC to capture and address these complaints.

Citizens also participate directly in the supervision of development programs for Small and Medium Enterprises through the Consultation Councils, which are bodies for orientation, promotion and supervision. They have been established in Mexico's 32 states, and there is one in California, USA. The Councils are made up of a minimum of five representatives of commercial, industrial and service sectors, as well as the Economic Development secretaries of each entity.

Professionalization of Personnel

Human Resources Planning. The Strategy for Transformation has made it possible to guide the action of employees in a manner consistent with achieving full customer satisfaction. This is not a casual process, but rather springs from the very nature of the strategy. Human resources planning is determined through a process of comprehensive education, as shown in figure 3.

Figure 3. Comprehensive Training Process

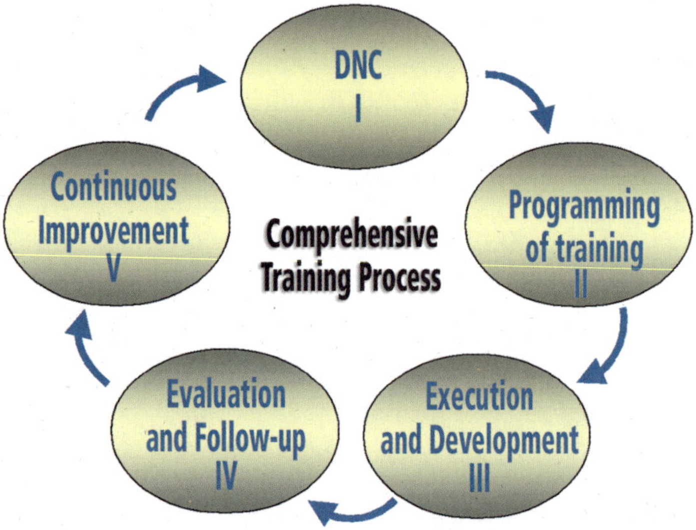

NAFIN has a Personnel Development System that makes it possible to design, develop, and implement training programs that are aligned with the Institution's strategic objectives and contribute to professional and personal development by building abilities, knowledge, skills, attitudes and new practices that facilitate the achievement of business results.

For development of abilities, a model has been implemented that identifies key competencies and critical personnel training needs in order to design a development program that contributes to performance improvement and achievement of goals. Among the model's benefits are that it:

- Identifies the abilities that processes require
- Creates a comprehensive approach to personnel development
- Clarifies improvements in performance
- Measures benefits more objectively
- More clearly focuses on improving abilities
- Improves the selection of development plans

The Strategy for Transformation has established three types of competencies that employees must develop in institutional, area and job dimensions. On the basis of the level of mastery in which the people involved in these processes find themselves, training and abilities development programs—krown as Detection of Competency Needs (DNC)—are determined.

A fundamental element for measuring the degree of satisfaction of human talent are assessments of the work climate which make it possible to define the degree of employee satisfaction with the immediate work environment. Through personnel performance assessment, their contribution to planned objectives is measured against established group and individual objectives and goals.

Quality

As has been stated, the Strategy for Transformation is designed to satisfy the needs of our customers. It is therefore of fundamental importance to understand their needs and their level of satisfaction with the services *Nacional Financiera* offers. During 2002, through its commercial intelligence system, the principal needs of customers were defined.

This information is vital for the design of products and services appropriate for satisfying these needs. In order to "close the circle" that begins with understanding customer needs, we defined how their satisfaction would be measured annually. This measurement is done through the Customer Service Center, which conducts a telephone survey. Figure 4 shows some of the results obtained from the survey conducted in May 2003.

Figure 4. Results of the Customer Satisfaction Survey

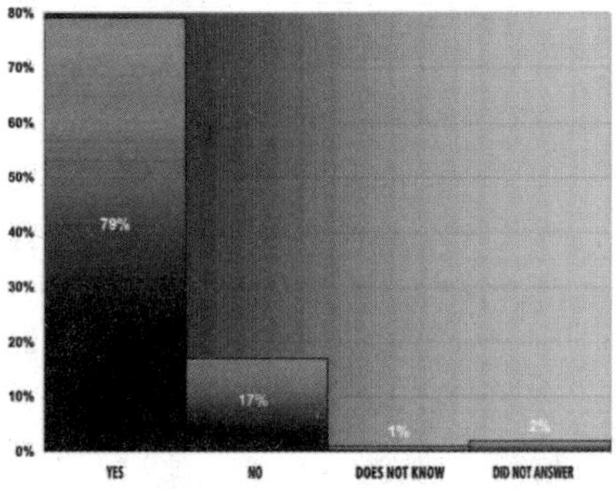

NAFIN support has enabled them to maintain jobs

NAFIN support has enabled them to increse their sales

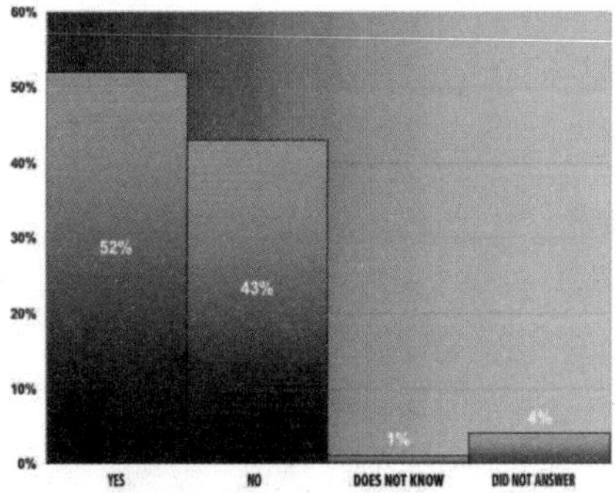

A fundamental aspect for applying the strategy is process redesign. The Strategy for Transformation established clear guidelines for process redesign, taking into account within its study guidelines that the macro-processes and the processes that comprise them should fulfill the following conditions:

- That they are aligned with NAFIN's mission and customer needs

- That they avoid duplication
- That they add value
- That they could be subcontracted by third parties
- That they represent a significant reduction in the cycle of processes

The progress obtained in redesign are shown in figure 5.

Figure 5. Progress in Processes Redesign

Product	Progress
Operations Manuals	100%
Work Flows	100%
Automation Processes	100%
Workloads	100%
Service Levels	100%
Management Indicators	100%

Quality Assurance/Certification System ISO 9001:2000

The Strategy for Transformation incorporates within its structure the requirements established in the ISO 9001:2000 quality standard as part of its methodology for implementation within the Institution's substantive processes.

From the institutional inventory of macro-processes, we have managed to achieve 100 percent certification. This is a major achievement, since it has been accomplished ahead of the President's schedule, which made a commitment to reaching the goal by 2006.

Electronic Strategy

Since 2001, the use of information technology to benefit customers has been one of the most important directives within the Strategy for Transformation. This philosophy of comprehensive attention to electronics is reflected in specific actions, which have included the conversion of products and services to electronic systems with outputs to portals where the customer can interactively conduct transactions rapidly, securely and efficiently. Portal operation results are compared to other systems worldwide in figure 6.

Figure 6. World Ranking of Development Internet Sites at World Level, after SBA

Worldwide	Ranking of Sites
SBA (USA)	3,214
NAFIN	43,159
KFW (Germany)	61,308
BNDES (Brazil)	69,546
BDC (Canada)	70,260
Pymarket (Spain)	87,401
CORFO (Chile)	123,479
ICO (Spain)	152,118
Mip/me (LA Regional)	331,258
Alpymes (LA Regional)	414,313

We are the second most important site for Development Banks worldwide, after SBA.

The above has made it possible to increase the supply of services and Internet transactions, with the results shown in figure 7.

Figure 7. Evolution of Electronic Services

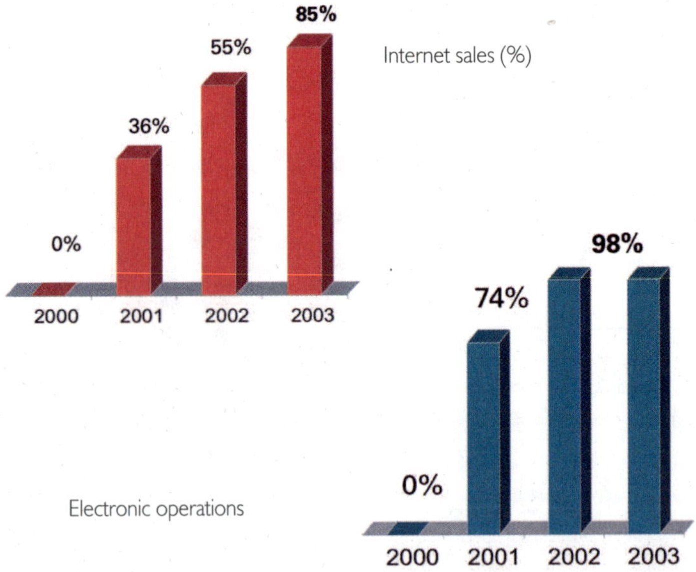

In addition, programs and projects needed for the conversion to electronic systems have been established to achieve the automation of 94 percent of processes through the development of informatics systems by the end of 2004 (fig. 8).

Figure 8. Evolution of Process Automation

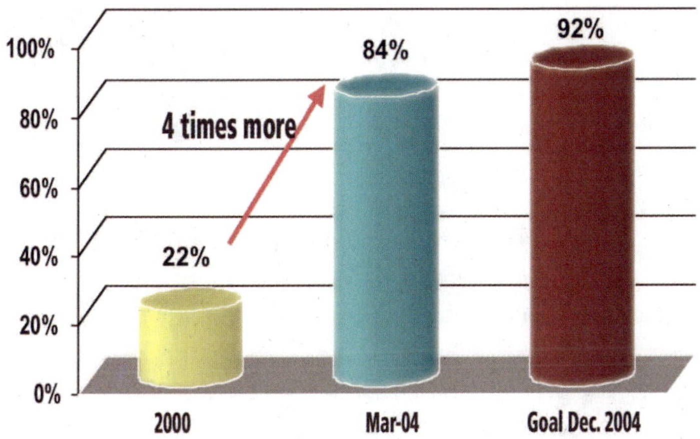

Deregulation

The Strategy for Transformation has created efforts which, within a framework of legal and operational certainty, have reduced the regulatory documentation involved in processes. This task began with process redesign, in which we clearly defined the minimum legal and operational regulations necessary to guarantee that products and services comply with customer requirements, as well as those defined by the authorities as mandatory.

In order to make the documentation of processes consistent, these have been edited in line with a uniform "Documentation Standard" which incorporates within its structure the description of the regulations applicable for carrying out the processes.

Application of this documentation standard has made it possible to reduce the number of pages of documentation by 74 percent, and the number of pages of regulations that apply to the operation have dropped from 24,000 to just 6,000 pages.

Another outstanding aspect is the editing of a single manual which brings together all the policies applicable to Human Resources, Material Resources, Information Technology and Expenditures, a manual now considered a best practice in the governmental sector.

One palpable result of this deregulation is the ease with which customer requests can be processed. The huge growth in electronic credit would not have been possible if the laws and policies in force had not been changed with regard to extending, maintaining and recovering credit with a view to increasing the legal and operational certainty of transactions, as mentioned previously.

NAFIN has conducted major efforts that are linked to and make possible the fulfillment of the objectives of the Presidential Good Government Agenda. In particular, in the case of *deregulated Government,* it is noteworthy that under the Strategy for Transformation, activities have been undertaken that support the strategy and make up a substantial part of the work done to achieve the improvement and optimization of the Institution's operations, with a clear focus on satisfying customer needs.

Savings

The Strategy for Transformation is based on the model of Business Profitability, defined within the Institution for the systematic evaluation of projects to meet new Operational, Organization and Technological requirements. This model offers a Shielding Mechanism that insures that the changes needed are solidly oriented toward fulfilling the Institution's Mission.

It bears mentioning that technology—owing to its relevance within the Strategy for Transformation—includes an evaluation system called Strategic Technology Planning (PET). This system makes it possible to evaluate the financial impact of any technological requirement on the business and its benefit for customers. Strategic Technology Planning has already been adopted as the standard in the Federal Government.

This has made it possible to shrink the Institution's structure and infrastructure, resulting in revenue of approximately 500 million pesos from the sale of real estate owing to the application of international standards for the use of space and computer equipment. Additional savings of 184 million pesos were obtained in associated current expenditures, the equivalent of 14 percent of the budget.

Another major savings has been achieved through the alignment of staffing with our operating model's current structures (fig. 9).

Figure 9. Reduction in Regular Staff

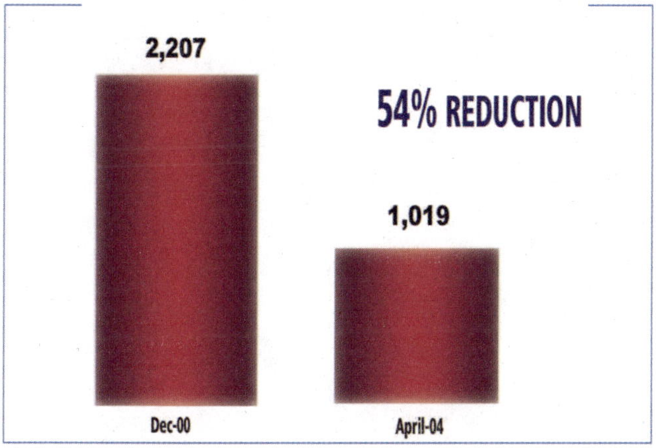

Furthermore, benefits for citizens have been achieved, since this has influenced the intermediation rates that the Mexican Banking System charges in general in models for financial resources delivery similar to those of NAFIN, with the reduction from TTIE+14 to TTIE+4 [TTIE: Interbank Balance Interest Rate]. This is directly attributable to the implementation of the strategy in benefit not only of our customers, but also of all small and medium-sized enterprises that use the banking system.

The Impact Made

As a comprehensive effort that extends throughout the Institution, the Strategy for Transformation has generated economic benefits in the Institution's operations and, above all, for its customers. Some of these benefits are outlined below.

5. Economic Benefits

Structures

- Fifty-two percent reduction in Total Staff from December 2000 to July 2003.

Organizational Standards

- The number of Organizational Levels has been reduced from 8/9 in 2000 to 45 in 2003.
- The Manager-to-Employee ratio changed from an average of one manager out of every two employees to one manager out of every six employees.
- The ratio of Business Area to Administrative employees changed from one-to-one to two-to-one.
- Human resources standards such as the following were established:
    - Secretarial Pool.
    - Pool of chauffeurs and messengers.

Productivity

- By the end of 2003, the loan volume per employee had increased more than elevenfold, rising from 8.6 million pesos to 98.4 million pesos per employee.
- The number of businesses served per employee had grown more than sixtyfold as of the end of 2003. In 2000, eight businesses were served per employee and 441 in 2003.

Material Resources

- In the year 2000, NAFIN offices occupied 71,247 m^2; in 2003 only 36,899 m^2 were needed, the equivalent of a 48 percent reduction.
- As of 2003, revenue from the sale of real estate had amounted to 490 million pesos.
- A new Financial Floor, a new Computer Center and a new Customer Service Call Center were built.
- Budget spending for Security, Real Estate Services and General Expenditures in 2002 was 145 million pesos—10 percent less than the 160 million pesos spent in the year 2000.
- During the same period, the number of security guards was reduced from 150 to 55.

Systems

- *Nafinsa.com* received more than 1 million hits in 2003, six times more than in 2001. Nine out of every ten customers were served by this means. The subjects of greatest interest were financing, entrepreneurial development and the network of businesses.
- In 2001, 7 electronic services were launched; today 26 services are offered electronically, or 52 percent of all those offered by the Institution.
- The informatics budget applied in 2002, which was the equivalent of 79 million pesos, is 39 percent less than the 128 million pesos applied in 2000.

Benefits in Institutional Operation

V. Process Redesign	VI. Process Certification
• 100% of Institution-wide processes were redesigned in 2003 • Processes whose Technological, Operational and Regulatory Structure had been aligned with the Mission of the Institution	• 100% of the Macro-processes were certified under the ISO 9001:2000 Standard • Goal achieved three months ahead of schedule

The Strategy's Financial Impact

Corruption among public officials is commonly cited in most developing countries, as is the indolence of the personnel directly serving citizens, as the major focal point for dissatisfaction with the government. The bureaucratization of public management of services and procedures is also cited as a real shortcoming which generally makes any interaction between citizens and government highly frustrating

The Strategy for Transformation has made it possible to bring about very important changes that have strengthened *Nacional Financiera*'s business indicators. The following graphs show this progress in the Institution's substantive indicators.

Net Profit (millions of pesos)

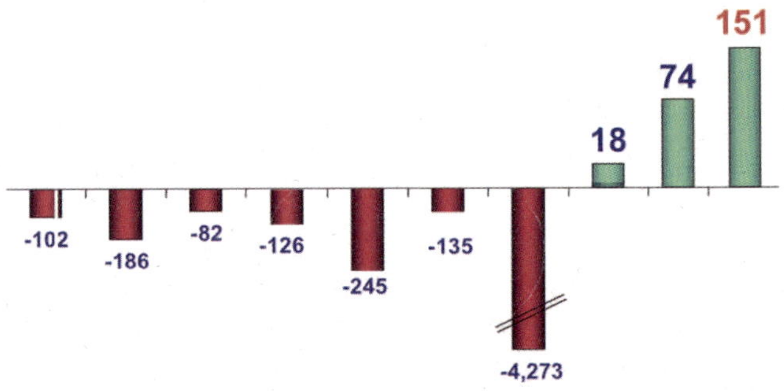

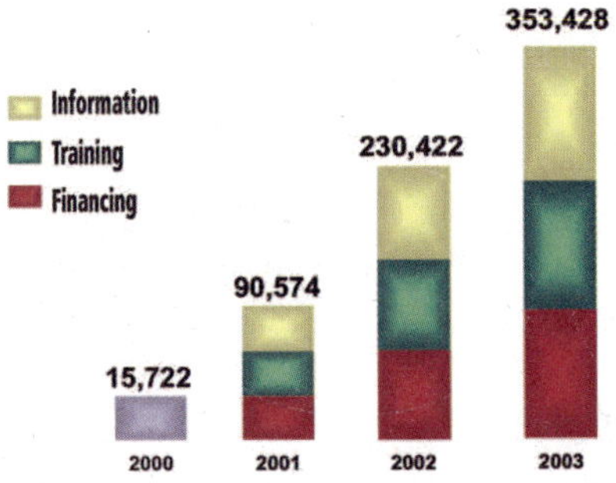

Enterprises Supported

Percentage of Past Due Portafolio

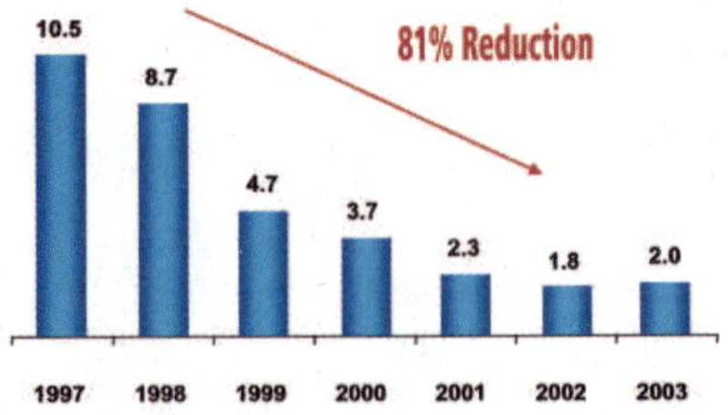

Conclusions

The Strategy for Transformation has made it possible to attack the goals set forth for the development of small and medium-sized enterprises. In the foreseeable future, the current changes may become long-term strategies, which will ensure the ongoing nature of this effort on behalf of *Nacional Financiera*'s customers: small and medium-sized enterprises.

4. International Awards

Ministry of Public Administration (SFP)

The Federal Government's Citizen Portal:
Toward a New, World-Class Model of Online Participation

Winner of the Stockholm Challenge Award

The Stockholm Challenge Award is an international award conferred by the city of Stockholm for the innovative use of Information Technology. It has been conducted since 1994 by Stockholm City Hall in collaboration with the European Commission and its task is to create a platform for the exchange of ideas and experiences, as well as to identify and reward examples of the innovative use of Information Technology in very different fields.

The projects compete in six different areas: electronic government, electronic business, environment, education, health and culture. Attention does not center on technique, but on its possible benefits for users.

Participants include cities, enterprises, organizations, governments, schools, researchers and other project promoters.

An international jury is in charge of rating the projects according to various criteria: degree of innovation, benefit for users, degree of application to other projects and accessibility. The competition rewards projects which, in addition to being innovative and focusing on the user, place importance on local development and are also so novel that they can work as models for other regions, cities and countries.

Around 900 projects from 107 countries in the world participated in the 2004 edition.

1. Innovation in Service Delivery: Can We Count on the Government?

In general, electronic government has become a strategic instrument of major public value when it has a well-defined, specific purpose and a clearly identified focus of attention.

Clearly, the rapid advance in Information and Communication Technologies (ICT) has led to a radical transformation in the behavior and performance of public and private organizations focusing on providing services. Thus, conventionally it is believed that private organizations with this service approach have been more successful and efficient than public agencies in achieving adequate satisfaction levels in users.

This view is consistent with the acknowledgment that public agencies face much more complex challenges in citizen service in comparison with private organizations as regards contact with customers: from the provision of education, health care and public security services, to processing all kinds of regulatory procedures and tax collection; without forgetting the delivery of resources and direct benefits to groups of society that live in conditions of vulnerability, to mention the most visible ones.

In all these cases, the experience of those who need to come into direct, personal contact with some authority or government service is also conditioned by a negative predisposition toward the government's capacity to respond satisfactorily. In general there is a feeling that the government is inward looking rather than looking toward the satisfaction of those who have entrusted it with the governance of the country: citizens and their families.

> Nonetheless, the creation and development of the Federal Government Citizen Portal (*www.gob.mx*) is a case of success in the provision of services to citizens, for reasons that are

worth carefully reviewing in order to appreciate its merits and encouraging scope.

2. The Citizen: the Great Unknown

As has been mentioned, there is a tradition of mistrust and skepticism about the government's effectiveness in dealing with the problems that most afflict citizens, not only in Mexico but in many countries. Suffice it to look at the various international surveys that periodically appear, both those sponsored by intergovernmental agencies and those promoted by private foundations and enterprises, as well as those furthered by the Non-Governnmental Organizations (NGOs).

Corruption among public officials is commonly cited in most developing countries, as is the indolence of the personnel directly serving citizens, as the major focal point for dissatisfaction with the government. The *bureaucratization* of public management of services and procedures is also cited as a real shortcoming which generally makes any interaction between citizens and government highly frustrating.

In this context, it is notable how the revolution in computer and Internet technologies has made customer service solutions in the private sector appear to move at the same pace or even ahead of the expectations of large masses of consumers and customers, whereas public agencies continue to be looked upon as mere users lagging behind in the utilization of ICTs.

It has therefore been important to become familiar with acquaintances', friends' and relatives' capacity for surprise in the face of advances in the efficiency of web sites that incorporate electronic transactions into their functions, at the same time as they develop a user profile for every visitor with all kinds of particular data on what satisfies them or what they like; also what would satisfy them or what they would like on future visits; all this in exchange for their preference over other service providers.

In parallel, this does not appear to happen, or at least it is not yet heard in daily conversations between individuals who have visited public agencies' web pages seeking information, without expecting levels of efficiency or service remotely resembling those of commercial and private sites. With regard to these visits on the Internet, the typical expression is "I went in looking for information," but not "I went in to solve a problem;" much less "I know if I go back to this site it will probably deal with needs or problems I might face tomorrow."

3. Governments out to Reconquer Citizens' Favor

However, it would be wrong to ignore various examples of websites of governments and their agencies around the world that have decisively undertaken the mission of reconquering the trust and favorable will of citizens and that have seen in the utilization of the Internet a powerful instrument for reversing the serious problem of governance involving the population's skepticism of the State's capacity.

Having focused their attention on the untapped possibilities of their presence on the Internet, the governments of countries as diverse as the United Kingdom (*Ukonline.gov; direct.gov.uk*), Singapore (*eCitizen Centre*) and Canada have placed online portals that once more accentuate addressing the needs and expectations of citizens and users in general, in order not only to provide them with information, but also to solve problems and make interaction with the government as free of complexity and as satisfactory as possible.

Thus, taking as a reference the leading countries in improvement of government portals, the international consulting firm *Accenture* has monitored and measured the international innovative impetus, identifying a clear trend of governments with greater initiative for adopting *"...the vision that the true value of eGovernment lies in [...] helping the government provide citizens and companies with improved services [...] to treating citizens and companies as customers and incorporating [customer relations management (CRM)] techniques into the delivery of government services."*[1]

In this regard, the same trend reveals four stages or moments

[1] *eGovernment Leadership: Engaging the Customer,* Accenture Government Executive Series, April 2003, p. 2.

In this regard, the same trend reveals four stages or moments of action:

First. Identifying correct services for the correct type of customer.

Second. Ensuring that the services selected are correctly introduced.

Third. Ensuring that they are properly used.

Fourth. Measuring success in service delivery within clearly defined parameters.[2]

4. President Fox's Vision: a Portal Furthered by Citizens

Since the outset of his administration, President Vicente Fox, through his Office for Government Innovation, incorporated the creation of a Citizen Portal as a key line of the Presidential Agenda for Good Government, under its fourth line of action, that of Digital Government, the objective of which is to make it possible for citizens, from the comfort of their homes or offices, to obtain government information and have access to its services.

This strategy reformulates the nature and internal and external functioning of the Government through Information and Communication Technologies, with four main objectives:

1. Offer a new way of governing, oriented completely to citizens' needs,
2. Make the Government competitive,
3. Reconsider the Government's relations with citizens and private companies, and
4. Comply with all the objectives of a Good Government.

Since the start we decided to build our own vision which, in response to Mexican reality, to the philosophy of government of

[2] Accenture, *ibid.*, p. 2.

President Vicente Fox and to the particularities of citizens' mentality, will succeed in uniting the dispersion of efforts that until then characterized government presence on the Internet. Due to this dispersion, it was to be expected that interaction between citizens and government online should be rather unsatisfactory, confusing and, in some cases, even frustrating. That was feasible as long as there was no inclusive but unifying model. The latter had to be capable, first of combining actions between units and agencies; then of coordinating them and, in the final analysis, optimizing the wealth of capacities and innovative talent within the government, in benefit of the citizen viewed as a customer seeking satisfaction.

As a result, an extensive analysis of the elements common to the best international practices in building government portals was carried out, on the basis of the following categories:

- Objectives
- Organization of contents
- Contents
- User profiles
- Efficiency
- Nature of the information
- Impact of services

As of this review we never lost sight of the fact that what we were seeking was to build our own paradigm of government online, summarized in the aim of using the new electronic media correctly to extend the frontier of the possible in satisfying citizens' needs and wishes by means of optimum utilization of the public resources entrusted to the government.

This, without sidestepping the importance of achieving an institutional synergy of different actors, coordinated from the Presidency of the Republic, through its Office for Government Innovation:

- Ministry of Public Administration, whose main task is that of overseeing correct execution of the Presidential Agenda for Good

Government; in this regard, it is the function of this agency to monitor the good performance of the Citizen Portal.

- Coordination Office of the e-Mexico National System, due to the fact that the Portal is also provided for within its strategy and this is from where it receives institutional, political, and even financial support.
- National Science and Technology Council (CONACYT), which provides financial resources and know-how on efficient use of technology in the public sector.
- The Public Center for Research and Technological Development (INFOTEC), which developed the technological platform, manages the Citizen Portal project, provides the services of highly qualified personnel and also conducts research on eGovernment, in order constantly to update and make innovations to the Portal.
- The totality of agencies and ministries in charge of high-impact public services, which were requested to participate in work teams which defined and reviewed the composition and topics of the Portal's 16 channels.

To carry out this initiative a work and collaboration network was established made up of 65 officers in charge of the different agencies and entities of the Federal Public Administration. At present an interdisciplinary team of 20 people participates in the administration and operation of *www.gob.mx*.

5. Construction of the Portal under an Innovative Paradigm

Since its launching in the fourth quarter of 2002, the Citizen Portal has positioned itself as a spearhead in government innovation through Information and Communications Technologies; but how was the efficiency the Portal should have, established? We began by responding to three criteria:

- The Portal should have horizontal reach with the resources of three levels of government.

- It should build the necessary capacity for citizens to find, from anywhere and at any time, the most important information for their relations with the Federal Government, in a single place and organized by the logic of users and not of the agencies.
- It should support the necessary functions for citizens to easily find comprehensive information related to their needs, according to basic topics in the "lifecycle" of persons and the community: employment, education, culture, family, business, health, security, transportation, rural sector, housing, sports, environment, tourism, foreigners and migrants.
- It should also have a technological platform for administration of contents and electronic services under open, universally accepted standards that incorporate technological solutions for the development, coordination and administration of government activities and that guarantee interoperability between electronic services of interest to citizens.

The Portal's specific goals should be: i) stimulate intensive use of ICTs in public-sector agencies that provide direct services to citizens; ii) encourage modernization initiatives within the government to digitize and improve the quality of services; iii) eliminate waste of resources due to excess procedures or personnel; iv) encourage citizens' involvement and participation in government decision-making; v) foster the development of new schemes for interaction with society among federal, state and local government levels.

6. Technological Platform of the Portal: Strategic Evolution

Traditionally, Federal Government agencies have adopted in their information technology architectures proprietary systems, have bought hardware, written or licensed applications and hired large human resources structures to keep said systems working and in operation. This approach has covered operative needs in an immediate manner; however, it has generated very high costs over years of purchases of "updates" or technological improvements in an attempt to maintain the vanguard, or simply the operation, adapting to technological conditions at a particular point in time, the result of which has been architectures with very complex interoperability due to their components.

Over the past decade the agencies' efforts in ICT have focused on consolidating these "data silos" by once again investing large sums of money in the adoption of Enterprise Resource Planning (ERP) systems, which offer applications interconnected with centralized repositories of related data (unified databases). The ERPs have certainly resolved some of the agencies' needs, without being a panacea: most government agencies continue to struggle with the technological diversity they have developed over the years, resulting in a new series of problems and barriers. The agencies have become relatively inflexible organizations, significantly complicating the ability to adopt and implement changes at the same pace as technology has been developing; likewise it is very complex to attain strategic restructuring processes, integration or inter-agency cooperation models.

The following chart summarizes the overall model shaping the Citizen Portal:

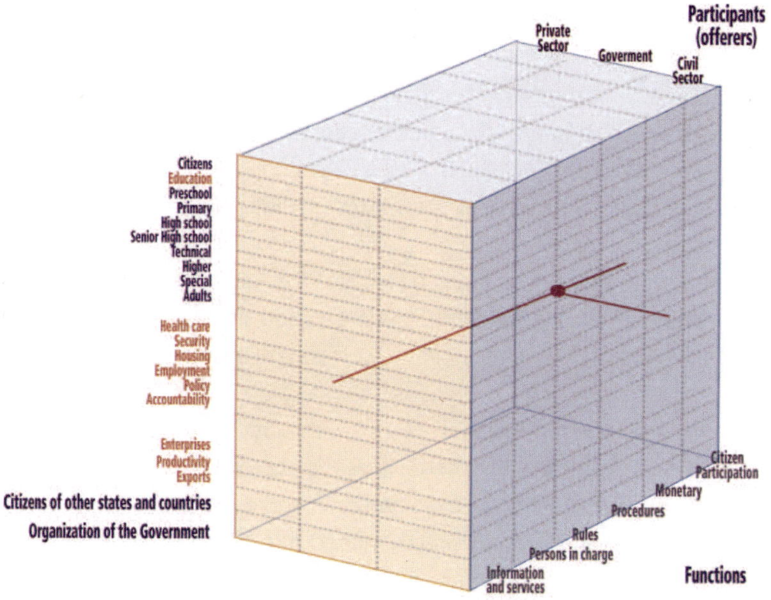

Although it is true that ERPs have resolved and integrated Fragmented Architectures, it is also true that they have not provided agencies with technological flexibility. The architecture of Electronic Services is a completely different paradigm. Based on the Internet, they are an open rather than proprietary architecture; based on standards adopted and recognized worldwide, instead of building and maintaining a specific structure for internal services, now the agencies have the opportunity to "rent" the functions they require in keeping with their context, whether data storage, processing power or specific applications, from external service suppliers.

At the base of the Electronic Services architecture there are standards for communication and data exchange protocols, such as XML or SOAP, which allow the information to travel easily between different applications. These tools provide universal languages that enable the applications to talk freely among themselves, exchanging information on demand. The standards significantly and dramatically simplify the flow of information administration, and the agencies do not have to develop long sequences of specific code every time they need to interact with a new application or orchestrate the exchange of data between a series of applications.

The service grid—The Intermediate Layer in the Architecture— is based on standards. Making an analogy with an electric power grid, the service grid provides a set of shared utilities—from security to the incorporation of third-party tools; from collection to electronic payments—which facilitates and makes possible the operation of critical mission functions as well as complete transactions through the Internet. In addition, the grid facilitates the transportation of messages (such as handling and filtering), identification of available services (such as directories or agents), in the certainty that data remain consistent and reliable (such as monitoring and resolution of inconsistencies). In short, this intermediate layer helps users and providers of Electronic Services to identify themselves and interact among themselves by creating environments of communication and exchange of reliable data, essential features in any service offered by the government.

A strong service grid is vital for the adoption, implementation and strengthening of the potential impact and value offered by Electronic

Services. The upper layer of this architecture is composed of a set of applied services, from processing of bank cards to the programming of services or events in citizens' lives. This makes possible the automation of some specific stages in processes and services. The upper layer is definitely the one with which citizens will have the most interaction on a daily basis; some services will be useful only for very specific contexts such as an industrial sector or some sector of the population, others will have an impact on larger groups. But in both cases, services can be combined to offer orchestrated services that involve the interaction of several government agencies, generating a great deal of value for citizens, saving resources for them, improving government performance, generating operative savings, fostering transparency and reducing corruption.[3]

In this regard the Citizen Portal is located in the last layer of the Electronic Services model, since it acts as the sole window where citizens will interact with the Federal Government.

The diagram on page 375 shows the model of architecture of Electronic Services on which the services offered by the agencies will be based. The model is unique in the world, since it involves the two main technological architectures, protecting the investments made by the Federal Government in information technology. It has been developed on the basis of identifying the best practices obtained from the result of similar implementation efforts in other countries, as well as on standards adopted and recognized worldwide by both governments and different industrial sectors.

7. User Profile and Scope of the Portal

Performance objectives

The Portal is aimed at 100 percent of the Mexican population with access to Internet, to the migrant population and to foreigners who wish to visit Mexico or do business in our country.

---

[3] Harvard Business Review Publishing Corporation, Your Next IT Strategy, John Hagel III and John Seely Brown, October 2001

There is an expected impact within the government. With regard to processes, the challenge posed by the Citizen Portal to all government agencies is enormous. Motivated by *www.gob.mx*, all of them are reviewing and reinventing their internal processes with the aim of providing better services with more quality to citizens. This obliges the government as a whole to be more efficient, providing higher added value in each of its actions.

With regard to the impact on the work and performance of employees of the public administration, the Citizen Portal furthers collaborative work by creating virtual work teams or communities of online collaboration where the main actors of IT and innovation in government participate, as well as those responsible for the creation, maintenance and improvement of the services the government provides to citizens.

Impact on Society

- The Citizen Portal offers a collection of public services, improving their accessibility and availability, which people can access from anywhere and at any time.
- Fosters transparency and access to government public information.
- The information made known through the Citizen Portal makes the relationship between government and citizens clearer, facilitating accountability.
- It is the tool that allows an improvement and increase in government efficiency and effectiveness by bringing procedures and services closer to citizens.
- It allows more active, clearer citizen participation in public decision-making.
- Reduces operating costs in government procedures, since it can be accessed through the Internet, avoiding material and human costs.

In analyzing the use habits of the Portal's users, it is possible to identify patterns of use that make it possible to continuously improve efficiency. The most visited channels are Education, Employment and

Technological Platform

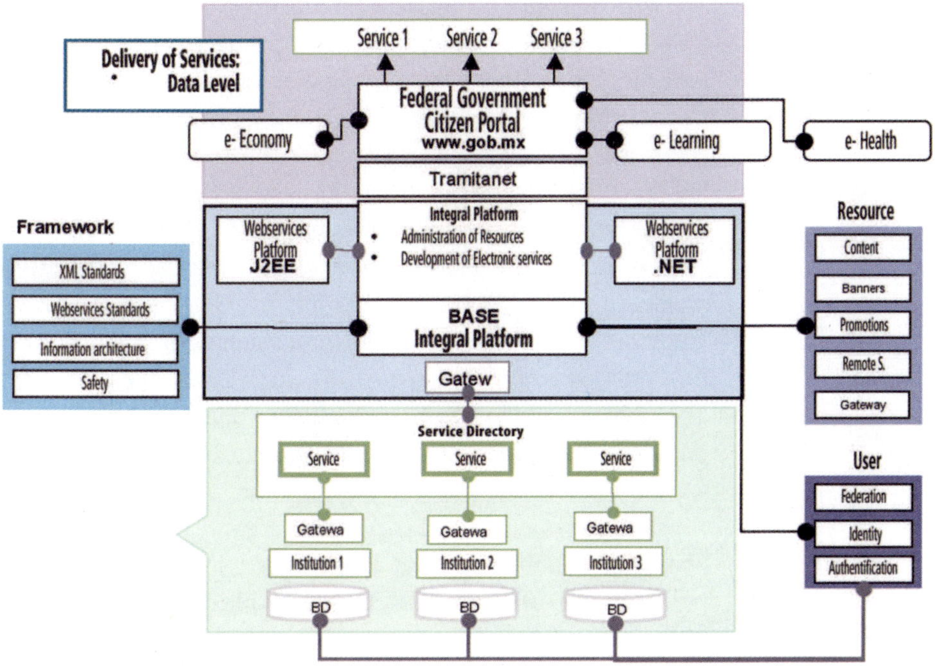

Family, which are of interest to the large majority of the population since employment, above all, is crucial to life in society.

A channel of major importance for the entire population, such as Employment, is visited at least once by all users seeking information and guidance on how to obtain employment. Around 6 percent of the population in Mexico have access to the Internet (approximately 6,478,788 inhabitants); of this percentage almost 70 percent use the Internet to check their e-mail, do some kind of research or interact with other users.

The total amount of accesses to the Portal has been maintained at between 800,000 and one million a month. The profiles of the users who most enter the site are directly related to the most visited channels.

The Family channel is a distinctive case, since it has contents (official identification documents, family health, entertainment, etc.) of common interest associated with various user profiles.

There is a clear, marked tendency to access the Portal from urban areas. This is mainly due to the lack of urbanization and expansion of technology to rural areas far from cities. Through future programs that make it possible to take in more areas and reach remote, non-urban communities a balance can be achieved in the type of areas that access the Portal, for which purpose the Ministry of Communications and Transportation is working on specific projects.

The requests for information for which citizens access the Portal are directly related to the search for information. This reinforces the Employment channel as one of the most visited. Citizens are entering the Portal expecting to be guided as to how to obtain employment. The other principal reason for access to the Portal is to carry out some procedure electronically—mainly the Sole Population Registry Code (CURP).

Gathering the information from the areas that access the Portal (mainly urban), the states that most access it are the states with the most urbanization (Federal District, State of Mexico). The central area of the country is the one that most accesses the Portal. The other states that have accessed the Portal are Nuevo Leon, Puebla, Tamaulipas, Veracruz, Baja California, Baja California Sur, Chiapas, Colima and Queretaro.

8. Recognition of a World-Class Effort

Just one year after the start of the Federal Government's Citizen Portal, there has been a wave of keen international interest in the innovations made by President Fox's government in the area of Digital Government. This is recognition that Mexico is effectively contributing innovative elements to the new world paradigm of good electronic government. It is worth giving an account of the expression of this international validation that we have evolved in the right direction.

OECD

A study is being made by the OECD on the development and evolution of Digital Government in Mexico, and to that end the key actors in its implementation in different sectors of the government have been selected in the following areas: social development, institutional-regulatory development and technological development. Surveys and interviews were carried out in order to establish a pattern of recent evolution of the best practices applied in the country to identify reference parameters with other OECD member countries, most of them advanced economies. This exercise will undoubtedly contribute elements of high strategic value for the future evolution of the Citizen Portal.

UN Recognition

In its World Report on the Public Sector 2003, the United Nations classified Mexico as one of the five developing countries with the greatest determination to offer transactional services online to its citizens, which also places it among the countries that have progressed more quickly and effectively than several of the most industrialized nations.

According to the same report, with regard to the criterion of overall performance Mexico stands in 30th place among around 200 countries and is in ninth position worldwide in e-participation, that is, in facilitating society's dialogue, in the use of public services, with its government. In addition, it occupies fourth place worldwide as regards sophistication and maturity of government information and services online, in view of the functional and technological development incorporated into service solutions.

Stockholm Challenge

The Federal Government's Citizen Portal (*www.gob.mx*) has obtained important international recognition by being declared last May 13 the winner in the category of Electronic Government of the Stockholm

Challenge Award 2003/2004, considered the "Internet Nobel," in which 900 projects from 107 countries participated, evaluated by 31 judges from 19 nations, in six categories.

This honorable distinction is added to others such as the INNOVA Recognition Award 2003, presented to the Portal last November by President Vicente Fox, and the fact of having also been the winner of the INNOVA Prize 2004, whose candidates were evaluated by the Office of the National Quality Award. In addition, the Citizen Portal was recognized as a finalist in the best of 2003 in the Government category by the Yahoo! Internet site.

9. Future Evolution of the Citizen Portal: Assuring a World-Class Quality Legacy in e-Government

Having obtained the Stockholm Challenge Award 2003/2004 in the category of Electronic Government places us in a position of great satisfaction, without this implying yielding in the strict demands that President Fox's administration has set itself. However, it is important to recognize that not only have the international standards of good government online been met, but in some areas they have been surpassed.

Thus, for example, the World Bank indicates that appropriate objectives for a good e-Government strategy should focus on three aspects of good government: capacity, efficiency and accountability.[4]

In this same regard, at present—together with our government's agencies and entities—the aim is to identify the services with the greatest impact on citizens which facilitate their use due to simplification or deregulation and which result in greater trust in the government and transparency.

This makes it necessary to promote the use of technology that allows standardization of data structures and better classification of information, which will make it possible to seek and find information in a more efficient and exact manner.

[4] *Information and Communication Technologies, Poverty and Development: Learning from Experience. Info Dev Annual Symposium,* World Bank, December 9/10, 2003.

Moreover, the ongoing challenge is to work with other levels of government so that, within a framework of cooperation and full respect for the authority of each one, information and services can be incorporated and exchanged in benefit of citizens, and that this results in being able to access, through the Citizen Portal, information, procedures and services of the three levels of government: municipal, state and federal.

In the Citizen Portal a space dedicated to transparency is being built, which will help to easily find all the information of a public nature and which will deal with requests for information made by individuals, in support of currently existing tools and within the framework of the Law on Transparency and Access to Government Public Information.

Despite the importance of these challenges, the greatest challenge will always be to broaden knowledge and response capacity in keeping with the degree of satisfaction of users of Citizen Portal services. In this regard, an immediate commitment is to count on precise methodologies to measure this degree of customer satisfaction, that is, citizens and their families.

As a pilot, the Ministry of Public Administration is measuring the satisfaction of the portal *www.gob.mx* against its US counterparts, obtaining comparable results. The US portal obtains satisfaction ratings approximately two points above or below the Mexican portal.

This shows that the government of Mexico offers its citizens a world-class portal. The measuring tool has provided Mexican authorities with specific information to improve the search and information management functions in the Portal.

Should the methodology be implemented in high-impact web sites in Mexico, the government can announce results in two months and show the world that Mexico's e-Government initiative is equal or superior to the services provided by the US government and the private sector.

The challenges of evolution of this portal will undoubtedly require new ideas, new efforts and new alliances to pave the way for a more responsive, flexible, comprehensive Portal of government services in keeping with the needs of each user, at any level of demand or need to be satisfied.

Date	Functionality	Image	Use Experience	Content	Surf	Search	Site's Functionality	Total
Up to August 9th	75	73	76	77	74	72	75	70
Up to August 11th	77	75	77	76	74	73	76	71
Up to August 13th	76	75	78	76	75	73	77	72

Citizen portal *firstgov.gov* (Average-21 June, 2004) General Services Administration (GSA)	In Spanish (United States) firstgov.gov website (Spanish) http://firstgov/Espanol/index.shtml 77
Citizen portal *firstgov.gov* General Services Administration (GSA)	firstgov.gov.govwebsite—***www.firstgov.gov*** 72

Ministry of Public Education (SEP)

José Martí Child Development Center (CENDI) 3

Winner of the Ibero-American Award for Quality

The Ibero-American Award for Quality is presented by the Ibero-American Quality Management Foundation (FUNDIBEQ), which is a non-profit institution founded in 1998 by various Ibero-American organizations.

Its objectives are:

- Promote self-evaluation, communication and training as basic tools for ensuring Continuous Improvement.

- Improve the utilization of available resources, with public and private organizations providing full satisfaction to customers.
- Develop stable exchanges in research, information and consultancy common to all the countries of the organizations that make up the Foundation, involving public and private educational organizations for both basic and specialized training.

The Award includes six categories: Small, Medium and Large Public Organization, on the one hand, and Small, Medium and Large Private Organization, on the other. This Award recognizes the organizations of Ibero-America which, following the principles of the Ibero-American Model of Excellence in Management, achieve excellent management and results. This international recognition endorses the soundness and competitiveness of the winning organization and converts into a world reference.

An International Jury concludes the Phases of the Awards Process. During this process more than 350 International Assessors from different Ibero-American countries take part in assessing the Management Accounts or Proceedings submitted by candidate organizations. Subsequently, the organizations that stood out in the first phases were visited by Teams of Assessors in order to verify and go more deeply into the evidence set forth in the Accounts. Finally, the Assessors prepare the Final Reports, which are evaluated by the International Jury.

CENDI 3 José Martí

Introduction

The CENDI 3 José Martí forms part of a pilot educational project called Child Development Centers of the "Land and Liberty" Popular Front. Since 1990 it offers an educational and specialized assistance service to boys and girls from marginalized areas from 45 days after birth to six years of age, children of working mothers who do not have labor benefits.

It belongs to the National Education System and shares the task of taking education and quality services to the most socially vulnerable children.

The CENDI is located to the north of Monterrey, capital of the state of Nuevo Leon, and caters comprehensively to slightly over 450 children through the coordinated actions of a multidisciplinary team that conducts the Institution's five key processes, which are: the Pedagogical, Health, Nutrition, Psychological and Social Work processes.

The purpose of the systemic conceptualization of the service is to address every aspect of the children's development and the social environment in which they develop. This is explained by the children's social, cultural and economic context, which has led the CENDI to create a network of systems and processes focusing on providing quality service with equity.

The fact that the communities attended to when the CENDI began its operations 14 years ago had acute economic and social problems indicated that performing educational work without taking into account the conditions and characteristics of the surrounding social milieu could perhaps make the educational function of the children's center unsuccessful

Situation of the CENDI in its Early Days

It has not been an easy road: the first few years were critical in view of parents' lack of information on the importance of early infancy, limiting their involvement in the teaching-learning process, the serious lags in the development of children from these areas and the lack of indicators to assess their development, as well as budget shortages and the uncertainty this causes among the staff. However, adversity itself led to designing the organizational structure and the systems and processes that helped to fulfill the mission and led to the proposal of considering continuous improvement as the only means to stay afloat, laying the foundations of what today is the culture of quality in the Institution.

The fact that the communities attended to when the CENDI began its operations 14 years ago had acute economic and social problems indicated that performing educational work without taking into account the conditions and characteristics of the surrounding social milieu could perhaps make the educational function of the children's center unsuccessful. The problems led to reflecting on how to integrate the community into the educational task and what means could be used to do make this function possible, which implied, first of all, modifying their behavior patterns, and secondly, getting them to play a role in favor of the work of the children's center.

A theoretical study was made of the particularities of the family and the community and of the methods and means of its education, to create a family and community action program which, along with the educational task of the children's center, would contribute to achieving the fundamental objectives of the educational process: to attain the maximum development of all the physical and psychic capabilities of the children that would attend the CENDI, by coordinating all the agents that could have a bearing on this.

Obviously the community's description produced a very unfavorable picture which indicated the need to carry out systematic, sustained actions of guidance to achieve the modification of factors that necessarily had an effect on the levels of development of the children who attended the CENDI.

Obviously the community's description produced a very unfavorable picture which indicated the need to carry out systematic, sustained actions of guidance to achieve the modification of factors that necessarily had an effect on the levels of development of the children who attended the CENDI

It was essential to carry out scientifically controlled parents' education with well-defined educational objectives, and execute diverse actions of community work that would imply changes and modifications in the immediate setting in which these households were located and that would consequently lead to transformations in the dynamics of the family itself.

> In this regard, the CENDI set itself the task of playing an active role in the community's social transformation and cease being a closed institution devoted exclusively to teaching work, so as to evolve toward an integrating educational model.

In 1997 the implementation of a Model of Quality Administration began, aligning efforts toward particular objectives incorporated in the Institution's strategic planning and ensuring that they comply with the needs and expectations of each customer, guaranteeing their satisfaction.

Implementation of the Quality System

The quality model was built on the basis of a series of values and concepts that were vital for the Institution, such as visionary leadership, education centered on learning, appreciation of individuals, administration for innovation, rapid, flexible response, commitment and social responsibility, creation of value toward the educational community, preventive, forward-looking approach and systems perspective. All these criteria helped in using resources more efficiently, improving organizational communication, productivity and effectiveness in reaching the strategic objectives set.

It should be stressed that the change toward quality management has not been exclusive to supervisory personnel but involved all the Institution's staff in important aspects such as labor relations, forms of hiring, distribution of benefits, distribution of responsibilities and participation in the setting of objectives; it was understood that the commitment to quality would only be possible by basing it on the principle that changes are made by people, not by organizations.

Undoubtedly, once everyone was quite clear about what they were doing and where the Institution wanted to go, the policies and values that would guide conduct were defined in order to take a firm step forward toward the construction of the culture of quality that was wanted.

As from then there was an understanding of the importance of diagnosis and the detection of needs as a tool for the design of any strategy, the importance of being familiar with the market and identifying users of the service. It was learned that it is necessary to commit oneself to people by achieving their satisfaction, their development and well-being, which contributes to creating an atmosphere of trust and commitment. The Institution focused on developing systems to assess the performance of key processes through indicators and understanding the importance of knowing the factors that have a bearing on the satisfaction of pupils, their parents and the community.

A planning process was also developed, measuring its effectiveness, creating information systems to help decision-making and increasing the required speed of response, as well as understanding the importance of fulfilling the commitment to the community.

Implementation of the INTRAGOB Model

One of the points in favor of the implementation of the Quality Model in 1997 and the subsequent incorporation of the guidelines of the INTRAGOB Model is that the criteria it uses are applied in the same way to any type of organization. It is likewise applicable if the institution is small, medium or large. The model is descriptive, not prescriptive. This afforded the possibility of creating the standards that the Institution determined as goals to be reached. Its approach concerns itself with the values of the Institution's organizational culture and its processes, which was and continues to be important.

Moreover, the model's components make it possible to identify the Institution's critical areas and provide it with a reference framework for establishing the development plan for a culture of educational quality that not only contains a program for the improvement of educational quality, but that also addresses the cultivation of a set of values to exercise a series of institutional practices and that make the process sustainable in the medium and long terms.

General Results

With regard to the impact of CENDI's processes and systems on citizens, it is worth highlighting the information from the comparative study carried out in the field in two stages, the first in 1996 and the second in 2001, which showed significant advances in quality of life (health and nutrition), community development (housing and social and ecological environment), education and reduction of social problems (less gang activity, prostitution, intra-family violence, drug addiction, etc.).

For example, with regard to the children's general development quotient, by way of comparison it should be stressed that in 1996 CENDI's children showed a development quotient of 94.8 which, although within the normal limits, was not particularly noteworthy. However, in the 2001 sample these children reflected a quotient of 107.6, which shows that in a period of just five years they achieved a favorable change of considerably more than ten points on the development scale.

In regard to attaining harmonious development in children, whereas in 1996 some 72.1 percent of those who attended the CENDI showed disharmony in their development, in the 2001 data this dropped to 58 percent, indicating advances in favoring proportional formation in all areas of development; currently less than 23 percent show disharmony.

Significance in the Community

CENDI's educational role has also achieved favorable changes in the family and community environment. The results of the interview conducted with parents of the community and key individuals, which was applied to a selected sample, reflects that the Institution has made substantial changes, although problems remain that are closely linked to the economic and social system that engenders them.

The majority of the residents of these marginalized areas consider that their community is safer than before (around 53 percent affirm this), that it is a good place to live (62.1 percent) and that it is appropriate for children's education (59.8 percent).

This shows that of the concepts that residents had of living in a highly dangerous place, at present most of them believe it is "regular" (61.2 percent), although those who still consider it dangerous or very dangerous reach 22 percent.

Likewise, there has been a significant reduction in street fights (only 3.2 percent underscore this as one of the main problems), which means that for more than four years there have been no murders in these marginalized areas, which used to be fairly frequent.

CENDI's Program of Community Action has had a great deal to do with this improvement, together with community actions and factors, and has been able to exercise effective educational actions, making possible evident transformations in the immediate social milieu, which have made themselves felt in children's development and in an improvement in family and social dynamics.

Recognitions

CENDI's policy of fostering the development and upgrading of its processes and systems has led it to obtaining the Nuevo Leon Award for Quality in 1998, in 1999 the National Quality Award and in 2002 the Ibero-American Quality Award.

Currently CENDI shares its culture of quality with other educational institutions through the educational encounters it organizes and interns it receives from the state of Nuevo Leon, from other states and other countries, since it is a reference model for marginalized urban areas in Latin America, considered so since 2001 by the Organization of American States (OAS) and considered by the World Bank one of the seven most successful educational projects for poor areas.

Federal Electricity Commission (CFE)

Winner of the Asia Pacific Quality Award International

The award is granted by the Asia-Pacific Quality Organization (APQO), founded in 1985, and is one of the most representative at international level, since it encompasses countries in two-thirds of the world's territory.

The APQO is a nonprofit organization that brings together the main professional quality associations in the countries bordering on the Pacific Ocean and Asian countries. The APQO's governing body includes representatives from Australia, China, India, Indonesia, Korea, Malaysia, Mexico, New Zealand, Philippines, Sri Lanka, United States and Vietnam.

The Asia-Pacific International Quality Award is granted by rating the following seven elements: leadership, strategic planning, customer and market approach, management of know-how, measurement and analysis, human resources approach, process management and business results. In addition, only organizations that have obtained the National Quality Award in their respective country can compete for this award. This is the case with the Center-West Division of the CFE which obtained it in the year 2000.

The categories under which this award is presented are:

- Manufacturing organizations. Small (less than 250 employees)
- Service organizations. Small (less than 250 employees)
- Manufacturing and services organizations. Large (more than 250 employees)

Center-West Division

To supply and market electric power, the Center-West Division is one of the country's 13 Divisions; its territorial sphere mainly encompasses the states of Michoacan and Colima, supplying a quality service with 1,864 workers.

During the current six-year term, the success factors have been working under a Quality Management System, uniting the efforts of the enterprise and the union, aligning processes, and allying them for competitiveness with visionary leadership.

Problems Encountered in 2000

To be competitive and transcend, processes were redesigned in order to generate value for customers and increase their satisfaction, and thus succeed in fulfilling commitments to customers, timely connections, no power cuts, no complaints, no illicit use, no occupational accidents, professional personnel, profitability, reliable suppliers, and being the best in the sector at world level in order to create a culture in Mexicans of respect for and pride in the CFE.

Not working under an organization centering on processes means that there would be very varied losses.

Customers would lose:

- receiving an invoice with meter readings to the day and always with the same date
- having an electrician who always provides service and solves any situation

- quality in supply, and
- not being connected when required

The personnel would lose:

- growing, professionalizing themselves by acquiring empowerment
- the opportunity to improve their wages and assure their jobs

The CFE would lose:

- achieving customer satisfaction
- achieving profitability, modernizing itself and being the best at world level

Solutions Applied

President Fox's administration has promoted quality by means of the six strategies for Good Government. To compete at world level the CFE redesigned its processes with a total customer approach, as an intelligent enterprise, with an integral team of leaders, and these are measured at present in terms of variation of results with the Six Sigma methodology.

APC Diagram, which includes eight criteria

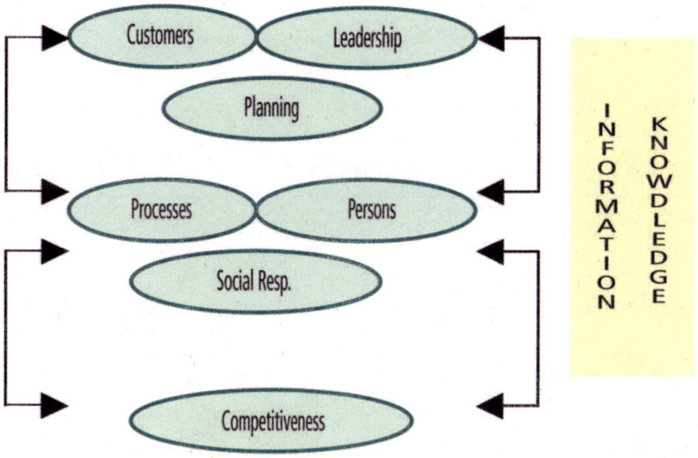

Mission

Satisfying customers' legitimate electricity needs and other services by complying with the commitments established to profitability, respect for nature, without adversely affecting third parties and guaranteeing the development of its collaborators and of the Division, through our Quality Management System.

Vision

Positioning the Center-West Division as a world-class electricity enterprise, diversified, with management autonomy, with a service and supply of electric power that surpasses society's legitimate needs and expectations, sustained by its processes, values and culture of quality of its personnel.

Philosophy

Working with pride for the customer's overall satisfaction.

1. Customers

To determine the critical factors of different groups of customers the following tools are used:

Structure of the Quality Council and Quality Committees

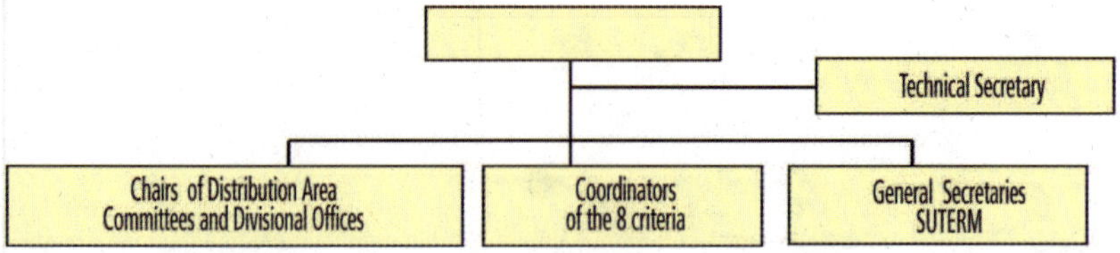

1. Customers

Determination of factors:

- —Market study
- —Customer surveys
- —Mailbox

Results: Customers' critical factors

Improvement of processes:

- —Customer service center
- —Center for control and continuity
- —Appointments agreed in situ
- —System of complaints

Results: Commitment to service and supply

Assessment of satisfaction:

- —System of surveys

Results: Measurement of value created

2. Leadership

An entrepreneurial leadership is exercised in keeping with a managerial leadership, exercised by professional leaders who create a culture of quality and have a vision of the future directed at the common good.

Leadership System

The Center-West Division evaluates overall performance with quarterly reviews at corporate level and monthly in each of the areas that compose it.

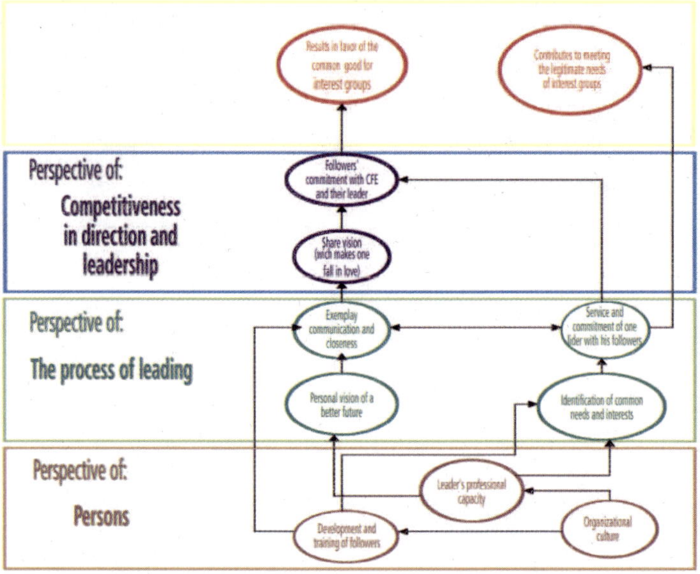

Every half year 360-degree surveys are carried out on personnel.

3. Planning

Strategic Objectives

1. Complying 95 percent with the quality requirements committed to customers, improving their satisfaction and loyalty to the CFE.
2. Complying 95 percent with the quality requirements committed to the persons who make up the Center-West Division, improving their satisfaction.
3. Supplying 98.5 percent of the inhabitants in the sphere of the Division with electric power.
4. Achieving results that sustain the development of our Division, reducing costs and increasing earnings.
5. Winning the Ibero-American Quality Award.

6. Consolidating ourselves as an Organization Centered on Processes.
7. Achieving world-class results.
8. Diversifying the goods and services offered.
9. Achieving innovations in our processes.
10. Strengthening the institutional image of an honest and transparent enterprise.

4. Information and Knowledge

The information is supported by Technologies and Communication, which facilitates its management for planning, evaluation, improvement and innovation of its services and processes. The Knowledge Management System identifies and generates knowledge with learning teams by means of practices of creativity and innovation.

5. Personnel

We have created the necessary conditions to favor the entry, training, education and development of personnel and improve their quality of life.

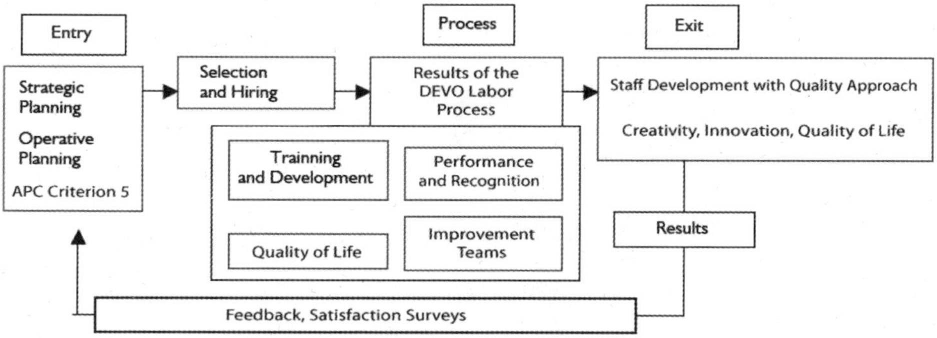

6. Processes

Based on commitments to customers, processes were created that anticipate needs and expectations.

The processes are aligned with customers' requirements. The High-Level Map on page 396 shows the interaction.

The purpose of the Business Processes is to deliver products and services that comply with customers' requirements. The three Advantage Creating Processes have been identified whereby the customer would prefer us and 19 Supplying Processes which manage resources.

Process	What Does the Customer Expect?
Advisory assistance and quotations	Written quotation. Information for decision-making. On-site visit. Fulfillment of agenda.
Promotion and incorporation of new supplies	Connection of the supply. Technical information. Commercial information.
Assurance of the supply pledged	Supply with fulfillment of commitment. Minor inspection of the customer's facilities. Advisory assistance for preventive maintenance. Periodic testing of voltage levels.
Marketing electric power of the quality contracted.	Minor inspection of the customer's facilities. Advisory assistance on energy saving.
Improvement of the supply and modifications at the customer's request	Modification of facilities. Supply according to needs. On-site visit. Fulfillment of agenda.

7. Social Responsibility

Promote the development of the community to improve its social and living conditions, as well as foster the culture of quality through the Alliance for Competitiveness, Consultative Councils, Suppliers, Federal Government, State Governments, among others.

Results

8. Competitiveness

Results are measured for customers, for personnel, for society and for the enterprise.

The trend of indicators such as power losses, interruption time per user, average connection time, disagreements, lags and frequency of accidents has substantially diminished.

Other indicators whose trend has been upward are compliance with the commitments established with customers, their satisfaction, the degree of electrification and the capacity of our people as professionals to provide world-class supply and service.

The change in the organizational culture has made it possible to raise productivity through efficient management based on producing more with less, reducing costs and increasing earnings, serving more customers with the same work force.

Time Line (Significant events in this Administration)

The above results have allowed us to obtain achievements and awards shown on the time line, such as state, national and international quality awards.

And to be a CFE recognized for its actions of transparency and combating corruption. Today the customer contracts the supply of electric power without making any payment to obtain the service. Once connected to the grid, the amount corresponding to the deposit for guarantee and use of the power supply will be charged on the first bill.

Another of the actions is the letter of guarantee that is delivered to the customers so that they aware of who is attending them, and should there be any anomaly, knows whom to report it to.

High-level map

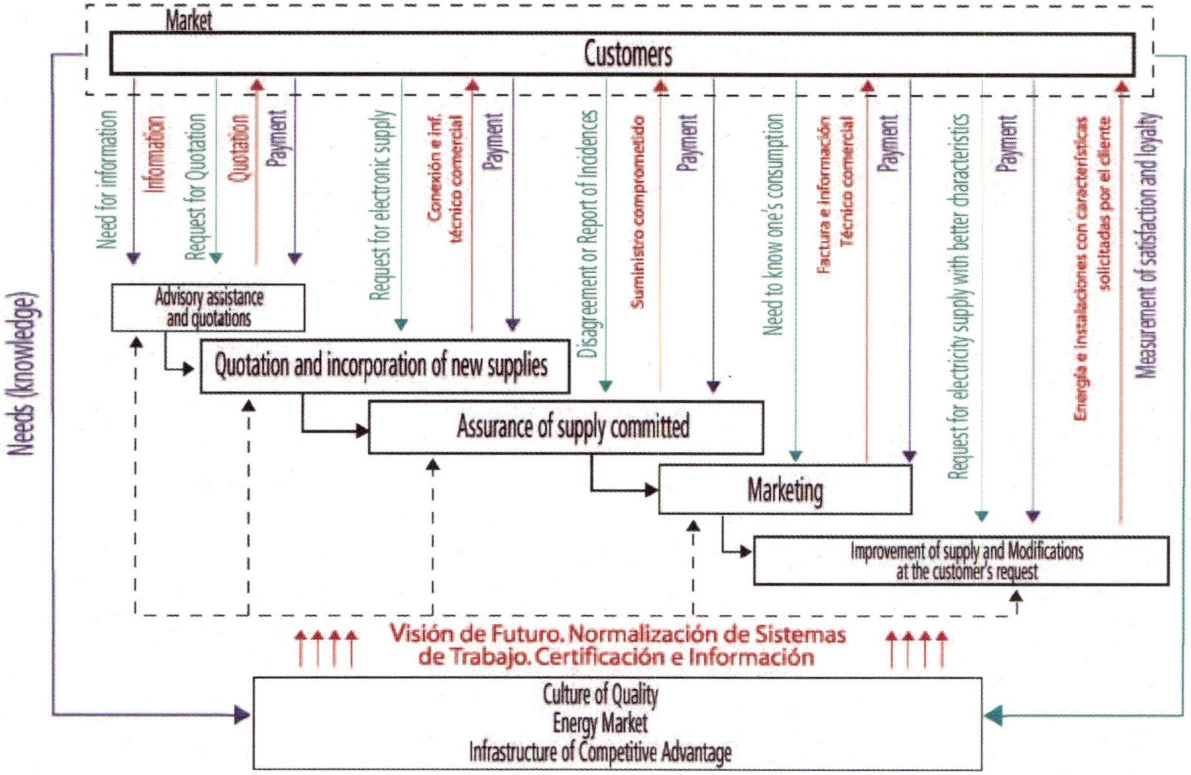

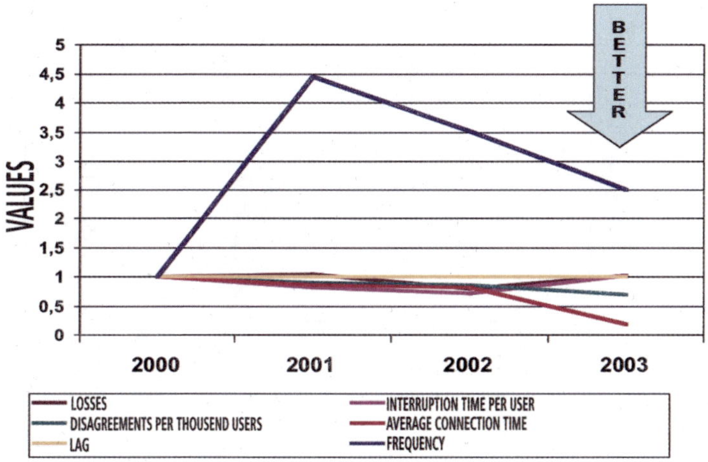

BETTER
5
4,5
4
3,5
3
2,5
2
1,5
1
0,5
0
VALUES
2000
2001
2002
2003
LOSSES
INTERRUPTION TIME PER USER
DISAGREEMENTS PER THOUSEND USERS
AVERAGE CONNECTION TIME
LAG
FREQUENCY

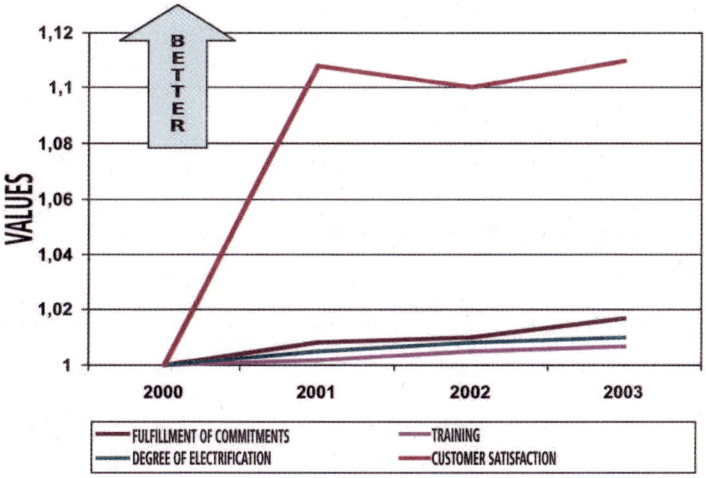

BETTER
1,12
1,1
1,08
1,06
1,04
1,02
1
VALUES
2000
2001
2002
2003
FULFILLMENT OF COMMITMENTS
TRAINING
DEGREE OF ELECTRIFICATION
CUSTOMER SATISFACTION

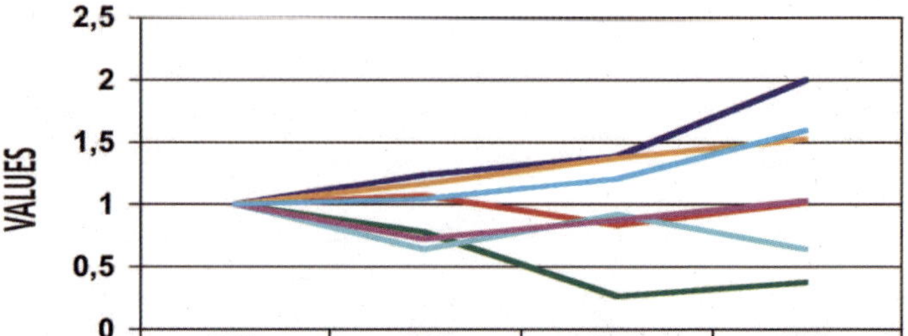

	2000	2001	2002	2003
Assek B.	1	0,78	0,26	0,37
Workers	1	1,07	0,83	1,01
CUDC	1	0,64	0,91	0,64
Vehicles	1	1,23	1,38	2
Users	1	1,17	1,37	1,53
GWH	1	0,71	0,87	1,02
Revenues	1	1,04	1,21	1,59

Annexes

Ibero-American Charter for Public Administration

PREAMBLE

In accordance with the Santo Domingo Declaration approved by the IV Ibero-American Conference of Ministers of Public Administration and Reform of the State, the State constitutes the greatest example of the articulation of social relationships. From the viewpoint of governance, economic progress and reducing social inequality, the State's role in contemporary societies, especially in the Ibero-American region, is fundamental to attaining increasing levels of collective well-being.

The professionalization of Public Administration is a necessary condition if we are to achieve a better State, which is an indispensable instrument for our countries' development. This is understood as the guarantee that public servants have a set of qualities, such as merit, capability, a calling for service, effectiveness in performance of their duties, responsibility, honesty and adherence to democratic principles and values.

For the purposes of this Charter, the term "Public Administration," with the meaning attributed to it in the first chapter, shall be understood to be the equivalent of "civil service," a term preferred in some Ibero-American countries. All allusions and references to the former shall therefore be considered as equally applicable to the latter term, with the consequent understanding that all positions of a political nature are excluded from the Charter.

Several studies conducted by international organizations provide evidence regarding the positive relationship between the existence of Public Administration or civil service systems that have such attributes and citizens' levels of confidence in public administration, government effectiveness and the fight against corruption, and a country's capacity for sustainable economic growth.

Furthermore, a professional Administration that incorporates these systems contributes to the institutional strength of nations and to the stability of a democratic system. For civil service systems of this kind to exist, the management of employment and human resources serving governments must incorporate the legal, organizational and technical criteria, as well as the political and practical ones, that characterize the transparent and effective management of human resources.

The effectiveness of management principles, procedures, policies and practices that comprise a Public Administration system requires that all of these elements be duly adapted to their context in the institutional environment into which they must be integrated and operate. The needs that derive from history, traditions, the socioeconomic context and the political framework of each nation's reality are factors that condition the specific forms of any generic model. Furthermore, the quality of the various national systems of government or civil service in the Ibero-American community is varied and heterogeneous.

Achieving a professional and effective Public Administration is, for any democratic society, an ongoing endeavor in which we always find many areas for improvement in the existing institutional arrangements. Moreover, we cannot ignore the obvious differences that different points of departure imply with regard to the content, scope and intensity of reforms needed in each case. Nonetheless, it is possible and advantageous to set forth a set of common foundations on which the design and operation of the various national systems of public administration in Ibero-American countries must be built.

The definition of these foundations and their adoption by governments will contribute, on the one hand, to provide a common focus of effort to improve national systems and, on the other hand, will make it possible to build a common language regarding Ibero-American Public Administration, thereby facilitating exchanges of all kinds and strengthening this field in the existing relations among our countries.

This is the objective of the Ibero-American Charter for Public Administration: that it may constitute for the countries that adopt it a common point of reference as regards Public Administration. The text defines a generic frame of reference, which is not binding, and which should be adapted in each case to each country's idiosyncrasies, history, culture, legal tradition and institutional environment. Its development will allow different normative and political manifestations, consistent with that heterogeneity.

CHAPTER ONE. THE CHARTER'S AIMS AND SCOPE

Objective

The Concept of Public Administration

The Ibero-American Charter for Public Administration has the following aims:

a) To define the bases that make up a professional and effective system of Public Administration, understood as a key component for the democratic governance of contemporary societies, and for good public management.
b) To configure a generic framework of guiding principles, policies and management mechanisms in order to build a common language with regard to Public Administration in the nations of the Ibero-American community.
c) To serve as a source of inspiration for concrete applications, regulations, development and reforms, which in each case would be appropriate for improving and modernizing national Public Administration systems in this sphere.

Public Administration comprises the group of institutional arrangements through which government employment is articulated and managed and through which individuals join government service in a given national context. These arrangements consist of written or informal standards, structures, cultural guidelines, explicit or implicit policies, processes, practices and various activities whose objective is to ensure the proper management of human resources within the framework of an effective and professional Public Administration that serves the public interest.

In the public arena, the goals of a system of human resources and employment management must make the objectives of effectiveness and efficiency compatible with the requirements for equality, a merit-based system and impartiality that are characteristic of professional administrations in democratic settings. The following are basic ideas for this concept:

a) Professional administration is understood to be a Public Administration directed and controlled by political forces that apply the principle of democracy, but in which politics does not act as the controlling element of its application, which requires preserving a sphere of independence and impartiality in its operation in order to serve the public interest.
b) The notion used is compatible with the existence of a variety of Public Administration models. The institutional arrangements that frame the access to government employment, the career paths of public employees, the powers of various people, and other aspects of employment and human resources management do not necessarily need to be the same in different national environments.
c) Public Administration systems may include one or more types of employment relationships between government organizations and their employees—relationships which may be more or less similar to the regular labor regime.

Public Administration in a country may have employment relations based on an appointment or a contract and may be regulated by public or private law, and its controversies may be heard by special legal bodies or before common courts of law. The existence and preservation of professional administration demands certain specific regulations governing public employment, which are different from those governing regular employment by others.

However, the concept of Public Administration in this Charter transcends the purely legal dimension of employment, since as reality often shows us, the mere existence of norms may not be sufficient to guarantee the effective articulation of the mechanisms that make professional administration possible. Only the effectiveness of this articulation in social practice enables us to properly speak of Public Administration. For the purposes of this Charter, Public Administration includes:

a) The various sectors of the political administrative system, including those like Education and Sanitation, among others, which may have unique personnel statutes or regulations.
b) The various levels of government and administration, which includes public employment corresponding to national governments, as well as employment in institutions at sub-national as well as intermediate levels, and where appropriate, local levels.
c) The various degrees of functional decentralization of management, including both central organs of government and decentralized agencies, whether or not they have their own independent legal status.

CHAPTER TWO. ORIENTING CONCEPTS AND GUIDING PRINCIPLES

Orienting Concepts

Public Administration is one of the key elements in articulating political-administrative systems. Therefore, modernization of public policies on management of employment and human resources constitutes a central element of public management reforms undertaken in recent decades by a significant number of governments around the world.

This Charter is positioned as an instrument to use in reform strategies that incorporate the concepts that inspired these modernization efforts, and the Charter promotes the adoption of reforms by civil service systems in Ibero-American countries. Specifically, these concepts have inspired those the Charter outlines:

a) The preeminence of individuals in assuring the proper functioning of public administrations, and the need for policies that guarantee and develop the greatest value in human capital available to governments and public sector organizations.
b) The professionalism of human resources serving in public administrations as a guarantee of higher quality services being delivered to citizens.
c) Stability in government employment and protection from arbitrary dismissal, regardless of the duration established, be it temporary or permanent in nature.
d) Flexibility in the organization and management of jobs.
e) Responsibility of government employees for the work performed and its results, as well as respect for them and their inclusion in development of the public policies governments define.
f) Observance by all personnel of the guiding principles, understood within the context of their application and of the ethical principles of public service: honesty, transparency, scrupulous care in managing public resources and constitutional principles and values.
g) The leading role of governmental senior managers and the internalization of their role as those principally responsible for the management of the employees they manage.
h) Promotion of communication, participation, dialogue, transaction and consensus oriented toward the public interest, as means of fostering the relationship between government employers and their personnel, with a view to achieving a more favorable working climate and the greatest degree of alignment between the organizations' objectives and the interests and expectations of their personnel.
i) The promotion of active policies to favor gender equality, protection and integration of minorities, and, in general, inclusion and non-discrimination for reasons of gender, social origin, ethnicity, disability or other causes.

The following are guiding principles of any public administration system, and they should inspire management policies on employment and human resources and in all instances should be safeguarded in actual personnel practices:

- The equality of all citizens, without discrimination on the basis of gender, race, religion, political tendency or others.
- Merit, performance and ability as the guiding criteria for hiring, career advancement and other human resources policies.
- Effectiveness and efficiency of governmental action and the policies and practices involved in managing jobs and individuals.
- Transparency, objectivity and impartiality.
- Fully subject to the law and respectful of rights.

CHAPTER THREE. BASIC CONCEPTS OF PUBLIC ADMINISTRATION

Public Administration as an Integrated System

In order to achieve the goals of this Charter, Public Administration must be designed and must operate as an integrated management system whose basic purpose or reason for existence is to create a fit between people and the strategy of the organization or multi-organizational system in order to produce results in accordance with those strategic priorities. The results sought by government organizations depend on their personnel in two ways:

1. Results are influenced by the degree to which human resources are of the appropriate dimension in quantitative and qualitative terms for the tasks to be done. Therefore, the provision of human capital must be adjusted in each case to organizational needs, avoiding both excessive and inadequate staffing and managing with as much agility as possible the necessary adjustment processes.
2. Results stem from conduct observed by people at work, which in turn are dependent on two basic variables:

   a) the abilities or sets of qualities possessed by the individuals, which determine how well-suited they are to perform the task; and

b) the motivation or level of effort that people are willing to apply to the performance of their work. Therefore, the standards, policies, processes and practices that comprise a Public Administration system must seek to develop a positive effect on the behavior of public servants, influencing, in the most appropriate sense in each case, the abilities and the motivation of the people performing the work.

Strategic Coherence. Situational Factors

Strategic coherence is an essential characteristic of any Public Administration system. This means that the quality of its instruments and interventions cannot be judged on the basis of a supposed technical or neutral standard separate from its connection with the strategy pursued by the organization in each case.

Employment and human resources management only creates value to the extent that it is consistent with organizational priorities and goals. The effectiveness of institutional arrangements that characterize Public Administration is impacted by conditions and variables present within or outside of the organization or multi-organizational system within which it operates. Although there are many situational factors, some deserve special mention owing to the degree of influence they have on the management of jobs and people:

- In the internal context, the organization's structure, or the group of forms used to divide and coordinate work; and the organization's culture, or the set of unspoken beliefs, values and mindsets that people share.
- In its environment, the legal framework of application, the political system and the labor markets are the primary situational factors. Mutual adjustments among the arrangements that are part of the Public Administration and this set of factors are a requirement for the success of the policies and practices for managing employment and human resources in any institutional setting.

CHAPTER FOUR. FUNCTIONAL REQUIREMENTS FOR PUBLIC ADMINISTRATION

Human Resources Planning

All Public Administration systems need to define methods for planning through which the organization studies its quantitative and qualitative human resource needs over the short, medium and long terms, compares the needs found with its ability to meet them internally, and identifies the actions that must be taken to make up the differences. Planning constitutes the obligatory link between organizational strategy and the set of policies and practices governing management of employment and people.

To ensure quality in human resources planning, it is essential to have data systems addressing human resources that make actual and current information on the quantitative and qualitative availability of human resources at present and foreseeable in the future, aggregated by sector, unit, organizational area, qualifications, age groups and any other classifications necessary to the proper management of human capital.

Human resources planning mechanisms and procedures should make it possible to:

- Optimize the quantitative and qualitative resources available.
- Flexibly adapt personnel policies and practices to changes occurring in the organization and its environment.
- Correctly distribute the resources available, flexibly redistribute people on the basis of organizational needs and appropriately divide the workload among the various organizational units and areas.
- Monitor and update its forecasts.
- Secure the active participation of senior managers in the planning process.

The Organization of Work

The organization of work requires human resources management tools for defining the characteristics and conditions of practice for conducting work (job descriptions), as well as the qualifications required of the individuals who would fill the jobs (qualifications profiles).

Job descriptions must include the position's mission, its location within the organization, its principal scope, duties and responsibilities assumed by the person holding it, and the aims or areas in which results are expected to be obtained. In each case, the job description will seek the proper balance between:

a) The precision with which the work is defined, so that the required skill specialization needed for the job in each case and the structure of responsibilities remain clear.
b) The flexibility essential for adapting the job as circumstances change. In particular, it must provide for the circumstance that the person holding the job may be called to confront unforeseen situations, as well as to behave in a cooperative way in responding to needs for teamwork.

The rapid evolution of social needs, technologies and work processes make frequent and flexible revision of job descriptions advisable. The qualifications profiles for those holding the positions must incorporate those key qualities or characteristics that are assumed to be critical for the person to be well-suited for the job and to be able to successfully perform the work. The formulation of qualifications profiles should be done with the following in mind:

- There should be consistency between the demands of the tasks, which are basically expressed through the aims for the positions, and the elements that comprise the profile of what qualifies the person occupying the position.
- The formulation of profiles must go beyond identifying specialized technical knowledge or experience performing similar work, and incorporate all those characteristics (skills, attitudes, self-concept, cognitive abilities, motivations and personality traits) that contemporary personnel management approaches consider relevant to achieving success in the position.
- Profiles must be the product of technical studies conducted by

people with the exact qualifications and knowledge of the work, and through use of tools capable of ensuring the reliability and validity of the result.

The classification of jobs should provide for orderly structures on the basis of the value of the contribution that is attributed to each job, and should have the flexibility to facilitate:

a) Functional and geographic mobility for people, motivated by personal or organizational interests, and
b) Recognition of professional improvement through the assignment of increasingly difficult tasks or increasing responsibility.

Managing the processes for access to public employment must be conducted in all cases in accordance with the following principles:

a) Publicity, understood as the effective diffusion of the calls for applications under conditions that enable these job listings to be known by all potential candidates.
b) Open competition, in accordance with some general access requirements for public employment and without restrictions other than those implied by the qualifications profile, which in all cases should correspond to the functional requirements of the job.
c) Transparent management and operation of recruitment and selection processes.
d) Specialization in the technical bodies in charge of managing and decision-making in hiring procedures, which requires professional qualifications on the part of their members derived from a knowledge of both the work and selection process tools.
e) Guaranteed impartiality on the part of the bodies in charge of managing and decision-making in hiring procedures, and in particular on the part of each of its members individually.
f) Proven reliability and validity of the tools used to verify the candidates' competency.

g) Selection of the best candidate consistent with the principles of merit and capability.
h) Effectiveness of the recruitment and selection processes in guaranteeing that the selected candidates are adequately matched to the jobs' profiles.
i) Efficiency and agility in recruitment and selection processes, without sacrificing observance of respect for each and every one of the guarantees that these should entail.

As regards the principles set forth, and always consistent with the profiles of the jobs to be filled, the bodies responsible for managing and decision-making in these procedures may use the following selection tools:

- Analysis of the candidates' biographical information and evaluation of their merits and references.
- Conduct of oral or written tests of knowledge.
- Application of tests of aptitude or cognitive abilities.
- Requirement to pass physical tests.
- Conduct of exercises and simulations demonstrating possession of skills and dexterity.
- Application of psychometric tests related to exploring personality traits or character.
- Requirement to pass a medical examination.
- Conduct of selection interviews.
- Conduct of selective training courses.
- Requirement to pass a probationary period or practice.

The effectiveness of the principles defined for access to public employment demands especially that Public Administration systems effectively protect the professionalism and impartiality of the bodies that manage and make decisions in these processes. To this end, it will be necessary to institute measures that guarantee:

- Accreditation of the necessary qualifications.
- The independence of the members of such bodies as regards

political power or other interest groups, which is assured by the standards that govern their appointment, tenure and termination.

- The avoidance of incompatibility owing to a direct interest in the proceedings.
- The possibility of challenging a decision for just cause on the part of one of the parties with a legitimate interest in it.

Performance Evaluation

The mechanisms of Public Administration in procedures for access to public employment should in all cases assure the effective application of principles of equality and non-discrimination, as well as of gender equity and inclusion of minorities requiring special protection, and where necessary should incorporate policies and active measures for positive discrimination or affirmative action. The principles and criteria adopted by this Charter as regards access to public employment are for application, regardless of any necessary adaptation, to any hypothetical incorporation of a job, whether it be from outside the public system or within it, through processes of mobility or promotion.

Performance evaluation of people employed must form part of the human resources management policies integrated throughout any civil service system. Making use of formal performance evaluation systems makes it possible to:

a) Obtain information necessary for decision-making in various areas of personnel management (compensation, promotion, training, discipline, . . .).
b) Validate human resources management policies and practices, including comparing and evaluating their impact on human behavior on the job.
c) Guide people's development and their professional growth.
d) Improve motivation and performance of individuals in their jobs.

Performance evaluation, whether individual or by group, requires using reliable and valid instruments. When evaluation is based on results, it should be based on the prior standardization of those results by outlining objectives consistent with the purposes of the job in question and identifying precise indicators.

When evaluation measures behavior at work, it should be based on the application of appropriate scales of conduct or other technically proven instruments. In all cases, the use of instruments that are ambiguous, of doubtful reliability, susceptible to bias in evaluation or favoring mere subjectivity or arbitrariness should be avoided.

Evaluation of personnel work performance, especially when done to motivate and improve performance, requires the active participation of senior managers who are immediate superiors to the people being evaluated. Training the evaluators so that they master the necessary technical skills and social abilities and make a meaningful commitment to these practices is crucial to the success of this effort.

Evaluation systems must incorporate mechanisms through which people may indicate their disagreement with the evaluation made and bring this disagreement to the attention of both their supervisors and higher-level managers. Care should be taken to avoid and punish improper use of evaluation in support of arbitrary or high-handed practices or those related to sexual harassment.

To the extent possible, and always in a manner consistent with the public organizations' internal culture, civil service systems should incorporate, especially for the purposes of developing and improving people's competence, 360-degree evaluation mechanisms or something similar through which people receive feedback on their performance from people who are affected by it in different ways, whether they be above, below or on a par in rank with the person being evaluated. All employment and personnel management systems need a compensation strategy.

Wage structures and remuneration policies and practices should respond to a set of priorities and objectives linked to the organization's strategy and the financial and budgetary circumstances, and should not be merely the result of inertia or of measures taken in reacting to individual or collective claims or labor conflict. Compensation policies should always seek to motivate public servants to work harder, achieve better individual or group results, acquire more training and develop their abilities.

Equity must be the guiding principle in designing compensation structures, as well as a basic characteristic of them. Equitable compensation is determined from both within and outside of the organization:

a) Internal equity is the quality that a structure has when individuals:
- In general have a perception that they receive compensation of all kinds from the organization in accordance with their own contribution, and
- perceive that the compensation received by other employees is fair when compared to what they themselves receive.

b) External equity brings together competitiveness and wage efficiency:
- A compensation system is competitive when it is adequate to attract, motivate and retain people with the necessary competence in the various types of positions that the organization requires.
- A compensation system is efficient when wage costs are not excessive in relation to those in the marketplace for any level or sector of positions.

Development

The wage range (the difference in total compensation received between the highest-paid and the lowest-paid employees) should be balanced: neither too compressed, because this reduces career incentives and the motivation to perform, nor too wide, which may be an indication that the system has been taken over by some elites and would reflect a greater or lesser degree of salary inequity.

If variable compensation is established in order to provide incentives for individual or group performance, its application should be linked to the prior definition of standards for results or effort and to reliable evaluation procedures, which must be defined ahead of time, known to all interested parties and administered in a way that guarantees the least possible degree of subjectivity.

Decisions regarding wage administration should in general be adopted in conjunction with coherent criteria and should be based on merit and individuals' capabilities.

Public Administration systems should incorporate mechanisms that protect compensation policies and practices from arbitrary decisions, seeking kickbacks, or political patronage. Non-monetary benefits incorporated into Public Administration systems should be equitable, effective in achieving their purposes and justifiable in cost-benefit terms.

The pension program for public employees should be adequate to ensure its goals of social support, have the necessary financial underpinnings, not create inordinate privileges with regard to other social groups and not place an excessive burden on State expenditures and countries' economies. Public Administration systems must incorporate mechanisms that foster and stimulate the growth of public employees' capabilities.

Labor Responsibility

Public employees' professional careers will be facilitated by flexible regulations that eliminate insofar as is possible formal barriers or limitations. Alternative formulas should be created to career paths that merely follow the hierarchy, formulas that should be based on recognition of professional growth and excellence, without requiring an increase in the formal authority of the person in question.

Promotion to higher-level positions should be based on performance assessment, analysis of the person's potential and development of capabilities. For this purpose, instruments endowed with the greatest objectivity possible should be used to reduce the risks of arbitrary action, nepotism or patronage in these processes.

Public employees should receive adequate training to complement their initial education or training at the time of hiring, in order to adapt to evolution in their work, to remedy performance deficits, to support professional growth and to cope with organizational changes. Training for public employees should be developed through plans designed to support the organization's clear priorities within the framework of comprehensive policies and should be based on reliable assessment of needs.

Investment in training must be subject to evaluation, which should extend to an assessment of the learning that took place, participant satisfaction, the relationship between the cost and results, and the impact on employees' performance in their jobs.

Public Administration systems must have mechanisms—through means appropriate in each case—that assure control of attendance, a full day's work, tools for reducing absenteeism and, in general, that ensure public employees fulfill their work duties. The necessary standards regarding incompatible activities should be established and applied in the strictest manner in order to prevent such conflicts from impinging on matters in which some interest might compromise their impartiality or bring the image of the Public Administration into question.

Disciplinary procedures must make it possible to correct effectively, quickly and in an exemplary manner inappropriate conduct on the part of public employees. The disciplinary system should be based on the categorization of infractions, proportional gradation of sanctions, impartiality on the part of the bodies that hear and decide on these procedures, their adversarial nature, and consistency between the proven facts and the decisions made. Those affected by a disciplinary procedure should have all the guarantees provided by the sanctioning law.

A mere change in administration or a concurrence of circumstances or decisions made on a purely discretionary basis shall not, in and of themselves, be sufficient cause to justify dismissal or termination of employment. In setting forth the possibility of termination owing to a clear lack of capability or poor performance, systems should create the mechanisms necessary to guarantee the objective documentation of these circumstances. By the same token, when there is the possibility of either individual or group lay-offs of public employees for technical, economic or organizational reasons that dictate the abolition of jobs, the joint occurrence of said causes should be objectively proven.

Necessary Human and Social Relations

Criteria used to orient labor relations in the Public Administration are as follows:

a) Public employees' right to defend their interests, within the frameworks and using the modalities that derive from national legislation in various cases.
b) Each of the parties in labor relations must—without overstepping their bounds—play the role assigned to them, and all sides must mutually recognize and accept this.
c) As regards establishing working conditions, it should be as the applicable national legislation provides in addressing which of the elements of those conditions should be subject to negotiation and which are governed by legal standards or the unilateral decision-making powers of the public employer.
d) The mechanisms and procedures established should facilitate labor relations oriented most commonly and preferentially toward interaction and agreement, thereby avoiding confrontation and discrediting the adversary.

Public Administration systems should incorporate the regulations and policies necessary to safeguard the rights of public employees as regards workplace health and security on the job. Public employers should make the effort to understand the labor climate in their organizations and to evaluate it periodically, taking these evaluations into account in order to review and improve their personnel management policies and practices. Internal communications policies and practices should be oriented toward organizing the human resources function:

a) To know the information, initiatives, suggestions, opinion and requests offered by public employees.
b) To accurately report on the decisions and directives of higher authorities and to ensure that information relevant to services and people circulates freely, using an open approach that limits only the information which by its very nature must remain confidential.
c) To strengthen the perception of belonging and the involvement of employees in the organization's overall purpose and in governmental strategies.

The key duties and responsibilities with regard to managing jobs and personnel require that public sector organizations and multi-organizational systems have specialized teams that have the corresponding technical qualifications. In the structural sense, these teams need to be located in positions of formal authority consistent with the high strategic value of their function. The basic mission of these teams or centralized departments is:

a) To formulate strategic directives for managing jobs and personnel consistent with organizational strategy and the monitoring and control of their application.
b) To promote and direct comprehensive personnel planning processes and the management of those human resources operations and processes, which because of their scale or specialization must be the responsibility of a central authority.
c) To study, analyze, evaluate and innovate in the field of human resource management policies and practices, and to promote the reforms needed to modernize them and adapt them to the changing requirements of public organizations.
d) To support the leadership of their organizations' chain of command in carrying out the duties incumbent upon them as managers of the people for whom they are responsible.

Without prejudice to the relevant functions of the centralized human resources teams or departments, civil service systems must assign to the front line of the units producing Public Administrations the predominant role in managing the people they supervise. This implies:

a) Decentralizing by transferring to front-line supervisors all those personnel decisions that the organization would not benefit from having centralized.
b) From the central authorities on down, playing a primary role of assisting, supporting and providing specialized technical services with regard to personnel to the group of senior managers.
c) Strengthening managers' abilities with regard to personnel management, providing ongoing training material addressing the

necessary knowledge and skills, and putting together the set of mechanisms for the Public Administration in such a way as to promote and stimulate greater involvement and more responsibility on the part of senior managers in this field.

CHAPTER FIVE. SPECIFIC CONSIDERATIONS REGARDING MANAGEMENT

Specific Regulations on Professional Management Functions

The Administration's requirements of professionalism, which are an integral part of Public Administration, extends to the senior or management level of political-administrative systems. This Charter understands this segment to be those management positions that report directly to positions filled by political appointment in governments, and those positions whose job it is to direct, under the strategic guidance and control of political appointees, the structures and processes through which public policies are implemented and public services are produced and provided. This is a function separate from both the political and the public professions that make up the ordinary Public Administration.

The proper definition and consolidation of public professional management are basic to the correct institutional design of contemporary public systems. Appropriate institutionalization of public professional management requires institutional arrangements that make possible:

a) A sphere of delegation in which it is feasible to exercise a margin of managerial discretion in the subject matter and decision-making being managed.
b) Effective systems of control and accountability that enable managers to take responsibility for their actions. The most appropriate control systems for the exercise of management duties are those that focus preferentially on results.

c) A catalogue of rewards and punishments linked to the responsibility held and given out on the basis of assessment of management results.
d) A set of common reference values, focusing on the rational handling of resources and on creating a greater degree of public value through the appropriate use of those resources. The nature of the public management function requires, in order to guarantee its professionalism, regulations specifically for the managerial function.

These regulations must define the universe of responsibilities considered part of professional public management, outlining both the political functions as well as the positions reserved for members of the Public Administration or ordinary civil service. These standards should be applied to filling management positions by people from Public Administration, as well as, when appropriate, the hiring of managers from other arenas. Whether forming a separate part of a single body of Public Administration legislation or through specific statute, regulations governing the management function should include:

- Requirements for professional qualifications that define the exact competencies needed for the performance of the positions, as well as acceptable means of accreditation of those qualifications.
- Rules governing assessment and accountability that define mechanisms for control by results, as well as the criteria for determining results.
- Rules governing candidacy for the position that guarantee professionalism through the use of criteria based on abilities and merit, which also makes possible the level of confidence required in each case owing to the nature of the duties.
- Rules governing tenure that link tenure to the results achieved by management, and rules that establish some type of protection from arbitrary dismissal.
- Incentives that encourage good management by linking a part of compensation, as well as, where appropriate, professional advancement, to results.

This Charter contains a set of elements that are considered integral parts of a Public Administration system capable of achieving the goals and meeting the challenges of contemporary Public Administrations. Development of this basic cluster of components and their realization through management regulations, structures, procedures, policies and practices allow diverse developments, which should be adapted to the history, traditions, cultures and other elements of the institutional environment in the various national circumstances in the community of Ibero-American countries. In particular, the guidance for management of employment and human resources serving public organizations adopted by this Charter allow for different models of Public Administration from the viewpoint of:

- The predominant types of systems for insuring and establishing professionalism that are used in qualifying candidates for public employment.
- The scale of system administration, which may range from a single model for a national system to a variety of managing structures and authorities as a function of criteria based on institutional articulation on a territorial level, by specific sector or using other criteria.
- The frameworks within which labor relations are conducted, which may include various degrees and forms of participation of social agents and may have more or less expansive arenas for negotiation of public employees' conditions of employment.

Regardless of the differences among national models for Public Administration, the full effectiveness of the criteria for managing jobs and human resources incorporated in this Charter require an institutional environment that enables them to be applied. The legal frameworks for public employment are relevant elements in that environment.

- The organization of professional careers for public employees and especially the possibility of opting for Public Administration systems of jobs or careers.

CHAPTER SIX. CONDITIONS FOR THE CHARTER'S EFFECTIVENESS

A Variety of Possible Development Paths

Legal Framework. Organizational Design

Structural design of public systems and their organizations, their internal capacity and the dominant cultural values. The guidance set forth in this Charter requires regulatory frameworks that ensure the professionalism and effectiveness of Public Administration. Therefore, it will be essential to introduce modifications and unique specialties different in some aspects from those that regulate employment in general.

Regulations for public employment should:

a) Guarantee the full enforcement of principles of equality, merit and ability in the array of public employment and personnel management practices for those working within it, providing them with protection from politicization, patronage, arbitrary action and being overtaken by private interests.
b) Limit the scope of single-purpose regulations to those elements essential to ensuring the professionalism of Public Administrations, without including special rules that create discrimination or privilege for public servants.
c) Avoid excessive uniformity in regulations that makes them unable to adapt to the extraordinary diversity and heterogeneity of contemporary political-administrative systems.
d) Incorporate the guidelines for flexibility which are indispensable for effective human resources management, and which have guided the reform of public employment systems undertaken in many countries throughout the past two decades.

In order to make effective Public Administration management possible, the structural design of public organizations should incorporate the following basic elements:

- Authorities specialized in management of jobs and human resources, endowed with powers.
- Formal internal capacity corresponding to the strategic value of its function and characterized by a three-pronged orientation toward:

    - Rational management of resources
    - Innovation in the policies and practices of personnel management
    - Support and assistance to line managers for the performance of their duties as managers of the people they supervise
- An approach that guarantees that the directors of centers and production units have the management attributes necessary to manage their personnel, including proper systems of control and accountability.

Administration of Public Administration systems in line with the orientation of this Charter requires that public organizations possess the essential areas of competence. These requirements are somewhat different for centralized bodies and for line management:

- Central authorities responsible for human resources should have a high level of professional qualifications, including multidisciplinary knowledge appropriate for personnel management, which requires combining in a balanced manner a collection of qualifications in the fields of law, economics, social psychology and Public Administration.
- Front-line managers of production units should have appropriate training for the development of the technical and social skills necessary for managing teams of people. In particular, their training in skills of an interpersonal and relational nature is fundamental.

Cultural Change

The effectiveness of the institutional arrangements that this Charter considers integral to Public Administration systems will require to a greater or lesser degree in the various national settings, adapting informal rules, mindsets and established guidelines for behavior that now characterize the functioning of public systems. In all cases, in order to achieve effective implementation of the model that is encouraged, the following will be required:

a) Internalization of models of Public Administration that preclude politics overwhelming the system and that assume the need for professional administrations using a merit-based system as indicators of solid democracies.
b) Overcoming bureaucratic conceptions of Public Administrations based on adopting standardized routines and repeating established procedures, and their replacement with approaches geared toward producing results, innovation and learning.
c) Adoption of flexible approaches to personnel management that are consistent with present-day trends in the workplace and reforms in public management.
d) Incorporation by the various institutional participants of the values inherent in serving the public, and in particular honesty in public behavior, austerity in the use of resources, transparency in decision-making, assessment and accountability, and the commitment to serve our citizens.

The Ibero-American Charter for Public Administration was Approved by the Fifth Ibero-American Conference of Ministers of Public Administration and Reform of the State in Santa Cruz de la Sierra, Bolivia, that took place on June 26-27, 2003. It was supported by the Thirteenth Ibero-American Summit of Heads of State and Government (Resolution No. 11 of the "Declaration of Santa Cruz de la Sierra"), Bolivia, November 14-15, 2003.

Latin American Center of Administration for Development (CLAD)
UN Department of Economic and Social Affairs (DESA)

Fifth Global Forum on Re-inventing Government: Innovation and Quality in the Government of the 21st Century
Mexico City, 3/6 November 2003
Mexico City Declaration

We, the participants of the Fifth Global Forum on Reinventing Government, held in Mexico City, Mexico, from 3 to 6 November 2003, on the theme of **"Innovation and Quality in the Government of the 21st Century"** have approved the following declaration:

1. Preamble

The Fifth Global Forum on Reinventing Government, organized by the Government of Mexico, in collaboration with the United Nations, brought together representatives of governments, international organizations, businesses and nongovernmental organizations (NGOs) to dialogue about governance in the 21st century from the perspective of innovation and quality. We began with two days of plenary sessions and panels where we heard from international organizations, including the UN, OECD, Transparency International, the World Bank and IDB, who shared international trends in reform and from country representatives who discussed reform efforts in their countries. We brought this knowledge to the seven interactive capacity development workshops that were organized by the UN Department of Economic and Social Affairs, UNDP, UN Habitat and partner institutions: American Society for Quality; Ash Institute for Democratic Governance and Innovation, Harvard University; World Bank Institute, International

Monetary Fund, Transparency International, and the World Bank, and funded by the Government of Italy.

The Fifth Forum followed events that began in 1999, when the USA partnered with Harvard in Washington, DC. In 2000, the Government of Brazil hosted an event in Brasilia. The Government of Italy held the 2001 event in Naples, and last December, the Government of the Kingdom of Morocco held the world-wide forum in Marrakech.

1.1 We recognize that governments across the globe are transforming themselves to deal with the challenges and opportunities of the 21st century. This transformation gives greater voice to citizens, calls for a re-thinking of government programmes and services and leadership paradigms. This forum discussed in detail the strategies of President Fox's Agenda for Good Government, namely, government that costs less; quality government; professional government; digital government; government with regulatory reform; and honest and transparent government.

1.2 The participants of the Fifth Forum would like to express their sincere gratitude to President Vicente Fox Quesada for his leadership and commitment to implementing good government initiatives. The participants also cordially thank the government of Mexico for the successful organization of this major global event and commend the United Nations and international organizations for their invaluable support.

2. General Recommendations

We agreed that the strategic pursuit of reform efforts is to create citizen centred governments. This requires that we call on all sectors of society to re-define the role of governance in this century. We also agreed that involvement of civil society will ensure the legitimacy and sustainability of systemic reform efforts. This approach is based on the Millennium Declaration, which takes a holistic view of development emphasizing not just economic growth but equity for sustainable development. The participants presented experiences and good practices from all over the world in the context of reform of the state and institutional development. We have listed our key recommendations and conclusions for the re-invention of government in the framework of the Fifth Global Forum:

2.1 Governments must attempt to create budgets that are responsive to national priorities, citizen driven and transparent, balancing costs with revenues. These reforms are about choices and decisions about the future. It is essential to review programs and policies developed in the last century, evaluate effectiveness, and eliminate outdated or redundant programs. It is important to ensure increased revenues through efficient tax and customs administration, and through public-private partnerships. Cost accounting, productivity studies and auditing are important tools in the process of creating governments that cost less. Citizens should be actively involved in all investment decisions. Options include deficit reduction, tax cuts, tax rebates or investing in social programs like education and health.

2.2 A crucial test of improved governance is citizen satisfaction with government services. Quality principles such as continuous improvement should underlie government innovation efforts. Surveys have shown that citizens are more satisfied with services delivered by empowered local governments, and with rules and regulations that are easily accessible and clearly understood. Governments should use independent tools to assess satisfaction such as citizen panels, focus groups, and customer surveys.

Citizens should have the right to be heard through feedback mechanisms such as ombudsmen and complaint procedures. Citizens should also have a voice in constructing performance measures that assess the quality and impact of services; the quality process should assess concrete results.

2.3 State capacity to respond to and manage change is essential to meeting the challenges of the 21st century and to improving quality of life for citizens. To undertake these efforts, governments need a professional civil service where employees and managers are recruited on merit, are trained for the jobs they carry out, are evaluated on programme results and promoted and paid for performance. It is important that recruitment is transparent and open to all sectors of society. Evaluating competencies necessary for 21st century governments is crucial. Governments with an established civil service must engage in efforts to reform their rules and regulations to make them responsive to the needs of citizens and competitive with private sector jobs. It is important to benchmark with the private sector about lessons learned in human resource management.

2.4 Now, more than ever, there is a critical need for governments to develop a policy framework for introducing e-government initiatives, including the creation of new strategies and legislation with the involvement of all stakeholders in society. E-government is justified if it enhances the capacity of Public Administration to increase the supply of public value i.e. things that people want. The transition to electronic delivery of services enables governments to better quantify cost effectiveness of electronic service delivery, and hence more effective use of limited resources, and improves accountability. E-government strategies also can improve commerce, democracy and transparency. With this in mind, states need to assess the potential for investing in e-government initiatives with a view to improving the cost effectiveness of the use of their increasingly stretched resources.

2.5 In many highly regulated countries, ineffective regulatory policies stimulate corruption and disempower citizens. Bad regulations distort the economic competitiveness of a nation; understanding the real cost of regulation is crucial to competitiveness in the global economy. While governments often think about the cost of implementing regulations, only a few are currently assessing the cost of complying with regulations on citizens and businesses. Few are also considering the need for capacity development in this area; it is essential that those who write regulations have proper training in understanding the importance and impact of their work. Regulatory programmes must balance the outcomes citizens want with the cost of their programmes. It is important for regulatory programmes to have strong enforcement capabilities. However, it is also crucial to look at how citizens, businesses and civil society groups can engage in leading compliance efforts. In particular, reform and enforcement of tax policy is often fundamental to healthy economies. Reforming the tax policy of a country is often an important first step in global competitiveness.

2.6 For innovations and reforms to grow strong roots, the role of ethics in public service and sensitivity towards and respect for citizens' needs cannot be ignored. It includes an accountable and transparent political and administrative system which ensures a citizen's fundamental right to information. Governments have to be willing to undertake anti-corruption measures through the creation of commissions or bodies that are willing to investigate inconsistencies and anomalies, and introduce innovations to improve integrity and transparency in the public sector. Access to public information is crucial to ensuring oversight, and that access must be guarded by independent autonomous bodies such as the ombudsmen. Programmes for the prevention of corruption should be installed and supported by the government and monitored by civil society. We agreed that the role of a national audit office is critical to internalizing assessment of transparency practices. Fiscal transparency and financial management tools are critical instruments that promote transparency and accountability.

2.7 Improving governance is often a function of decentralization and citizen participation. Decentralization of the administrative, financial and political aspects of government is critical to the process of reform. It requires a legal framework that entails transfer of authority and resources to local governments and instituting checks and balances between central and local governments. At all levels, governments should aim to instill higher professional standards, ethics, and values as part of the good government agenda, and, ultimately, to set the standard for society at large.

3. Follow up

3.1 Reiterating our deepest appreciation to the government of Mexico, the participants recommended appropriate action to ensure the follow-up to the above recommendations among world leaders, international organizations, NGOs, and actors of civil society. We also recommend that the government of Mexico present the report of the Fifth Global Forum to the General Assembly of the United Nations.

3.2 Participants urge the governments represented in the Forum, civil society organizations and the private sector to promote partnerships to foster innovation and quality in the public sector, e-government development, access to services, decentralization and local governance, and accountability and transparency.

3.3 The participants appreciated the strong technical support provided by the United Nations to the Fifth Global Forum and urged the United Nations to continue such support for future forums, including the establishment of a network of innovators and reformers in order to capitalize on the results of the previous global forums. The participants welcomed the statement of the representative of the Government of Italy to continue to provide financial support for the next forum, for which they expressed great appreciation.

4. Sixth Global Forum

The participants welcomed with appreciation the kind invitation of the Government of the Republic of Korea, extended by His Excellency, Goh Kun, Prime Minister, to host the Sixth Global Forum in Seoul in 2005.

Bibliography

Adame Miranda, Julián. *México: Satisfacer o superar las expectativas de los ciudadanos en los servicios que se les brindan.* Fifth Global Forum on Reinventing Government, Mexico, 2003. See *Revista de Política Digital,* No. 13, November, 2003: p. 38.

Australian Public Service Commission. *The Australian Experience of Public Sector Reform.* Australia, 2003.

Bassanini, Franco. *Un paradigma de calidad para la reinvención de los gobiernos.* Fifth Global Forum on Reinventing Government, Mexico, 2003. See *Revista de Política Digital,* No. 13, November, 2003: p. 39.

Bertucci, Guido. *La innovación gubernamental en el mundo: Retos y perspectivas.* Fifth Global Forum on Reinventing Government, Mexico, 2003. See *Revista de Política Digital,* No. 13, November, 2003: p. 8.

Bobbio, Norberto. *El futuro de la democracia.* Mexico: FCE, 1984.

Carillo, Fernando (ed.). *Democracia en déficit.* Washington, D.C.: Inter-American Development Bank, 2001.

Csikszentmihaly, Mihaly. *Creatividad. El fluir y la psicología del descubrimiento y la invención.* Barcelona: Paidós Ediciones, 1998.

Dahrendorf, Ralf. *Después de la democracia.* Barcelona: Crítica, 2002.

De Dommartin, Alain. *El Modelo de Calidad Total en los gobiernos.* Fifth Global Forum on Reinventing Government, Mexico, 2000. See *Revista de Política Digital,* No. 13, November, 2003: p. 42.

Fernández Santillán, José. *Filosofía política de la democracia*. Mexico: Fontamara, 2002.

Giddens, Anthony. *La tercera vía*. Mexico: Taurus, 1998.

Huntington, Samuel. *The Third Wave*. USA: University of Oklahoma Press, 1993.

Interministerial Committee on Public Management. *Experiencias innovadoras en la Gestión Pública.* Chile, 1999.

Kamarck, Elaine C. *Innovación global del gobierno.* Fifth Global Forum on Reinventing Government, Mexico, 2003. See *Revista de Política Digital, Estudios I*, No. 13, November, 2003.

Kaplan, Robert D. "Was Democracy Just a Moment?" In *Globalization and the Challenges of a New Century*, Patrick O'Meara, H.D. Melinger, and M. Krain (eds.). USA: Indiana University Press, 2000.

Kemp, Tim. *Cuatro claves para el cambio en Gran Bretaña.* Fifth Global Forum on Reinventing Government, Mexico, 2003. See *Revista de Política Digital,* No. 13, November, 2003: p. 66.

Majone, Giandomenico. "*Avatares de la reforma regulatoria en la Unión Europea.*" Fifth Global Forum on Reinventing Government, Mexico, 2003. See *Revista de Política Digital,* No. 13, November, 2003: p. 98.

Mickletwai, John, and A. Wooldridge. *A Future Perfect.* New York: Random House, 2000.

Miles, Marc A., E.J. Feulner Jr., M.A. O'Grady, and A.I. Eiras. *Índice de Libertad Económica 2004.* The Heritage Foundation, USA: The Wall Street Journal and others, Dow Jones & Company Inc., 2004.

Mosgaller, Thomas J. *Hacia una definición operativa de Gobierno de Calidad.* Fifth Global Forum on Reinventing Government, Mexico, 2003. See *Revista de Política Digital,* No. 13, November, 2003: p. 10.

OECD. *The e-Government Imperative.* OECD, 2004.

OECD. "Managing Conflict of Interest in the Public Service." In *Guidelines and Country Experiences,* OECD, 2003.

Office of the Presidency of the Mexican Republic. *Conference Book.* Second Forum on Innovation and Quality in Public Administration. Mexico: Office of the Presidency of the Mexican Republic, 2002.

Paiva, Paolo. *La persona en el centro de la gestión fiscal.* Fifth Global Forum on Reinventing Government, Mexico, 2003. See *Revista de Política Digital,* No. 13, November, 2003: p. 30.

Pasha, Hafiz. *Perspectivas y posibilidades de la calidad total en los gobiernos.* Fifth Global Forum on Reinventing Government, Mexico, 2003. See *Revista de Política Digital,* No. 13, November, 2003: p. 48.

Przeworski, Adam, *et al. Democracia sustentable.* Buenos Aires, Mexico City: Paidós, 1998.

Public Governance Committee. *Meeting the Challenges of Public Governance.* OECD, March 2004.

Public Sector Management Committee. *Public Sector Modernization: Changing Organizations.* OECD, October 2003.

Sartori, Giovanni. *¿Qué es la democracia?* Mexico: Nueva Imagen, 1997.

Smith, Trevor. *Normas internacionales para la calidad gubernamental.* Fifth Global Forum on Reinventing Government, Mexico, 2003. See *Revista de Política Digital,* No. 13, November, 2003: p. 50.

Touraine, Alain. *¿Podremos vivir juntos?* Mexico: FCE, 1997.

Zakaria, Fareed. "The Rise of liberal Democracy." In *Globalization and the Challenges of a New Century*, Patrick O'Meara, H.D. Melinger, and M. Krain (eds.). USA: Indiana University Press, 2000.

Acronyms

Agencia Federal de Investigación	AFI	Federal Investigation Agency
Asociación Nacional de Universidades e Institutos de Educación Superior	ANUIES	National Association of Universities and Institutes of Higher Education
Mecanismo de Cooperación Económica Asia Pacífico	APEC	Asia-Pacific Economic Cooperation Mechanism
Administraciones Portuarias Integrales	API	Integral Port Administrations
Organización para la Calidad Asia-Pacífico	APQO	Asia-Pacific Quality Organization
Aeropuertos y Servicios Auxiliares	ASA	Airports and Auxiliary Services
Sociedad Estadounidense para la Calidad	ASQ	American Society for Quality

Banco del Ahorro Nacional y Servicios Financieros	BANSEFI	National Savings and Financial Services Bank
Banco de México	BANXICO	Bank of Mexico
Instituto Británico de Estándares	BSI	British Standards Institute
Comisión de Avalúos de Bienes Nacionales	CABIN	National Assets Appraisal Commission
Centro de Apoyo al Desarrollo Rural	CADER	Rural Development Support Center
Marco Común de Evaluación	CAF	Common Assessment Framework
Caminos y Puentes Federales de Ingresos y Servicios Conexos	CAPUFE	Federal Toll Highways and Bridges and Related Services
Centro Comunitario Digital	CCD	Digital Community Center
Certificado de Vivienda de Interés Social	CEDEVI	Low-Cost Housing Stock Market Certificate
Clínica de Especialidades de la Mujer	CEM	Women's Specialties Clinic
Centro de Desarrollo Infantil	CENDI	Child Development Center
Centro de Servicio INFONAVIT	CESI	INFONAVIT Service Center

Comisión Federal de Electricidad	CFE	Federal Electricity Commission
Coordinación General de Apoyos	CGA	General Coordination of Supports
Coordinación General de Empleo	CGE	General Coordination of Employment
Clave de Identificación Electrónica Confidencial	CIEC	Confidential Electronic Identification Code
Comisión Intersecretarial para la Transparencia y el Combate a la Corrupción	CITCC	Inter-Ministerial Commission for Transparency and the Fight against Corruption
Centro Latinoamericano de Administración para el Desarrollo	CLAD	Latin American Center for Administration for Development
Consejo Mexicano del Café	CMC	Mexican Coffee Council
Modelo de Madurez de Capacidades	CMM	Capability Maturity Model
Comisión Nacional del Agua	CNA	National Water Commission
Comisión Nacional de Derechos Humanos	CNDH	National Human Rights Commission
Comisión Federal de Mejora Regulatoria	COFEMER	Federal Commission on Regulatory Improvement

Comisión Federal de Telecomunicaciones	COFETEL	Federal Telecommunications Commission
Comisión de Fomento Minero	COFOMI	Mining Development Commission
Comités de Mejora Regulatoria Interna	COMERI	Internal Regulatory Improvement Committees
Sistema Electrónico de Contrataciones Gubernamentales	COMPRANET	Electronic Government Procurement System
Consejo Nacional de Ciencia y Tecnología	CONACYT	National Science and Technology Council
Colegio Nacional de Educación Profesional Técnica	CONALEP	National College for Professional Technical Education
Comisión Nacional de Libros de Texto Gratuitos	CONALITEG	National Commission on Free Textbooks
Comisión Nacional de Arbitraje Médico	CONAMED	National Commission on Medical Arbitration
Consejo Nacional de Población	CONAPO	National Population Council
Compañía Nacional de Subsistencias Populares	CONASUPO	National Popular Subsistance Company

Admistración de Relaciones con el Cliente	CRM	Customer Relations Management
Clave Única de Registro de Población	CURP	Sole Population Registry Code
Dirección General de Administración	DGA	General Directorate of Administration
Sistema Nacional para el Desarrollo Integral de la Familia	DIF	National System for Integral Family Development
Dirección Metropolitana Norte (LICONSA)	DMN	Northern Metropolitan Directorate (LICONSA)
Detección de Necesidades de Competencias	DNC	Detection of Competency Needs
Fundación Europea para la Gestión de Calidad	EFQM	European Foundation for Quality Management
Entidad Mexicana de Acreditación	EMA	Mexican Accreditation Entity
Planeación Empresarial de Recursos	ERP	Enterprise Resource Planning
Unión Europea	EU	European Union
Fuerza Aérea Mexicana	FAM	Mexican Air Force

Fiscalía Especializada para la Atención de Delitos Electorales	FEPADE	Specialized Inspector's Office for Attention to Electoral Offences
Fideicomiso de Formación y Capacitación para el Personal de Marina Mercante Nacional	FIDENA	Trust for National Merchant Marine Personnel Education and Training
Fideicomiso de Fomento Minero	FIFOMI	Mining Development Trust
Fondo de Inversión en Infraestructura	FINFRA	Infrastructure Investment Fund
Fuerzas, Oportunidades, Debilidades y Amenazas	FODA	Strengths, Opportunities, Weaknesses and Threats
Administración Pública Federal (APF)	FPA	Federal Public Administration
Fundación Iberoamericana para la Gestión de Calidad	FUNDIBEQ	Ibero-American Quality Management Foundation
Producto Interno Bruto (PIB)	GDP	Gross Domestic Product
Red Internacional de Gobiernos en Línea	GOL	Governments Online International Network
Sistema de Posicionamiento Global	GPS	Global Positioning System

Planeación Gubernamental de Recursos	GRP	Government Resource Planning
Administración General de Recursos	GSA	General Services Administration
Instituto para la Conectividad en las Américas	ICA	Institute for Connectivity in the Americas
Organización de Aviación Civil Internacional (OACI)	ICAO	International Civil Aviation Organization
Institutos de Capacitación	ICAP	Training Institutes
Tecnologías de la Información y Comunicación	ICT	Information and Communication Technologies
Banco Interamericano de Desarrollo (BID)	IDB	Inter-American Development Bank
Instituto Federal de Acceso a la Información Pública	IFAI	Federal Institute for Access to Public Information
Instituto Federal Electoral	IFE	Federal Electoral Institute
Instituto Mexicano del Seguro Social	IMSS	Mexican Social Security Institute

Instituto Mexicano del Transporte	IMT	Mexican Transportation Institute
Instituto Nacional de Ciencias Penales	INACIPE	National Criminal Sciences Institute
Instituto Nacional para el Federalismo y el Desarrollo Municipal	INAFED	National Institute for Federalism and Municipal Development
Instituto Nacional de las Personas Adultas Mayores	INAPAM	National Institute for Older Adults
Instituto Nacional para la Educación de los Adultos	INEA	National Institute for Adult Education
Instituto Nacional de Estadística, Geografía e Informática	INEGI	National Institute of Statistics, Geography and Informatics
Instituto del Fondo Nacional de la Vivienda para los Trabajadores	INFONAVIT	National Institute of the Workers' Housing Fund
Centro Público para la Investigación y el Desarrollo Tecnológico	INFOTEC	Public Center for Research and Technological Development
Premio Nacional de Innovación en la Administración Pública	INNOVA PRIZE	National Award for Innovation in the Public Administration

Índice Nacional de Precios al Consumidor	INPC	National Consumer Price Index
Instituto Panamericano de Alta Dirección de Empresas	IPADE	Pan-American Institute of Senior Business Mananagement
IMSS desde su Empresa	ISDE	IMSS from your Company
Organización Internacional para la Estandarización	ISO	International Organization for Standarization
Instituto de Seguridad y Servicios Sociales de los Trabajadores del Estado	ISSSTE	Social Security and Services Institute for Government Workers
Expediente Clínico Electrónico del ISSSTE	ISSSTEMED	ISSSTE's Electronic Clinical Record
Indicador de Seguimiento de Transparencia	IST	Transparency Follow-up Indicator
Instituto Tecnológico Autónomo de México	ITAM	Autonomous Technological Institute of Mexico
Instituto Tecnológico de Estudios Superiores de Monterrey	ITESM	Monterrey Technological Institute of Higher Studies
Laboratorio de Pruebas de Equipos y Materiales	LAPEM	Equipment and Materials Testing Laboratory

Ley Federal de Transparencia y Acceso a la Información Pública Gubernamental	LFTAIPG	Federal Law on Transparency and Access to Public Government Information
Leche Industrializada CONASUPO, S. A. de C. V.	LICONSA	CONASUPO Industrialized Milk
Ley del Servicio Profesional de Carrera	LSPC	Law of the Professional Career Civil Service
Medicina Familiar	MF	Family Medicine
Índice de Mortalidad de Fetos	MFT	Fetus Mortality Indicator
Modelo Integral de Calidad	MIC	Integral Quality Model
Sistema de Expedición Múltiple de Documentos de Identidad	MIDIS	Multiple Identity Document Issuing System
Sistema de Cumplimentación Multicapa	MLIS	Multi-layer Infilling System
Índice de Mortalidad de Recién Nacidos	MNT	Newborn Mortality Indicator
Nacional Financiera	NAFIN	Nacional Financiera
Norma Oficial Mexicana	NOM	Official Mexican Standard

Organización de Estados Americanos (OEA)	OAS	Organization of American States
Órgano Interno de Control.	OIC	Internal Control Office
Organización para la Cooperación y el Desarrollo Económico (OCDE)	OECD	Organisation for Economic Co-operation and Development
Organización No Gubernamental (ONG)	NGO	Non-Governmental Organization
Portable Document File	PDF	Portable Document File
Presupuesto de Egresos de la Federación	PEF	Expenditures Budget of the Federation
Petróleos Mexicanos	PEMEX	Petroleos Mexicanos (Mexican Oil Company)
Pemex Exploración y Producción	PEP	PEMEX Exploration and Production
Planeación Estratégica de la Tecnología	PET	Strategic Technology Planning
Procuraduría General de la República	PGR	Office of the Attorney General of the Republic
Programa Institucional de Comunicación Motivacional	PICOM	Institutional Program for Motivational Communication

Proyectos de Infraestructura Productiva con Impacto Diferido en el Registro del Gasto	PIDIREGAS	Productive Infrastructure Projects with Deferred Impact on the Expenditures Register
Instituto para la Administración de Proyectos	PMI	Project Management Institute
Programa Nacional de Auditorías Ambientales	PNAA	National Program of Environmental Audits
Premio Nacional de Calidad	PNC	National Quality Award
Programa Nacional de Combate a la Corrupción, Transparencia y Desarrollo Administrativo	PNCTDA	National Program for the Fight Against Corruption and Promotion of Transparency and Administrative Development
Plan Nacional de Desarrollo	PND	National Development Plan
Programa Operativo Anual	POA	Annual Operative Program
Programas Operativos para la Transparencia y el Combate a la Corrupción	POTCC	Operative Programs for Transparency and the Fight Against Corruption

Proyectos para la Prestación de Servicios	PPS	Service Delivery Projects
Planeación de Recursos Institucionales	PREI	Institutional Resource Planning
Partido Revolucionario Institucional	PRI	Institutional Revolutionary Party
Procuraduría Federal de Protección al Ambiente	PROFEPA	Office of the Federal Attorney for Environmental Protection
Programa de Separación Voluntaria	PSV	Voluntary Termination Program
Registro Nacional de Población	RENAPO	National Population Register
Registro Federal de Contribuyentes	RFC	Federal Taxpayers Register
Registro Federal de Trámites y Servicios	RFTS	Federal Register of Procedures and Services
Región Marítima del Suroeste	RMSO	Southwestern Maritime Region
Residuos Peligrosos Biológico Infecciosos	RPBI	Hazardous Biologically Infectious Wastes
Registro Único de Personas Acreditadas	RUPA	Sole Register of Accredited Persons

Registro Único de Servidores Públicos	RUSP	Sole Register of Public Servants
Secretaría de Agricultura, Ganadería, Desarrollo Rural, Pesca y Alimentación	SAGARPA	Ministry of Agriculture, Livestock, Rural Development, Fisheries and Food
Sistema de Abasto Institucional del IMSS	SAI IMSS	Institutional Supply System of the IMSS
Sistema de Atención de Quejas Médicas	SAQMED	System for Attention to Medical Complaints
Sistema de Apertura Rápida de Empresas	SARE	System of Rapid Start-up of Enterprises
Servicio de Administración Tributaria	SAT	Tax Administration Service
Suprema Corte de Justicia de la Nación	SCJN	Supreme Court of Justice of the Nation
Secretaría de Comunicaciones y Transportes	SCT	Ministry of Communications and Transportation
Secretaría de la Contraloría y Desarrollo Administrativo	SECODAM	Ministry of the Comptroller and Administrative Development
Secretaría de la Defensa Nacional	SEDENA	Ministry of National Defense

Secretaría de Desarrollo Social	SEDESOL	Ministry of Social Development
Secretaría de Gobernación	SEGOB	Ministry of the Interior
Servicios Estatales de Empleo	SEE	State Employment Services
Secretaría del Medio Ambiente y Recursos Naturales	SEMARNAT	Ministry of the Environment and Natural Resources
Servicios a la Navegación del Espacio Aéreo Mexicano	SENEAM	Mexican Air Space Navigation Services
Secretaría de Educación Pública	SEP	Ministry of Public Education
Sistema Estratégico de Resultados	SER	Strategic System of Results
Secretaría de la Función Pública	SFP	Ministry of Public Administration
Sistema de Gestión de Calidad	SGC	Quality Management System
Secretaría de Hacienda y Crédito Público	SHCP	Ministry of Finance and Public Credit
Sistema Integral de Administración	SIA	Integral Administration System

Sistema Integral de Administración Financiera Federal	SIAFF	Integral Federal Financial Administration System
Sistema de Afiliación, Recaudación y Fiscalización	SIAREFI	Affiliation, Collection and Oversight System
Sistema Institucional de Calibraciones y Homologaciones	SICH	Institutional Calibration and Standarization System
Sistema Comercial de CFE	SICOM	CFE Commercial System
Sistema de Información de Medicina Familiar	SIFM	Family Medicine Information System
Sistema de Información Geográfica	SIG	Geographical Information System
Sistema Institucional de Metrología de la CFE	SIMCFE	CFE Institutional Metrology System
Sistema Metrológico del Sector Eléctrico	SIMESE	Metrological System for the Electric Power Sector
Sistemas de Solicitud de Información	SISI	System of Requests for Information
Pequeñas y Medianas Empresas (PyMEs)	SME	Small and Medium-Sized Enterprises
Servicio Militar Nacional	SMN	National Military Service

Servicio Nacional de Empleo	SNE	National Employment Service
Sindicato Nacional de Trabajadores del Seguro Social	SNTSS	National Union of Social Security Workers
Sociedad Financiera de Objeto Limitado	SOFOL	Limited-Purpose Financial Company
Sistema de Planeación Estratégica / Sistema de Alineación Digital-Gobierno	SPE/DAS-G	Strategic Planning System/Digital Alignment System-Government
Secretaría de Relaciones Exteriores	SRE	Ministry of Foreign Affairs
Secretaría de Salud	SSA	Ministry of Health
Secretaría del Trabajo y Previsión Social	STPS	Ministry of Labor and Social Welfare
Teléfonos de México	TELMEX	Telefonos de Mexico
Tesorería de la Federación	TESOFE	Treasury of the Federation
Tasa de Interés Interbancaria de Equilibrio	TIIE	Interbank Balance Interest Rate
Tiempo de interrupción por usuario	TIU	Downtime per User

Veces el Salario Mínimo (VSM)	TMW	Times the Minimum Wage
Administración de Calidad Total	TQM	Total Quality Management
Universidad Autónoma de Nuevo León	UANL	Autonomous University of Nuevo Leon
Universidad de Monterrey	UDEM	University of Monterrey
Unidad de Especialidades Odontológicas	UEO	Dental Specialties Unit
Unidades de Medicina de Familia	UMF	Family Medicine Unit
Organización de las Naciones Unidas (ONU)	UN	United Nations
Universidad Nacional Autónoma de México	UNAM	National Autonomous University of Mexico
Programa de las Naciones Unidas para el Desarrollo	UNDP	United Nations Development Programme
Estados Unidos (de América)	US(A)	United States (of America)
Impuesto al Valor Agregado	VAT	Value-Added Tax

The printing and binding of *Government Innovation. The Good Government Paradigm in the Administration of President Vicente Fox* was finished in April 2005, in the workshops of Impresora y Encuadernadora Progreso, S. A. de C. V. (IEPSA), Calz. San Lorenzo 244, 09830 Mexico, D. F.

The edition consists of 1 000 hardcover copies.